MARRIAGE

BY

THE BOOK

WHAT PROSPECTIVE COUPLES SHOULD KNOW
BEFORE THEY SAY I DO

MARK HOBAFCOVICH

NERA HOUSE
PUBLISHING

Marriage By The Book: What Prospective Couples Should Know Before They Say I Do

With Mark Hobafcovich

Published by Nera House Publishing, Athens, Georgia, USA

Printed in the United States of America
ISBN: (paperback) 978-1-968541-06-4
ISBN: (hardcover) 978-1-968541-07-1
ISBN: (ebook) 978-1-968541-08-8
Library of Congress Control Number: 2025925496

Dedication

Marriage, a sacred covenant instituted by God, unites two souls in love, faith, and purpose. It is a journey marked by both joy and challenge, demanding commitment, grace, and an unwavering trust in God's divine design. The book Marriage by the Book: What Prospective Couples Should Know Before They Say I Do was written to guide couples in building a Christ-centered marriage—one rooted in biblical truth and prepared for a lifetime of shared devotion. This work is born from a profound desire to see marriages flourish as reflections of God's glory.

Over the years, I have developed the content within these pages, and together with my wife, Christine, we walked along with new couples through biblical teachings and shared the wisdom and principles that have profoundly shaped our own journey.

For more than four decades, Christine has been my wonderful companion and a profound blessing throughout our journey. Her love, dedication, and tireless support for our family and the advancement of God's Kingdom have been the very heartbeat of our shared life. Christine has beautifully exemplified the virtues of a godly wife, embodying the principles cherished in this book with remarkable grace and strength.

With gratitude and love, this book is dedicated to Christine for walking hand in hand with me, for reflecting the love of Christ within our home, and for being a true partner in our shared journey. May our lives together continue to inspire others to pursue marriage according to God's design, all to His glory.

Acknowledgments

First and foremost, I give thanks to God, who designed marriage as a reflection of Christ's relationship with His church and who continues to teach me daily about covenant love, grace, and faithfulness.

I am deeply grateful to my wife, whose support made my ministry possible. Your willingness to walk this journey with me has been invaluable. Many of the principles in these pages were born in our lives as we journeyed together for over four decades.

My heartfelt appreciation goes to the late Pastor Anatoly (Tolly) Jaloshin in Melbourne, State of Victoria, Australia, for the premarital counselling and mentoring us in our marriage, and the congregation of Bethel Baptist Church in Brisbane, Queensland Australia for their prayers and support as we learned together as young couples how to grow our own marriage as well as ministering to the new congregation.

I am grateful to the many authors and teachers whose works have influenced my understanding of biblical marriage. I stand on the shoulders of these and many other faithful servants who have gone before us.

I am deeply grateful to my editorial and publishing team for their dedication and support in bringing this book to completion. Their efforts have transformed my vision into the finished work you hold today.

Special thanks to John William Halladay for his specialized editorial work, meticulous attention to detail, and ability to strengthen every aspect of this manuscript. I am equally grateful to Lucas Herrington for his editorial expertise and professionalism, which have greatly contributed to the quality and clarity of this project.

I am also deeply thankful to Marcus Lewis for his publishing expertise, strategic guidance, and commitment to excellence that has ensured this project reached its full potential. His professional expertise and support have been instrumental in this book's success.

Your combined professionalism and dedication have made this work possible.

Contents

Preface

A Word from My Heart

As I look at the world around us, with so many different ideas about life and love, I see God's plan for marriage as an unwavering truth. It's a special promise, a journey He designed not just to make us happy (though happiness is a wonderful part of it!) but to show His glory and help us grow closer to Him. When you decide to marry, to share your life so closely with someone else, it's one of the biggest choices you'll ever make. It's a path that can bring great joy, deep friendship, and a unique kind of teamwork. But, if we're not careful to build on a strong foundation with good advice, it can also be a path with unexpected problems and disappointments. Many of us start out on this journey with hopeful hearts but soon find we're in new territory without a good guide to lead us. I've written this book because I want to offer you that reliable compass, one that's based on the never-changing truth of God's Word.

Challenging Views of Marriage

We live in a time when people often question what marriage even means. Sometimes, carnal notions that focus on quick feelings instead of covenant vows or on what we can get instead of what we can give can weaken the foundations of marriage. The stories our culture tells about love and marriage can sound exciting, but they often lead us away from the eternal verities we find in the Bible. The idea of a perfect, easy romance, the stress of planning a flawless wedding, or the hope of finding a partner who meets our every need can give us a wrong idea of what marriage is really like. These worldly views can make marriage seem like something we try out, and if it doesn't make us happy right away, we can just give up on it. They don't see it as a sacred covenant we make to care for and protect. Because of this, many couples start their marriage without being fully ready. They have romantic dreams, but they don't have the practical wisdom or the spiritual strength to handle the ups and downs of a lifelong partnership. I wrote this book to help fight against these common ideas by offering a strong, biblical paradigm for marriage.

The Purpose of This Book

It's because I see this great need for clear, Bible-based advice that I wrote Marriage by the Book: What Prospective Couples Should Know Before They Say I Do. This book is more than just another set of tips for relationships; it's my heartfelt invitation to you to start your marriage journey with your eyes open, your heart ready, and your spirit resting on the solid wisdom of God's Word. I wrote this book because I truly believe, after many years of serving in ministry and from my own marriage, that a strong, Christ-focused marriage isn't just a nice idea – it's what God truly wants for every couple who chooses to build their life together on His plan. My goal is to help you look past all the confusing advice out there, which often gives easy answers to hard problems, and to point you, whether you're about to be married or just starting out, back to the divine precepts that have helped marriages last for thousands of years. You'll find my passion for this on every page; it's my sincere wish to help couples avoid common mistakes and instead build marriages that are strong, joyful, and honor God.

The Biblical Foundation of Marriage by the Book

What makes Marriage by the Book different is that I always point back to the Bible as the ultimate authority on marriage. In a world where people often think truth can change, this book holds onto the belief that God's Word gives us eternal counsel that works for everyone in every part of life, including marriage. From the first chapters, where I talk about God's divine design for creating us and for marriage – a plan that's often forgotten or ignored today – to the practical talks about how to communicate, solve problems, and be close to each other, everything I share is carefully based on what the Bible teaches. I don't offer quick fixes or simple tricks. Instead, I go deep into what it means to love like Christ loved the church, to talk with kindness and honesty, and to build a partnership that shows who God is. This book doesn't avoid the deeper spiritual truths about marriage; it celebrates them! I want to show you how understanding God's big plan for you can change every part of your life together. It's my invitation to you to move past a shallow idea of love and commitment and to embrace the kind of agape love, a covenant fidelity, that is at the center of a true, truly biblical marriage – a love that's like God's own faithful love for us.

Topics for a Strong Union

One of the main things I believe makes this book strong is how it covers so many important parts of getting ready for marriage. I know that a good marriage isn't built on just one thing but on many things working together: understanding what marriage is about, learning good relationship skills, and growing spiritually. So, in this book, I've tried to bring together a rich collection of topics, and I believe each one is very important for the journey you're about to take. I start by helping you build a strong foundation by looking at God's divine purpose for why He created us and the special place marriage has in that plan. When you see marriage this way, it becomes more than just a personal choice; it becomes a sacred vocation that can advance God's kingdom. This view helps us remember that our marriage is meant for something much bigger than just our own happiness.

Exploring Biblical Love

After that, I spent a good amount of time talking about what biblical love really is – something that our world today often gets wrong or makes seem less important. I use Bible passages like 1 Corinthians 13 to carefully explain what it means to love with patience, kindness, and a willingness to put others first. I show how this "agape" love is so different from the love we often see in the world, which can change quickly and depend on how we feel. I also explore the wonderful ways different kinds of love work together in marriage: agape (love that is unconditional and sacrificial), phileo (the love between good friends), storge (the natural affection in a family), and eros (romantic and physical love). I explain how each of these when we grow them according to God's plan, helps make a marriage strong and able to last.

As you prepare for marriage, I want to give you useful advice on the practical side of building a life together. The chapters on communication are, I believe, especially helpful. I offer biblical principles to help you talk openly, honestly, and with understanding for each other. These skills are so important for any healthy relationship, but they are absolutely key in the close relationship of marriage. I also know that arguments will happen in any close relationship, even one that is focused on Christ. So, I give you a way to work through disagreements that will make your marriage stronger, not weaker. This means learning to listen well, trying to understand each other, and working towards peace with a humble and gracious heart. The topic of intimacy, which can sometimes be hard to talk about, is handled with care and clear biblical teaching. I address not just physical intimacy as a gift from God within marriage but also the very important ways we connect emotionally, intellectually (with our minds), and spiritually. These connections help create a marriage that is strong in every way. I also strongly encourage premarital counseling. I don't see it as something for couples who are already having problems but as a smart, proactive way to invest in a healthy future. It's a chance to build a strong foundation before life's challenges come along. Beyond these, in Marriage by the Book, I also share wisdom on the challenges of raising children as a team, managing money together, and handling relationships with your extended families. These are all common areas where couples can face big problems if they are not ready.

I've tried to look at each of these areas with a good understanding of the pressures that couples face today, offering Bible-based advice that is both enduring and pertinent for this generation.

Lessons from Ministry

As I share these ideas with you, I'm not just talking about theories. I try to fill this book with practical wisdom that I've learned from my many years in ministry and from my own marriage of over forty years. When I dedicate this book to my wife, Christine, in the opening pages, it's a heartfelt way of showing that the ideas in this book are real and have been lived out. This personal experience, along with what I've learned from respected Christian writers and counselors, helps make the advice I offer both relatable and trustworthy. I'm not afraid to talk about the ways our culture often presents wrong ideas about love and marriage, and I want to help you learn to tell the difference between what's just a passing trend and what is abiding truth. I understand the real-life problems couples face: being too busy to connect in meaningful ways, carrying hurts from the past that can make it hard to be close, or feeling commitment fade in a world that often doesn't value staying together for the long haul. For all these, I offer biblical hope and real steps you can take to overcome them. I haven't written this book from a distant, perfect place, but from right in the middle of real life and real ministry, offering you both understanding and encouragement.

Standing on the Shoulders of Giants

I can hardly claim originality in this book or any of my other writings. As I consider the wisdom contained in these pages, I'm humbled by the realization that I stand on the shoulders of our forefathers and other giants of faith who endured, learned, wrote, and experienced so that we might have their example as we follow Christ in our generation. The writer of Ecclesiastes wisely noted that "there is no new thing under the sun"

(Ecclesiastes 1:9), and I claim that truth in this instance as well as we embark on this journey together. The principles of godly marriage have been established since the Garden of Eden, refined through the wisdom literature of Scripture, illuminated by the teachings of Christ, and applied by faithful believers throughout church history. I don't have the courage to call myself the author of this work, but I have humbly noted that this book title includes "with" myself rather than identifying me as the author of it. The notes throughout these pages underline the fact that we are relying on the work that so many others have done before us. Hebrews 13:7 instructs us to "Remember them which have the rule over you, who have spoken unto you the word of God: whose faith follow, considering the end of their conversation." This remembrance includes not only acknowledging those who have gone before us but also learning from their examples and teachings. The wisdom of these spiritual giants provides a foundation upon which we can build our understanding of God's design for marriage in our own time and context.

Aspirational Principles, Not Perfect Practice

As I present these biblical principles for marriage, I must acknowledge with humility that many of these teachings remain aspirational for my own marriage rather than fully lived realities. Like all believers, I am on a journey of sanctification, growing in grace and knowledge day by day. The apostle Paul's words in Philippians 3:12-14 resonate deeply with me: "Not as though I had already attained, either were already perfect: but I follow after if that I may apprehend that for which also I am apprehended of Christ Jesus."

Vision for Your Marriage: Hope

The main message I want you to take from Marriage by the Book is one of great hope. I want to encourage you to be intentional – to understand that a marriage that honors God doesn't just happen by accident. It's something you build, day by day, choice by choice, by staying committed to God's divine ordinances and to each other. I also want to emphasize that marriage is a journey where you keep learning and growing. When challenges come, I don't want you to see them as roadblocks that can't be overcome. Instead, see them as chances to grow more like Christ and to depend more on God. This way of looking at things is especially encouraging if you feel a bit scared about getting married or if you've seen other marriages struggle. This book will reassure you that, with God's divine favor and your willingness to follow His Word, a happy and lasting marriage is definitely possible. I encourage you to see your marriage not as something that stays the same but as a living relationship that needs constant care, effort, and a shared desire to grow in your faith together.

Addressing Life Challenges

One of the things I believe is most helpful about this book is how it deals directly with the real problems that couples face today. I don't try to paint a perfect picture of marriage without any troubles. Instead, I acknowledge the difficulties and pressures that can put a strain on even the best relationships. Whether it's learning to live with your different personalities, managing money worries in an unsure world, dealing with hurts from your past (from family or other relationships), or just trying to cope with how busy life is today, this book offers biblical wisdom and practical application to handle these things. Because it's realistic, the advice I offer is both relevant to your life and something you can actually use. I hope you'll appreciate that I try to be both understanding and firm, encouraging you to face problems head-on, using the Scriptural truth and the support of a loving church community. This book gives you tools not just to get through these challenges but to use them to become closer to each other and to rely more on God.

Your Marriage: A Testimony to God's Glory

In the end, Marriage by the Book is my call to you to aim for a bigger vision for your marriage – one that's about more than just your own happiness but about magnifying the glory of God. I want to remind you that marriage, when it's lived out God's way, is a testament to God's steadfast love. It's a vivid portrayal of Christ's devotion to His bride, the Church. When a husband and wife commit to loving each other as God planned, their marriage becomes a powerful testimony to everyone around them, showing them a little bit of the divine order and steadfastness that comes from following God's ways. This book will help you not just to survive in your marriage but to truly thrive. And by doing that, you'll bring glory to God, who created this special bond in the first place. I want to encourage you to see your marriage as a ministry, a way you can show the transformative power of the gospel in how you treat each other every day.

Embarking on Your Marriage Journey

This preface is just a small taste of the divine wisdom I've endeavored to impart into these pages. As you read Marriage by the Book, I hope you'll be ready to have some of your old ideas challenged, to be encouraged as you dream of a pious union, and to get the tools you need to build a covenant that endures and yields spiritual fruit. Whether you're just starting to think about engagement, are newly married and figuring things out, or want to make your long-term marriage even stronger by going back to foundational precepts, the ideas I share here can change how you see and experience marriage. It's my sincere hope that this book will be a faithful companion on your pilgrimage, guiding you to a marriage that is not only built by the Book but is also an abundant blessing to you, your spouse, and everyone you know. May you start this wonderful adventure with fortitude, discernment, and unwavering faith in the Sovereign God who ordained marriage for His divine glory and for our spiritual welfare. The path to a truly scriptural marriage is one of revelation, steadfastness, and divine grace, and I believe this book is an invaluable compass for every segment of that journey. Embrace its precepts, apply its wisdom with diligence and supplication, and watch as the Lord establishes your marriage as a beautiful testament to His unfailing love and covenant faithfulness – a clear demonstration of God's truth in a world that truly needs to see what authentic love manifests in actions.

Introduction

The Purpose And Importance Of Marriage Preparation

In today's rapidly changing world, the institution of marriage faces unprecedented challenges. Cultural shifts, evolving social norms, and competing worldviews have created an environment where many couples enter marriage unprepared for its demands and unaware of its divine purpose. Marriage by the Book: What Prospective Couples Should Know Before They Say I Do seeks to address this critical need by providing a comprehensive, biblically-grounded approach to marriage preparation that honors God's design while equipping couples with practical wisdom for their journey together.

The Current State Of Marriage

The landscape of marriage in contemporary society presents a troubling picture. Divorce rates, though slightly declining in recent years, remain alarmingly high, with nearly half of all marriages ending in dissolution. [1] Beyond these statistics lies a deeper reality: many marriages that remain intact suffer from dysfunction, disappointment, and disconnection. The prevalence of unhappy marriages suggests that simply avoiding divorce does not constitute success in God's eyes. As Marriage by the Book emphasizes throughout, God desires not merely the preservation of marriage as an institution but the flourishing of marriages that reflect His character and purposes.

What accounts for this troubling state of affairs? Several factors contribute to the fragility of modern marriages. First, many couples enter marriage with unrealistic expectations, influenced by romantic notions from media and entertainment rather than biblical wisdom. [2] The idea that marriage primarily exists for personal fulfillment and happiness sets couples up for disappointment when inevitable challenges arise. When difficulties

12

emerge—as they always do—couples lacking a biblical foundation may question the marriage itself rather than their expectations of it.

Second, our culture increasingly views marriage as a temporary arrangement rather than a lifelong covenant. The concept of "no-fault" divorce has normalized the breaking of marital vows when relationships become difficult. [3] This perspective stands in stark contrast to God's design for marriage as a permanent union that reflects His faithfulness to His people. The casual attitude toward marital commitment undermines the very stability that makes marriage a safe haven for vulnerability, growth, and intimacy.

Third, many couples receive inadequate preparation before marriage. The focus often centers on planning the wedding day rather than preparing for the marriage itself. [4] Without intentional preparation addressing biblical foundations, communication skills, conflict resolution, and other essential areas, couples lack the tools needed to build and maintain a God-honoring marriage. Marriage by the Book contends that this lack of preparation represents one of the most significant yet addressable factors in marital distress. Fourth, the increasing secularization of society has diminished understanding of marriage's spiritual dimensions. Many couples approach marriage as a purely human arrangement governed by personal preference rather than divine design. [5] Without recognizing marriage as a covenant established by God, couples miss the spiritual resources and biblical guidance that sustain marriages through difficulties. This book seeks to restore this spiritual foundation while providing practical applications.

The Biblical Vision For Marriage

In contrast to cultural confusion about marriage, Scripture presents a clear and compelling vision. From the opening chapters of Genesis to the closing pages of Revelation, the Bible portrays marriage as a divinely ordained institution with profound significance. Marriage by the Book is founded on the conviction that returning to this biblical vision provides the only solid foundation for marital success.

Genesis 2:24 establishes the fundamental nature of marriage: *"Therefore a man shall leave his father and his mother and hold fast to his wife, and they shall become one flesh."* [6] This passage reveals several key truths. Marriage involves leaving prior primary relationships, forming an exclusive bond with one's spouse, and experiencing a profound unity that encompasses all dimensions of human existence—physical, emotional, and spiritual. This "one flesh" union creates a new family unit distinct from the families of origin while maintaining appropriate honor toward parents.

Beyond this foundational text, Scripture develops a rich theology of marriage. In Ephesians 5:22-33, Paul reveals that marriage serves as a living picture of Christ's relationship with the Church. [7] This metaphor elevates marriage from a merely human arrangement to a sacred covenant with eternal significance. When husbands and wives fulfill their biblical roles, they participate in displaying the gospel to a watching world. This perspective transforms daily marital interactions from mundane exchanges to opportunities for spiritual witness.

The Bible also addresses the practical dimensions of marriage. Proverbs offers wisdom for daily marital life, emphasizing qualities like faithfulness, kindness, and mutual respect. [8] The Song of Solomon celebrates the beauty of physical intimacy within marriage's protective boundaries. [9] Throughout Scripture, we find guidance for navigating the joys and challenges of married life according to God's design. Marriage by the Book draws from this rich biblical tradition to provide couples with both theological understanding and practical application.

Scripture also acknowledges marriage's challenges in a fallen world. Jesus recognized that the hardness of the heart affects marital relationships

(Matthew 19:8), and Paul addressed specific marital difficulties in his letters to early churches. [10] The Bible never presents an idealized version of marriage that ignores human sinfulness and its relational consequences. Instead, it offers realistic guidance while pointing to God's grace as the ultimate resource for marital healing and growth.

Why Marriage Preparation Matters

Given both the cultural challenges facing marriage and the high calling of biblical marriage, preparation becomes not merely helpful but essential. Marriage by the Book contends that thorough preparation significantly increases the likelihood of building a marriage that honors God and brings joy to both spouses.

Research supports this conviction. Studies consistently show that couples who participate in comprehensive premarital education experience higher marital satisfaction and lower divorce rates than those who do not. [11] One landmark study found that couples who completed a structured premarital program were 31% less likely to divorce over a five-year period compared to couples without such preparation. [12] While statistics alone cannot capture the full value of marriage preparation, they confirm what Scripture suggests: wisdom before marriage contributes to flourishing within marriage.

Beyond statistical benefits, marriage preparation matters for several theological reasons. First, it acknowledges marriage as a divine institution deserving careful stewardship. Just as we would not approach other significant spiritual responsibilities without preparation, we should not enter marriage without thoughtful readiness. [13] Marriage by the Book emphasizes that honoring God through marriage begins before the wedding day, with intentional preparation that recognizes marriage's sacred character.

Second, preparation recognizes human fallenness and its impact on relationships. Since the Fall, all human relationships—including marriage—bear the effects of sin. Selfishness, pride, and poor communication do not magically disappear when couples say, "I do." [14] Effective preparation helps couples identify potential problem areas and develop strategies for addressing them from a biblical perspective. This realistic approach prevents disillusionment when marital challenges inevitably arise.

Third, preparation honors the covenant nature of marriage. Unlike casual relationships, marriage involves solemn vows made before God and witnesses. [15] These promises deserve serious consideration and preparation. Marriage by the Book emphasizes that understanding the weight of marital commitment before entering it leads to greater faithfulness in fulfilling that commitment. Preparation helps couples count the cost of covenant commitment and embrace it with full awareness.

Fourth, preparation establishes patterns that will serve couples throughout their marriage. The habits of communication, conflict resolution, and spiritual intimacy developed during engagement often carry into marriage. [16] By intentionally establishing healthy patterns before marriage, couples create a foundation for continued growth after the wedding. Marriage by the Book guides couples in developing these patterns through practical exercises and biblical reflection.

Effective Marriage Preparation

What constitutes effective marriage preparation? While many approaches exist, Marriage by the Book advocates a comprehensive framework addressing several key components.

First, couples need a solid theological foundation. Understanding God's purpose for marriage provides the necessary framework for everything else. [17] Without this foundation, couples may build their relationship on shifting cultural sands rather than biblical bedrock. This book begins with theological foundations precisely because they inform and shape all other aspects of marriage. When couples grasp God's design for marriage, practical decisions flow from this understanding rather than from cultural assumptions.

Second, couples must develop practical relationship skills. Communication patterns established during dating and engagement often carry into marriage. [18] Learning to communicate effectively, resolve conflicts biblically, and build emotional intimacy prepares couples for the daily work of marriage. These skills do not develop automatically but require intentional learning and practice. Marriage by the Book provides specific guidance for developing these skills within a biblical framework.

Third, couples benefit from exploring specific topics relevant to married life. Financial management, sexual expectations, family planning, and relationships with extended family represent just a few areas where unexamined assumptions can lead to significant conflict. [19] Addressing these topics before marriage allows couples to identify potential differences and develop shared approaches. This book guides couples through conversations about these crucial topics, offering biblical principles for each area.

Fourth, couples should seek wisdom from experienced mentors. While books and formal programs provide valuable information, the guidance of mature Christian couples offers unique benefits. [20] These mentors can share their experiences, provide accountability, and model what a God-honoring marriage looks like in practice. Marriage by the Book encourages readers to supplement their study with mentoring relationships. The wisdom gained from those who have walked the marriage path for decades proves invaluable for those just beginning the journey.

Finally, couples must nurture their spiritual lives individually and together. The strength of a marriage correlates strongly with the spiritual vitality of the spouses. [21] Developing habits of prayer, Bible study, and worship—both separately and as a couple—establishes patterns that will sustain the marriage through future challenges. Throughout this book, couples will find guidance for growing spiritually together, recognizing that a marriage centered on Christ stands on the strongest possible foundation.

The Role Of The Church

While individual couples bear primary responsibility for their preparation, the church plays a vital supporting role. Throughout history, Christian communities have recognized their responsibility to prepare and support couples for marriage. [22] Marriage by the Book affirms this historical commitment and calls churches to renewed engagement with marriage preparation.

Churches contribute to marriage preparation in several ways. First, they provide biblical teaching about marriage through sermons, classes, and counseling. [23] This teaching helps form a congregation's understanding of marriage according to God's design rather than cultural patterns. When pastors and teachers present a consistent biblical vision of marriage, they create a context where healthy marriages can flourish.

Second, churches offer structured premarital counseling programs. Many congregations require couples to complete such programs before performing their weddings. [24] These programs typically include assessment tools, discussion of key topics, and practical guidance for building a strong marriage. Marriage by the Book can serve as a resource for such programs, providing a comprehensive curriculum grounded in Scripture.

Third, churches provide community support for marriages. When couples belong to a congregation that values marriage, they gain access to examples, encouragement, and accountability. [25] This community context proves especially valuable during difficult seasons when couples might otherwise isolate themselves. The church offers a counter-cultural environment where covenant marriage receives honor and support rather than the casual treatment often found in broader society.

Fourth, churches connect couples with resources for ongoing marriage enrichment. Marriage preparation does not end with the wedding day but continues throughout the marriage journey. [26] Churches that offer marriage retreats, small groups for couples, and counseling services help couples continue growing together. Marriage by the Book encourages couples to remain connected to such resources throughout their marriage, recognizing that growth requires ongoing investment.

Overcoming Resistance To Marriage Preparation

Despite its importance, many couples resist thorough marriage preparation. Several factors contribute to this resistance. Some couples, caught up in wedding planning, simply fail to prioritize preparation for the marriage itself. [27] Others feel confident in their relationship and see no need for formal preparation. Still, others fear that addressing potential problem areas might reveal incompatibilities or create conflict.

Marriage by the Book acknowledges these concerns while gently challenging couples to overcome their resistance. The book emphasizes that preparation represents an investment in the marriage's future health rather than an unnecessary burden. [28] Just as wise builders would not construct a house without proper planning and materials, wise couples should not build a marriage without adequate preparation. The time invested before marriage often prevents years of struggle afterward.

For couples already engaged in wedding planning, this book offers practical suggestions for integrating marriage preparation into their schedule.

[29] The investment of time before marriage often saves countless hours of conflict resolution later. Furthermore, the book reassures couples that identifying differences before marriage provides an opportunity to address them constructively rather than a reason to panic. Discovering areas of potential conflict before marriage allows couples to develop strategies for handling these differences within the safety of premarital preparation.

Some couples resist preparation because they believe their love will naturally overcome any obstacles. While romantic love provides an important emotional connection, it cannot substitute for intentional preparation. [30] Marriage by the Book helps couples understand that preparing for marriage demonstrates love rather than undermining it. By investing in preparation, couples show their commitment to building a relationship that will thrive for a lifetime.

The Approach In This Book

Marriage by the Book offers a distinctive approach to marriage preparation grounded in biblical truth and practical wisdom. Unlike some resources that focus narrowly on either theological foundations or practical skills, this book integrates both dimensions. Each chapter builds on a biblical foundation while providing concrete applications for daily married life.

The book's organization follows a logical progression. It begins with God's purpose for marriage, establishing the theological framework for everything that follows. [31] Subsequent chapters address specific aspects of marriage: biblical love, biblical foundations, communication, conflict resolution, intimacy, premarital counseling, parenting, spiritual growth, extended family relationships, and maintaining a healthy marriage long-term. This comprehensive approach ensures that couples receive guidance for all major dimensions of married life.

Throughout these chapters, Marriage by the Book maintains several commitments. First, it remains firmly grounded in Scripture, recognizing the Bible as the ultimate authority for understanding and practicing marriage. [32] Second, it speaks with a pastoral voice, offering encouragement alongside instruction. Third, it provides practical guidance that couples can immediately apply to their relationships. This combination of biblical fidelity, pastoral sensitivity, and practical application distinguishes Marriage by the Book from many other marriage resources.

The book serves several audiences. Engaged couples will find it a comprehensive guide for marriage preparation. Dating couples considering marriage can use it to evaluate their readiness and compatibility. Newly married couples can benefit from its wisdom as they establish patterns for their life together. Even long-married couples may discover fresh insights for strengthening their relationship. While primarily written for those preparing for marriage, the principles apply throughout the marriage journey.

Using This Book Effectively

Readers should approach it with intentionality and commitment to gain maximum benefit from Marriage by the Book. Several suggestions may enhance the learning experience.

First, read the book with your partner rather than alone. Marriage preparation works best as a shared journey of discovery. [33] Schedule regular times to read and discuss the content together, creating space for honest conversation about the topics addressed. These discussions often reveal important insights about yourselves and your relationship that might otherwise remain undiscovered.

Second, engage with the reflection questions at the end of each chapter. These questions move beyond theoretical understanding to personal application. [34] Take time to consider your responses individually before discussing them together, allowing for both personal reflection and mutual sharing. Writing down your thoughts often leads to deeper insights than mental reflection alone.

Third, supplement your reading with conversations with mature Christian couples. Their lived experience provides valuable context for the principles discussed in the book. [35] Consider asking such a couple to meet with you regularly as you work through the material, providing guidance and accountability. Their perspective can help you apply the book's principles to your specific relationship circumstances.

Fourth, view this book as the beginning rather than the end of your marriage preparation. The topics introduced here deserve ongoing exploration throughout your relationship. [36] Use the recommended resources to continue learning in areas particularly relevant to your relationship. Marriage preparation represents a lifelong process rather than a one-time event completed before the wedding.

Fifth, practice the skills described in this book. Knowledge about communication or conflict resolution has little value without implementation. [37] Set aside time to practice these skills in low-stress situations so they become natural when you face real challenges. Like any important ability, marital skills improve with consistent practice and feedback.

Finally, approach this journey with prayer. Marriage preparation involves not merely acquiring information but seeking God's wisdom and grace. [38] Pray individually and together for God to guide your preparation and bless your future marriage. Recognize your dependence on Him for understanding and applying the principles in Marriage by the Book.

Conclusion

The journey toward a God-honoring marriage begins long before the wedding day. Through intentional preparation, couples lay a foundation that will support their relationship through the joys and challenges of married life. Marriage by the Book: What Prospective Couples Should Know Before They Say I Do provides a roadmap for this crucial preparation process.

In the chapters that follow, we will explore God's design for marriage and the practical implications of that design. We will examine biblical principles for love, communication, intimacy, and other vital aspects of marriage. We will address common challenges and guide navigating them successfully. Throughout this exploration, our goal remains consistent: to help couples build marriages that reflect God's character, advance His purposes, and bring joy to both partners.

Your investment in marriage preparation now will yield dividends throughout your life together. By understanding God's purpose for marriage and developing the skills needed to fulfill that purpose, you position yourselves for a relationship that honors Him and blesses you. May God guide you on this journey of preparation for one of life's most sacred covenants.

Chapter 1

God's Purpose For Creation And Marriage

Why Did God Create Us?

God didn't need us. Before time began, He existed in perfect fellowship as Father, Son, and Holy Spirit. Yet, out of His abundant love, He chose to create us. Not because He was lonely or incomplete, but for His glory and our joy.[1]

Isaiah puts it beautifully when he writes that God created everyone *"called by my name for my glory."* Think about that for a moment. You were created to display God's glory! This isn't about God having an ego—it's about Him sharing His goodness with us.[2]

Jesus prayed about this glory before His crucifixion: "Father, glorify me in your own presence with the glory that I had with you before the world existed." This eternal glory wasn't meant to be kept private—Jesus wanted us to experience it too: "Father, I desire that they also, whom you have given me, may be with me where I am, to see my glory."[3]

The Westminster Shorter Catechism captures this truth succinctly when it asks, "What is the chief end of man?" The answer: "Man's chief end is to glorify God and enjoy Him forever." This dual purpose—glorifying and enjoying—defines our existence and gives meaning to all human relationships, especially marriage.[4]

As John Piper explains, "God created us to live for His glory, and He created marriage to display that glory in a unique way." When we understand that our primary purpose is to glorify God, it transforms how we approach every aspect of life, including our marriages.[5]

24

Our Purpose: Glory and Joy

So what does this mean for our everyday lives? Simply put, we're here to glorify God and enjoy Him forever. These two purposes—glorifying and enjoying—go hand in hand.

Paul reminds us in 1 Corinthians 10:31 to *"do all to the glory of God,"* whether eating, drinking, or anything else. This includes our marriages! When we understand that even our most ordinary activities can honor God, it transforms how we view our relationships. As John Piper notes, *"God is most glorified in us when we are most satisfied in Him."* [6]

But God doesn't just want our dutiful obedience—He wants us to find joy in Him. Jesus said, "I came that they may have life and have it abundantly." David discovered this joy in God's presence: "In your presence, there is fullness of joy; at your right hand are pleasures forevermore."[7]

Have you experienced this? When we begin to grasp how wonderful God truly is, our hearts naturally respond in worship. We want to love Him with everything we have—"heart, soul, mind, and strength." As Augustine famously said, our hearts are restless until they find rest in God. [8]

R.C. Sproul emphasizes that "the pursuit of God's glory and the pursuit of our joy are not at odds. They are one and the same pursuit." This understanding is crucial for marriage. When we seek God's glory in our marriages, we discover the deepest joy possible in human relationships.[9]

The Relationship Between Glory and Joy

This connection between glorifying God and enjoying Him deserves deeper exploration, especially as it relates to marriage. Many Christians mistakenly believe that glorifying God means denying themselves any pleasure or joy. They think that the more miserable they are, the more God is glorified. But this couldn't be further from the truth.[10]

God designed us to find our deepest satisfaction in Him. When we delight in God, we glorify Him by demonstrating that He is the source of true joy. As C.S. Lewis famously observed, "God is most glorified in us when we are most satisfied in Him." Our joy in God magnifies His worth, just as our enjoyment of a magnificent sunset honors the beauty of God's creation.[11]

In marriage, this means that God is glorified when husbands and wives find deep joy in their relationship—not a shallow, self-centered happiness, but a profound delight that flows from living according to God's design. When a couple builds their marriage on biblical principles, they experience the joy God intended, which in turn brings glory to Him as the designer of marriage.[12]

As Timothy Keller writes, "Marriage was designed to be a reflection of the covenant love between Christ and the church. When that design is honored, both joy and glory result." Our marriages are meant to be signposts pointing to God's goodness and wisdom in creating this unique relationship.[13]

Three Pillars of Society

In His wisdom, God established three foundational institutions for human society: the family, government, and church. Each plays a vital role in His design. Wayne Grudem explains that "these three institutions have different spheres of authority, and each is directly responsible to God."[14]

Understanding these divine institutions helps us see marriage in its proper context. Marriage isn't just a personal arrangement between two individuals—it's part of God's larger design for ordering society and reflecting His character.

The Family: God's First Institution

The family came first. Before sin entered the world, before nations formed, and before the church began—God created marriage and family. Remember His assessment in Eden? *"It is not good that the man should be alone; I will make him a helper fit for him."*[15]

This was the only time God looked at His creation and said something wasn't good! Adam needed Eve—not just for companionship but to fulfill God's purposes for humanity. Together, they formed the first family unit. As Andreas Köstenberger observes, "Marriage and the family are institutions under siege in our world today, and only a return to the biblical foundation will reverse the decline of marriage and the family in our culture."[16]

Marriage and family aren't human inventions or social constructs that evolve with the times. They're divine institutions with specific purposes. Throughout Scripture, God provides guidance for family relationships:

"Wives, submit to your husbands. Husbands, love your wives as Christ loved the church. Children, obey your parents" (Ephesians 5:22, 25; 6:1).

"Train up a child in the way he should go; even when he is old, he will not depart from it" (Proverbs 22:6).[17]

The family is where faith, character, and values are nurtured and passed down. It's where we first learn about love, trust, forgiveness, and sacrifice— the very qualities that reflect God's nature. Voddie Baucham emphasizes that "the family is the first and most fundamental of all human institutions that God ordained."[18]

In God's design, the family serves several crucial purposes:

1) **Procreation and child-rearing:** *"Be fruitful and multiply and fill the earth"* (Genesis 1:28). Through marriage and family, God designed

for humanity to continue and for children to be raised in stable, loving environments.[19]

2) **Companionship and mutual support:** *"It is not good that the man should be alone"* (Genesis 2:18). God created us for a relationship, and marriage provides the most intimate human relationship possible.[20]

3) **Character development:** Family life, with all its joys and challenges, shapes us in profound ways. As James Dobson notes, "Nothing reveals character like marriage and parenthood." The daily give-and-take of family relationships develops patience, selflessness, and love.[21]

4) **Spiritual formation:** Deuteronomy 6:6-7 instructs parents to teach God's commands diligently to their children. The family is God's primary context for passing faith to the next generation.[22]

5) **Social stability:** Strong families create strong communities. When marriage and family break down, society suffers. As R. Albert Mohler observes, "The family is the most basic unit of society. When it functions according to God's design, it provides the stability necessary for human flourishing."[23]

The Primacy of the Family

It's worth emphasizing that the family was God's first institution—established before civil government or even formal religious structures. This primacy speaks to its fundamental importance in God's design for human society. As Herman Bavinck notes, "The family is not founded by the state or the church, but precedes both and has its own sovereign sphere."[24]

This has profound implications for how we view the relationship between family, government, and church. While all three institutions are ordained by God, the family has a unique priority. The government and church should support and strengthen families, not undermine or replace them.[25]

In our culture, this order is often inverted. The state increasingly encroaches on family authority, particularly in education and child-rearing. Even churches sometimes create programs that inadvertently separate family members rather than equipping families to function as God designed.[26]

As Christians preparing for marriage, we need to reclaim this biblical understanding of the family's primacy. Our marriages and future families aren't just private arrangements but vital building blocks of God's design for society. When we build strong, God-honoring marriages, we contribute to the health of both church and society.[27]

The Government: God's Second Institution

After the family, God established a civil government. Romans 13:1-7 teaches that governing authorities are *"instituted by God"* and serve as His *"servants"* for maintaining order and justice. The government's primary role is to protect citizens, punish evildoers, and create conditions where people can live peacefully.[28]

Government relates to marriage in several ways:

1. **Legal recognition:** The government provides a legal structure for marriage through laws regarding marriage licenses, property rights, inheritance, etc.
2. **Protection:** The government should protect the institution of marriage and family from harmful influences.
3. **Boundaries:** While the government has legitimate authority in the civil realm, it should respect the God-given autonomy of the family.[29]

As Christians, we're called to honor governing authorities (Romans 13:1-7; 1 Peter 2:13-17) while recognizing that their authority is limited and derived from God. When government oversteps its boundaries—particularly in matters of faith and family—we must *"obey God rather than men"* (Acts 5:29).[30]

The Church: God's Third Institution

The church, established by Christ (Matthew 16:18), is God's community of believers. It serves as the *"pillar and foundation of the truth"* (1 Timothy 3:15) and the body of Christ on earth (1 Corinthians 12:27).[31]

The church relates to marriage in several important ways:

1. **Teaching:** The church teaches God's design for marriage and equips couples to build strong, Christ-centered relationships.
2. **Accountability:** The church provides community support and accountability for marriages.
3. **Restoration:** When marriages struggle, the church offers counsel, support, and pathways to healing.[32]

As Bryan Chapell notes, "The church doesn't create marriage, but it does have a sacred responsibility to uphold God's design for marriage and to support couples in living out that design." The church's role is not to replace the family but to strengthen it.[33]

The Harmony of God's Institutions

God designed these three institutions—family, government, and church—to work in harmony, each fulfilling its unique role. Problems arise when one institution usurps the authority of another or fails in its responsibilities.[34]

For example, when families abdicate their responsibility to raise and educate children, the government or church may step in to fill the gap. While this may be necessary in some cases, it's not ideal. Similarly, when government overreaches into family matters or when churches fail to teach biblical truth about marriage, the harmony is disrupted.[35]

As you prepare for marriage, consider how your future family will relate to the government and church. How will you honor governing authorities while maintaining your family's God-given autonomy? How will you engage with the church in ways that strengthen rather than fragment your family?[36]

The Biblical Foundation for Marriage

Having explored God's purpose for creation and His establishment of family, government, and church, let's now focus specifically on marriage. What is God's design for this unique relationship?

Marriage Defined: One Man and One Woman in Covenant

From the very beginning, God designed marriage as a covenant relationship between one man and one woman. Genesis 2:24 states, *"Therefore a man shall leave his father and his mother and hold fast to his wife, and they shall become one flesh."* Jesus affirmed this definition when He quoted this passage and added, *"What therefore God has joined together, let not man separate"* (Matthew 19:4-6).[37]

Several key elements define biblical marriage:

1. **Gender complementarity:** Marriage unites male and female, who are equal in value but different in role and function. As John MacArthur explains, "God created male and female with equal dignity but with different and complementary roles. These differences are not cultural but divinely designed."[38]

2. **Covenant commitment:** Marriage is not merely a contract but a covenant—a binding relationship established by solemn vows before God. As Michael Horton notes, "A covenant differs from a contract in that it creates a relationship bond rather than merely an exchange of services."[39]

3. **Permanence:** God intended marriage to be lifelong. While Scripture allows for divorce in limited circumstances (Matthew 19:9; 1 Corinthians 7:15), this is a concession to human sinfulness, not God's original design.[40]

31

4. **Exclusivity:** Marriage is an exclusive relationship. The command against adultery (Exodus 20:14) underscores God's requirement for sexual fidelity within marriage.[41]

5. **Sexual union:** Physical intimacy is an essential aspect of marriage. Paul teaches that spouses' bodies belong to each other and encourages regular sexual relations within marriage (1 Corinthians 7:3-5).[42]

This biblical definition stands in stark contrast to our culture's evolving views of marriage. Today, marriage is often seen as a temporary arrangement based on emotional fulfillment rather than a lifelong covenant. As R. Albert Mohler observes, "The modern concept of marriage as primarily a vehicle for personal happiness and self-fulfillment is a radical departure from the biblical understanding."[43]

The Distortion of Marriage in Our Culture

Our culture's understanding of marriage has undergone dramatic changes in recent decades. These changes didn't happen overnight but resulted from gradual shifts in worldview and values. Understanding these distortions helps us recognize how countercultural biblical marriage has become.[44]

Several key distortions have undermined marriage in our society:

1. **Individualism:** Our culture prioritizes individual fulfillment over commitment and sacrifice. Marriage is viewed primarily as a means of personal happiness rather than a covenant relationship that reflects God's character.[45]

2. **Redefinition:** The legal definition of marriage has been expanded beyond one man and one woman, contradicting God's design established in creation.[46]

3. **Devaluation:** With the rise of cohabitation, no-fault divorce, and other alternatives to traditional marriage, the institution itself has been devalued. Marriage is now often seen as just one lifestyle option among many rather than the foundation of family and society.[47]

4. **Confusion of roles:** Biblical teaching about distinct yet complementary roles for husbands and wives has been rejected in favor of interchangeable roles or complete role reversal.[48]

5. **Separation from procreation:** Contraception, reproductive technologies, and changing attitudes have separated marriage from its procreative purpose, making children optional rather than integral to marriage.[49]

As James Dobson writes, "The institution of marriage represents the very foundation of human social order. Everything of value sits on that base. Institutions, governments, religious fervor, and the welfare of children are all dependent on its stability."[50]

The consequences of these distortions are evident in rising divorce rates, declining marriage rates, increasing numbers of children born outside marriage, and widespread confusion about gender and sexuality. These trends affect not just individuals but society as a whole.[51]

As Christians preparing for marriage, we must recognize how deeply our cultural context has been shaped by these distortions. Building a God-honoring marriage requires swimming against the cultural current and intentionally embracing biblical principles that may seem countercultural or even offensive to contemporary sensibilities.[52]

God's Purposes for Marriage

Why did God create marriage? What purposes did He intend this unique relationship to serve? Scripture reveals several divine purposes for marriage:

1. Companionship

God's first statement about human need was, *"It is not good that the man should be alone"* (Genesis 2:18). He created Eve as a "helper fit for" Adam—someone corresponding to him, suitable for him, his counterpart. Marriage addresses our deep need for intimate companionship.[53]

This companionship involves friendship, partnership, and mutual support. As Gary Thomas observes, "God designed marriage to be a place where two people help each other become all that God intended them to be." In marriage, we find someone to share life's joys and sorrows, someone who knows us deeply and loves us anyway.[54]

The companionship of marriage provides a safe haven in a broken world. As Ecclesiastes 4:9-12 beautifully expresses: *"Two are better than one... For if they fall, one will lift up his fellow. But woe to him who is alone when he falls and has not another to lift him up!... And though a man might prevail against one who is alone, two will withstand him—a threefold cord is not quickly broken."*[55]

This companionship aspect of marriage addresses the fundamental human need for belonging and connection. God created us as relational beings, and marriage provides the most intimate human relationship possible. As Timothy Keller notes, "Marriage is a unique kind of friendship that meets our deep need to be known and loved."[56]

2. Procreation and Child-Rearing

God's first command to humanity was to *"be fruitful and multiply and fill the earth"* (Genesis 1:28). While not every marriage results in children, procreation is one of marriage's fundamental purposes. Marriage provides the ideal context for bringing children into the world and raising them.[57]

Children benefit tremendously from being raised by their biological mother and father in a stable, committed marriage. Decades of social science research confirm what Scripture has always taught—that God's design for the family best serves children's needs. As Andreas Köstenberger notes, "Children need both a mother and a father, each contributing unique and complementary qualities to their development."[58]

Marriage creates the stable environment children need to flourish. It provides them with a sense of identity, security, and belonging. It gives them daily examples of how men and women relate to each other in healthy ways. And it creates the context for passing on faith and values to the next generation.[59]

The procreative purpose of marriage doesn't mean that couples who cannot have children have "failed" or have less valuable marriages. Infertility is a painful reality for many couples, and Scripture provides examples of godly marriages that were childless (like Abraham and Sarah for many years). Yet the general pattern God established is for marriage to be the context for bearing and raising children.[60]

3. Sanctification

While not often discussed, one of God's key purposes for marriage is our sanctification—our growth in holiness and Christlikeness. Marriage reveals our selfishness and sin, as few other relationships can. It then provides the context for addressing these issues and growing in godly character.[61]

As Gary Thomas provocatively asks in his book *Sacred Marriage*, "What if God designed marriage to make us holy more than to make us happy?" This doesn't mean marriage shouldn't bring happiness—it certainly should. But its ultimate purpose is even higher—to conform us to the image of Christ.[62]

Marriage serves as a "laboratory of sanctification" where we learn to love sacrificially, forgive repeatedly, serve humbly, and persevere faithfully. The daily challenges of living with another imperfect person provide countless opportunities to develop patience, kindness, gentleness, and self-control—the very qualities that reflect Christ's character.[63]

Dave Harvey observes, "God didn't create marriage just to give us a pleasant means of repopulating the world and providing a steady societal institution to raise children. He planted marriage among humans as yet another signpost pointing to His own eternal, spiritual existence."[64]

This sanctifying purpose of marriage explains why marriage can be simultaneously so challenging and so rewarding. The very difficulties that test us are often God's tools for shaping us into the people He wants us to become.[65]

4. Sexual Fulfillment

God designed sexual intimacy to be expressed exclusively within marriage. Paul writes in 1 Corinthians 7:2-5:

"But because of the temptation to sexual immorality, each man should have his own wife and each woman her own husband. The husband should give his wife her conjugal rights, and likewise, the wife to her husband... Do not deprive one another, except perhaps by agreement for a limited time, that you may devote yourselves to prayer; but then come together again, so that Satan may not tempt you because of your lack of self-control." [66]

This passage reveals that one purpose of marriage is to provide a legitimate context for sexual expression. God created sexual desire, and He provided marriage as the exclusive relationship for fulfilling that desire. As Ed Wheat explains, "Sexual intimacy in marriage is not just permitted but celebrated in Scripture as a good gift from God." [67]

The Song of Solomon celebrates the beauty and pleasure of physical intimacy within marriage. Far from viewing sexuality negatively, Scripture presents it as God's good gift to married couples—a gift that brings pleasure, creates bonding and potentially leads to the blessing of children.[68]

This sexual dimension of marriage serves several purposes:

- It creates a unique bond between husband and wife
- It provides pleasure and delight
- It potentially leads to procreation
- It meets legitimate physical needs
- It protects against temptation[69]

As C.J. and Carolyn Mahaney write, "God designed sexual intimacy not just for procreation but for pleasure, protection, and profound union." When expressed according to God's design, sexual intimacy enhances and complements the other dimensions of marital love.[70]

5. Reflection of Christ and the Church

Perhaps the most profound purpose of marriage is to reflect the relationship between Christ and His church. Paul reveals this mystery in Ephesians 5:31-32: "'Therefore a man shall leave his father and mother and hold fast to his wife, and the two shall become one flesh.' This mystery is profound, and I am saying that it refers to Christ and the church." [71]

Marriage serves as a living parable of the gospel—a visible representation of Christ's covenant love for His people. As Ray Ortlund explains, "Every human marriage is meant to reflect something of the beauty, love, and faithfulness between Jesus and His bride, the church."[72]

This purpose elevates marriage from a merely human institution to a divine portrait. When a husband loves his wife sacrificially as Christ loved the church, and when a wife respects and submits to her husband as the church does to Christ, their marriage becomes a powerful testimony to the gospel.[73]

This reflection works in both directions. Not only does marriage reflect Christ and the church, but Christ and the church provide the pattern for marriage. Husbands learn how to love their wives by looking at Christ's love for the church. Wives learn how to relate to their husbands by considering how the church relates to Christ.[74]

As Timothy Keller observes, "Marriage was designed to be a reflection of the covenant love between Christ and the church. When that design is honored, both joy and glory result." Our marriages are meant to be signposts pointing to God's goodness and wisdom in creating this unique relationship.[75]

The Complementary Roles in Marriage

Having explored God's purposes for marriage, let's now consider the distinct yet complementary roles He designed for husbands and wives. This topic has become controversial in our culture, but Scripture provides clear guidance.[76]

Equal in Value, Different in Role

The biblical teaching on marriage roles begins with the fundamental equality of men and women. Genesis 1:27 states that God created both male and female in His image. Galatians 3:28 affirms that in Christ, there is *"neither male nor female,"* indicating equal standing before God.[77]

This equality of value and dignity is essential to understand before discussing different roles. As Wayne Grudem explains, "The Bible teaches both the equality of men and women as persons before God and the distinct roles that God has given to men and women in marriage. These two truths complement rather than contradict each other."[78]

Difference in role does not imply a difference in worth, just as the different roles within the Trinity don't imply that the Son is less divine than the Father. Jesus submitted to the Father's will yet remained fully God. Similarly, when wives submit to their husbands, they do so as equals in personhood and value.[79]

The Husband's Role: Loving Leadership

Ephesians 5:23 states, *"The husband is the head of the wife even as Christ is the head of the church."* This headship is not about domination or superiority but about loving leadership and responsibility.[80]

What does this headship involve? Paul elaborates in Ephesians 5:25-29:

"Husbands, love your wives, as Christ loved the church and gave himself up for her, that he might sanctify her, having cleansed her by the washing of water with the word, so that he might present the church to himself in splendor, without spot or wrinkle or any such thing, that she might be holy and without blemish. In the same way, husbands should love their wives as their own bodies. He who loves his wife loves himself. For no one ever hated his own flesh, but nourishes and cherishes it, just as Christ does the church."[81]

This passage reveals several aspects of a husband's role:

1. **Sacrificial love:** The husband is called to love his wife as Christ loved the church—sacrificially, putting her needs before his own. As John MacArthur notes, "The husband who loves his wife as Christ loved the church will give up everything he has for her, including his life if necessary."[82]

2. **Spiritual leadership:** The husband has responsibility for the spiritual well-being of his family. This doesn't mean he's spiritually superior but that he's accountable for leading his family in following Christ.[83]

3. **Provision and protection:** Just as Christ nourishes and cherishes the church, husbands are to provide for and protect their wives. 1 Timothy 5:8 states, *"If anyone does not provide for his relatives, and especially for members of his household, he has denied the faith and is worse than an unbeliever."[84]*

4. **Servant leadership:** Jesus modeled leadership as service (Mark 10:42-45). Similarly, a husband's headship is expressed through serving his wife, not lording authority over her.[85]

This biblical model of headship stands in stark contrast to both domineering authoritarianism and passive abdication. A husband's authority is always to be exercised in love, with his wife's best interests at heart.[86]

The Wife's Role: Respectful Submission

Ephesians 5:22-24 instructs: *"Wives, submit to your own husbands, as to the Lord. For the husband is the head of the wife even as Christ is the head of the church, his body, and is himself its Savior. Now, as the church submits to Christ, so also wives should submit in everything to their husbands."*[87]

This submission is often misunderstood in our culture. Biblical submission is not:

- Inferiority or lesser value
- Blind obedience
- Absence of influence or input
- Applicable only to wives (all Christians are called to submit in various contexts)
- Permission for abuse or mistreatment[88]

Rather, biblical submission involves:

1. **Voluntary respect and honor:** Ephesians 5:33 calls wives to "respect" their husbands. This respect acknowledges the husband's God-given responsibility as head of the family.[89]
2. **Support and cooperation:** Submission means working with, not against, the husband's leadership. As Carolyn Mahaney explains, "Submission is the divine calling of a wife to honor and affirm her

husband's leadership and help carry it through according to her gifts."[90]

3. **Recognition of order:** Submission acknowledges God's created order for the family. This doesn't diminish the wife's intelligence, capabilities, or worth but recognizes the structure God designed for family harmony.[91]

4. **Influence through wisdom:** A submissive wife still offers counsel, perspective, and wisdom. Proverbs 31 describes a wife of noble character who speaks with wisdom and provides valuable input to her husband.[92]

The biblical pattern of wifely submission is modeled on the church's relationship to Christ—willing, loving, and respectful. It's never forced or demanded but freely given out of reverence for God's design.[93]

Mutual Submission and Service

While Scripture teaches distinct roles for husbands and wives, it also emphasizes mutual submission and service. Ephesians 5:21 instructs believers to *"submit to one another out of reverence for Christ,"* establishing the context for the specific instructions that follow.[94]

This mutual submission is expressed in different ways according to each person's role, but the attitude of humility and service should characterize both husband and wife. As Peter writes, *"All of you, clothe yourselves with humility toward one another"* (1 Peter 5:5).[95]

In practice, this means:

1. Both spouses put the other's needs before their own (Philippians 2:3-4).
2. Both seek to serve rather than be served (Mark 10:45).
3. Both contribute their gifts, strengths, and perspectives to the marriage.
4. Both show honor and respect to each other (Romans 12:10).[96]

As Bryan Chapell observes, "The dance of marriage requires both partners to make movements of grace toward each other. The husband leads with love; the wife responds with respect. Both submit to Christ and serve one another."[97]

Preparing for Biblical Marriage Roles

As you prepare for marriage, it's important to discuss and align your expectations regarding roles. Our culture offers many competing models of marriage, and even within Christian circles, there are different interpretations of these biblical principles.[98]

Consider discussing these questions with your future spouse:

1. What does headship look like in practical terms? How will decisions be made?
2. How will you balance career and family responsibilities?
3. What examples of biblical marriage roles have you observed? Which do you want to emulate?
4. How might your family background influence your expectations about roles?
5. In what areas might role confusion or conflict arise? How will you address these?[99]

Remember that growing into these roles is a lifelong process. Few couples perfectly embody biblical ideals from day one. With grace, communication, and commitment to Scripture, you can develop a marriage that increasingly reflects God's design.[100]

Conclusion: Building on God's Design

As we conclude this exploration of God's purpose for creation and marriage, let's summarize the key principles we've discovered:

1. God created us for His glory and our joy. These purposes are not in conflict but are fulfilled together as we delight in Him.
2. God established three foundational institutions—family, government, and church—each with distinct but complementary roles in society.
3. Marriage is God's design for the union of one man and one woman in a covenant relationship that reflects Christ's relationship with the church.
4. God's purposes for marriage include companionship, procreation, sanctification, sexual fulfillment, and reflecting Christ and the church.
5. God designed husbands and wives with equal value but different, complementary roles that, when embraced, lead to harmony and flourishing.[101]

These biblical foundations provide the framework for building a God-honoring marriage. When we align our understanding and expectations with Scripture rather than culture, we position ourselves for a marriage that brings glory to God and joy to us.[102]

As you prepare for marriage, I encourage you to:

1. Study Scripture together to deepen your understanding of God's design.

2. Seek mentoring from couples who exemplify biblical marriage principles.

3. Discuss your expectations about roles, responsibilities, and decision-making.

4. Commit to building your marriage on God's unchanging truth rather than shifting cultural trends.[103]

In the next chapter, we'll explore the nature of biblical love and how it forms the foundation for a lasting, fulfilling marriage. We'll discover how love, as defined in Scripture, differs dramatically from our culture's understanding and how we can cultivate this kind of love in our relationships.[104]

Chapter 2
Understanding Biblical Love

What Is Love?

Love. Perhaps no word in the English language has been more misused, misunderstood, and misapplied. Our culture bombards us with messages about love—from romantic comedies and love songs to dating apps and relationship advice columns. We're told to "follow our hearts" and that "love conquers all." But what is love, really?[1]

As Christians preparing for marriage, we need a biblical understanding of love that goes far beyond the shallow, feeling-based definitions our culture offers. The stakes couldn't be higher. Without a proper understanding of biblical love, marriages crumble under the weight of unrealistic expectations and self-centered desires.

In this chapter, we'll explore what the Bible teaches about love—not just romantic love, but the multifaceted, rich concept of love that God reveals in His Word. We'll examine different types of biblical love, contrast them with cultural counterfeits, and discover how understanding biblical love transforms our approach to marriage.[2]

The Four Greek Words for Love

The English language has just one word for love, which we use for everything from "I love pizza" to "I love my spouse." This limitation makes it difficult to distinguish between different types of love. The ancient Greeks, however, had four distinct words for love, each capturing a different dimension of this complex emotion and commitment.[3]

Understanding these four Greek words—storge, philia, eros, and agape—helps us grasp the richness of biblical love and how it applies to marriage. While the New Testament was written in Greek, it's important to note that these categories aren't explicitly taught in Scripture. Rather, they provide a helpful framework for understanding the different aspects of love described throughout the Bible.

Storge: Family Affection

Storge (pronounced STOR-gay) refers to family love or natural affection. It's the instinctive bond between parents and children, siblings, and extended family members. While the word storge doesn't appear in the New Testament, the concept is present in passages about family relationships.[4]

Romans 12:10 instructs believers to *"be devoted to one another in brotherly love,"* using the term philostorgos, which combines philia (friendship) with storge (family affection). This suggests that Christian relationships should have the natural warmth and commitment typically found in healthy families.

In marriage, storge manifests as comfortable familiarity and the deep affection that develops through shared experiences and history. It's the love that makes your spouse feel like "home." As Gary Thomas notes, "Storge is that feeling of familiarity and comfort that makes a healthy marriage a safe haven in a chaotic world."[5]

This aspect of love grows gradually over time as couples build a life together. It's not the exciting, passionate love of early romance but the warm, secure attachment that sustains a relationship through decades. Couples who've been married for many years often describe this comfortable affection as one of marriage's greatest blessings.

Philia: Friendship Love

Philia (pronounced FIL-ee-ah) describes the warm affection, loyalty, and camaraderie between friends. It's based on mutual respect, shared interests, and genuine enjoyment of one another's company. The city of Philadelphia gets its name from this word—"the city of brotherly love."[6]

Jesus demonstrated the importance of philia when He called His disciples friends: *"I no longer call you servants... Instead, I have called you friends"* (John 15:15). The deep friendship between David and Jonathan in the Old Testament exemplifies philia love, described as Jonathan loving David *"as his own soul"* (1 Samuel 18:1).

In marriage, philia is essential. Spouses should be best friends who genuinely enjoy spending time together, share common interests, and respect each other's thoughts and opinions. As Tim Keller observes, "Friendship is a deep oneness that develops when two people, speaking the truth in love to one another, journey together to the same horizon."[7]

Many marriage experts consider friendship the foundation of lasting marriages. Research by the Gottman Institute found that couples who describe their spouse as their best friend report significantly higher levels of marital satisfaction. When romantic passion naturally ebbs and flows, friendship provides stability and connection.

To nurture philia in marriage:

- Develop shared interests and activities
- Engage in meaningful conversations beyond household logistics
- Support each other's goals and dreams
- Make time for fun and laughter together
- Show genuine interest in your spouse's thoughts and feelings

As C.S. Lewis wisely noted, "Friendship is unnecessary, like philosophy, like art... It has no survival value; rather, it is one of those things which give value to survival."[8]

Eros: Romantic and Sexual Love

Eros (pronounced AIR-ohs) refers to romantic and sexual love—the passionate attraction between spouses. While the word eros doesn't appear in the New Testament, the concept is clearly affirmed throughout Scripture, particularly in the Song of Solomon, which celebrates the beauty of physical intimacy within marriage.[9]

God designed eros as a good gift to be enjoyed within the covenant of marriage. The Bible speaks positively about sexual desire between husband and wife: *"May you rejoice in the wife of your youth... may you ever be intoxicated with her love"* (Proverbs 5:18-19). Far from the prudish stereotype sometimes associated with Christianity, Scripture presents a healthy view of sexuality as part of God's good design.

In marriage, eros provides a unique bond that distinguishes the relationship from all others. Physical intimacy is designed to nurture closeness, provide pleasure, and strengthen the marital bond. As Ed Wheat explains, "Sexual intimacy in marriage is the deepest level of communion between two human beings—the ultimate expression of love that God designed to be a foretaste of the joy that awaits us in our eternal union with Christ."[10]

However, our culture has distorted eros by separating it from covenant commitment. When physical intimacy is pursued outside marriage or becomes the primary focus within marriage, it loses its intended meaning and power. True eros is not just about physical pleasure but about expressing and deepening the comprehensive love between husband and wife.

Agape: Sacrificial, Unconditional Love

Agape (pronounced ah-GAH-pay) is the highest form of love—selfless, sacrificial, and unconditional. Unlike the other types of love, which arise somewhat naturally, agape is a deliberate choice to value another person's well-being above your own, regardless of feelings or circumstances.[11]

This is the love most frequently mentioned in the New Testament and the love that God has for us: *"For God so loved (agapao) the world that he gave his one and only Son"* (John 3:16). It's also the love that Christians are commanded to have for God, for one another, and even for enemies (Matthew 5:44).

In marriage, agape is essential because feelings fluctuate and circumstances change. There will be seasons when you don't particularly like your spouse or feel romantically inclined toward them. In those moments, agape love continues to act for their good, regardless of feelings.[12]

Paul's famous description of love in 1 Corinthians 13:4-7 describes agape: *"Love is patient, love is kind. It does not envy, it does not boast, it is not proud. It does not dishonor others; it is not self-seeking; it is not easily angered; it keeps no record of wrongs. Love does not delight in evil but rejoices with the truth. It always protects, always trusts, always hopes, always perseveres."*

As John Piper explains, "Agape love is the backbone of marriage. It's the commitment that holds everything together when emotions falter and circumstances turn difficult." This doesn't mean romantic feelings aren't important, but they cannot be the foundation of a lasting marriage.[13]

The Interplay of the Four Loves in Marriage

A healthy marriage incorporates all four types of love. They complement and strengthen each other, creating a multidimensional relationship that can weather life's challenges and grow deeper over time.

Imagine a marriage with only eros but no philia—physical attraction without friendship. Or consider a relationship with Storge and Philia but no agape—comfortable affection and friendship without sacrificial commitment. Such imbalanced relationships eventually falter.[14]

Gary Chapman, author of *The Five Love Languages*, notes: "The most successful marriages blend all aspects of love. They have the warm affection of Storge, the companionship of philia, the passion of eros, and the enduring commitment of agape." When all four types of love are present, marriages thrive even through difficult seasons.

Understanding these different dimensions of love helps us set realistic expectations for marriage. No single aspect of love can bear the weight of an entire relationship. When we expect our spouse to fulfill all our needs through just one dimension of love (usually eros), disappointment inevitably follows.[15]

Cultural Counterfeits of Love

Our culture offers several counterfeits of biblical love that can damage our marriages if we embrace them. Let's examine some of these distortions and contrast them with biblical truth.

Counterfeit #1: Love as Mere Feeling

Perhaps the most common cultural distortion is reducing love to an emotion or feeling. We hear phrases like "follow your heart" and "love at first sight" that suggest love is primarily about emotional response. While feelings are certainly part of love, biblical love goes far deeper.[16]

In Scripture, love is consistently portrayed as action and commitment, not just emotion. Jesus said, *"If you love me, keep my commands"* (John 14:15). John wrote, *"Let us not love with words or speech but with actions and in truth"* (1 John 3:18). Biblical love certainly includes feelings but it's fundamentally about choices and behaviors.

When couples base their relationship primarily on feelings, they build on shifting sand. Emotions naturally fluctuate based on circumstances, health, stress levels, and countless other factors. A marriage built on feelings alone cannot withstand these natural variations.[17]

As Francis Chan observes, "The world says love means accepting someone as they are and not trying to change them. Jesus says love means speaking truth and calling people to change." Biblical love isn't just affirming; it's transformative. It seeks the highest good for the beloved, even when that requires difficult conversations or confrontation.

Counterfeit #2: Love as Self-Fulfillment

Another cultural counterfeit presents love as primarily about personal happiness and self-fulfillment. We're told that the right relationship should make us feel complete, fulfilled, and consistently happy. When it doesn't, we're encouraged to move on.[18]

This self-centered view directly contradicts biblical love, which is fundamentally other-centered. Jesus defined love at its highest as laying down one's life for others (John 15:13). Paul instructed husbands to love their wives *"just as Christ loved the church and gave himself up for her"* (Ephesians 5:25).

Timothy Keller addresses this counterfeit directly: "In the world's version of love, we fill our cup from others. In the biblical version, our cup is filled by God so we can pour ourselves out for others." When we enter marriage primarily seeking our own fulfillment, we set ourselves up for disappointment and conflict.[19]

This doesn't mean marriage shouldn't bring joy and fulfillment—it often does. But these come as byproducts of giving ourselves in love, not as the primary goal. As Jesus taught, *"It is more blessed to give than to receive"* (Acts 20:35). Paradoxically, we find our greatest fulfillment when we stop seeking it directly and focus instead on loving and serving our spouse.

Counterfeit #3: Love Without Boundaries

Our culture often portrays love as accepting and affirming everything about another person without judgment or expectations. While unconditional acceptance is part of love, biblical love also includes appropriate boundaries and expectations.[20]

God's love for us is unconditional in that it's not based on our performance or worthiness. However, God doesn't affirm everything we do. He loves us enough to discipline us (Hebrews 12:6) and call us to repentance when we sin. His love seeks our transformation, not just our comfort.

In marriage, healthy love includes both grace and truth. We accept our spouse unconditionally as a person while also maintaining appropriate expectations for behavior. As Henry Cloud and John Townsend explain in their book *Boundaries in Marriage*, "Love without boundaries isn't really love at all, but enabling and codependency."[21]

Biblical Love in Action: 1 Corinthians 13

The most comprehensive description of biblical love appears in 1 Corinthians 13, often called the "love chapter." While this passage is frequently read at weddings, its implications for daily married life deserve deeper exploration.[22]

Paul begins by emphasizing love's supreme importance: *"If I speak in the tongues of men or of angels, but do not have love, I am only a resounding gong or a clanging cymbal"* (1 Corinthians 13:1). Without love, even the most impressive spiritual gifts and accomplishments are meaningless.

Let's examine each characteristic of biblical love and its application to marriage:

Love Is Patient

The Greek word for patience (makrothumia) literally means "long-tempered"—the opposite of having a short fuse. Patient love endures irritations, delays, and disappointments without becoming angry or resentful.[23]

In marriage, patience means:

- Giving your spouse time to grow and change
- Not interrupting or finishing their sentences
- Waiting calmly when they're running late
- Responding gently when they make mistakes
- Listening fully before responding

As James Dobson notes, "Patience in marriage isn't about gritting your teeth and enduring; it's about giving your spouse the gift of time and grace." This patience reflects God's patience with us, as He gives us time to grow and doesn't demand instant perfection.

Love Is Kind

Kindness (chrestotes) goes beyond mere niceness to active goodwill that seeks opportunities to bless others. Kind love looks for ways to make life better for the beloved.[24]

In marriage, kindness means:

- Noticing and meeting needs before being asked
- Speaking encouraging words daily
- Performing small acts of service
- Giving the benefit of the doubt
- Expressing appreciation regularly

Gary Chapman observes, "Many marriages die not from a lack of love but from a lack of kindness. Daily kindness is the soil in which love grows." Simple acts of kindness—making coffee, leaving an encouraging note, offering a back rub—build a culture of love in marriage.

Love Does Not Envy

Envy (zeloo) means resentment over another's advantages, success, or possessions. Love celebrates the beloved's blessings rather than feeling threatened by them.[25]

In marriage, freedom from envy means:

- Celebrating your spouse's successes wholeheartedly
- Supporting their dreams and goals
- Not competing for recognition or achievement
- Being secure in your own identity and calling
- Wanting the best for them, even when you don't benefit

Timothy Keller writes, "In a healthy marriage, spouses want more for each other than they want from each other." This generous spirit creates an atmosphere where both partners can flourish without fear of resentment.

Love Does Not Boast, Is Not Proud

Boasting (perpereuomai) and pride (phusioo) both involve self-exaltation at others' expense. Love doesn't need to prove its worth or superiority.[26]

In marriage, humility means:

- Admitting mistakes readily
- Listening to your spouse's perspective
- Being willing to learn from them
- Not keeping score of who does more
- Serving without recognition or reward

C.S. Lewis described pride as "the complete anti-God state of mind." Pride damages marriages by creating competition instead of cooperation. Humble love, by contrast, creates safety and intimacy.

Love Does Not Dishonor Others

To dishonor (aschemoneo) means to behave inappropriately or indecently toward someone, treating them with disrespect or contempt. Love treats the beloved with dignity and respect.[27]

In marriage, honor means:

- Speaking respectfully, even during disagreements
- Not criticizing your spouse in front of others
- Valuing their opinions and preferences
- Treating them as an equal partner
- Respecting their boundaries

Emerson Eggerichs, in his book *Love and Respect*, emphasizes that "without honor, intimacy cannot thrive." When spouses honor each other, they create an environment where love can flourish.

Love Is Not Self-Seeking

Self-seeking love (zeteo ta heautou) puts personal desires and needs first. Biblical love, by contrast, considers others' needs as important as—or even more important than—one's own.[28]

In marriage, selflessness means:

- Considering your spouse's preferences in decisions
- Willingly sacrificing for their well-being
- Listening to understand, not just to respond
- Serving without expecting immediate reciprocation
- Finding joy in meeting their needs

As John MacArthur observes, "The essence of love is self-sacrifice. Self-centeredness is the opposite of love." This doesn't mean completely neglecting your own needs, but it does mean refusing to make them the relationship's primary focus.

Love Is Not Easily Angered

Being easily angered (paroxuno) means being quickly provoked to irritation or wrath. Love maintains emotional stability and doesn't react harshly to every provocation.[29]

In marriage, emotional control means:

- Responding calmly to frustrations
- Taking a timeout when emotions run high
- Not using anger to control or intimidate
- Distinguishing between minor irritations and serious issues
- Addressing problems without attacking character

Gary Thomas notes, "Your ability to remain calm when your spouse is not may be the most powerful relational skill you can develop." This doesn't mean suppressing legitimate concerns but addressing them with self-control rather than reactive anger.

Love Keeps No Record of Wrongs

Keeping a record of wrongs (logizomai to kakon) means mentally tallying offenses to use as ammunition later. Love forgives completely and doesn't resurrect past failures.[30]

In marriage, forgiveness means:

- Truly letting go of past hurts
- Not bringing up forgiven offenses in future arguments
- Refusing to use the phrase "You always..."

- Extending grace for human imperfection
- Remembering your own need for forgiveness

Lewis Smedes wrote, "To forgive is to set a prisoner free and discover that the prisoner was you." Marriages thrive when both partners practice regular, genuine forgiveness rather than stockpiling grievances.

Love Does Not Delight in Evil But Rejoices with the Truth

Delighting in evil (chairo epi te adikia) means finding satisfaction in wrongdoing—either one's own or others'. Love takes no pleasure in what is wrong but celebrates truth and righteousness.[31]

In marriage, this means:

- Not enjoying your spouse's failures or mistakes
- Refusing to participate in or condone sinful behavior
- Celebrating growth in godly character
- Speaking truth with gentleness and love
- Finding joy in integrity and honesty

R.C. Sproul emphasizes that "love never celebrates another's sin. True love cannot be divorced from truth." This aspect of love may require difficult conversations, but always with the goal of restoration, not condemnation.

Love Always Protects, Trusts, Hopes, and Perseveres

The final characteristics of love form a powerful quartet of enduring commitment:

- Protects (stego): covers, bears, supports, shields
- Trusts (pisteuo): believes the best, gives the benefit of the doubt
- Hopes (elpizo): maintains optimism about the future
- Perseveres (hupomeno): endures difficulties without giving up

In marriage, these qualities mean:

- Defending your spouse's reputation and dignity
- Choosing to believe the best about their motives
- Maintaining hope for growth and positive change
- Committing to the relationship through all circumstances[32]

As John Piper notes, "These four qualities form the backbone of covenant love—the kind that doesn't depend on feelings or circumstances but on commitment to the beloved's good." This enduring love reflects God's faithful love for His people.

Love Never Fails

Paul concludes his description with the triumphant declaration that *"love never fails"* (1 Corinthians 13:8). The Greek word for "fails" (ekpipto) means to fall away or become ineffective. While prophecies, tongues, and knowledge will pass away, love remains eternally.[33]

In marriage, this means that love—true biblical love—has staying power. It doesn't depend on changing circumstances or feelings but endures through every season of life. As couples grow older together, external beauty fades, and health may decline, but love can continue to deepen and strengthen.

This doesn't mean that every marriage will succeed, as human sinfulness and hardness of heart can resist even the most faithful love. But biblical love itself never fails—it remains effective and powerful when genuinely practiced.

The Source of Biblical Love: God Himself

As we consider these characteristics of biblical love, an important question arises: How can we possibly love like this? The standard seems impossibly high for imperfect humans.[34]

The answer lies in recognizing the true source of biblical love. The apostle John tells us plainly: *"God is love"* (1 John 4:8). Love isn't just something God does; it's who He is. And the love we're called to demonstrate comes from Him, not from our own limited resources.

John continues: *"This is love: not that we loved God, but that he loved us and sent his Son as an atoning sacrifice for our sins... We love because he first loved us"* (1 John 4:10, 19). Our capacity to love flows from experiencing God's love for us in Christ.[35]

As Tim Keller explains, "The gospel is this: We are more sinful and flawed than we ever dared believe, yet more loved and accepted than we ever dared hope." When we grasp the depth of God's love for us despite our unworthiness, it transforms our ability to love others, including our spouse.

This means that growing in your relationship with God is essential for loving your spouse well. The more deeply you experience God's love, the more that love will overflow into your marriage. As Jesus taught, *"Remain in me, as I also remain in you... apart from me you can do nothing"* (John 15:4-5).[36]

Practical Steps for Growing in Biblical Love

Understanding biblical love intellectually isn't enough; we need to put it into practice daily. Here are some practical steps for growing in biblical love toward your spouse or future spouse:

1. Study God's love regularly. Spend time meditating on passages that reveal God's love, such as Romans 8, Ephesians 3, and 1 John 4. Ask God to help you grasp the height, depth, width, and breadth of His love for you.[37]

2. Practice the "one another." The New Testament contains over 50 "one another" commands that describe how Christians should treat each other. Apply these specifically to your marriage: love one

another, serve one another, bear with one another, forgive one another, etc.

3. Identify your love blockers. What specific attitudes or behaviors prevent you from loving well? Common blockers include pride, selfishness, unforgiveness, fear, and busyness. Ask God to help you recognize and address these obstacles.

4. Develop love habits. Create daily rituals that express love to your spouse: a morning blessing, a thoughtful text during the day, a genuine question about their experiences, a physical expression of affection. Small, consistent actions build a culture of love.[38]

5. Love when you don't feel like it. Choose to act in loving ways even when emotions don't cooperate. Often, loving actions eventually rekindle loving feelings. As C.S. Lewis noted, "Do not waste time bothering whether you 'love' your neighbor; act as if you did."

6. Receive love from God daily. You cannot give what you haven't received. Make time each day to receive God's love through prayer, Scripture, worship, and the Christian community. Let His love fill your heart until it overflows to others.

7. Seek accountability and support. Share your journey of growing in love with trusted friends who can encourage you, challenge you, and pray for you. Consider mentoring from a couple with a strong, loving marriage.[39]

Biblical Love in Different Seasons of Marriage

As you prepare for marriage, it's important to understand that love will look different in various seasons of your relationship. Each stage brings unique challenges and opportunities for love to deepen and mature.

The Newlywed Season

In the early years of marriage, love often feels easy and natural. Romantic feelings are strong, and the joy of building a life together creates a sense of excitement and possibility. This is a wonderful season, but it's also a crucial time to establish healthy patterns of biblical love.

During this season, focus on:

- Establishing habits of communication and conflict resolution
- Learning to balance independence and togetherness
- Building a foundation of spiritual intimacy through prayer and Scripture
- Creating shared traditions and memories
- Practicing selflessness when it's tempting to insist on your own way

As Dennis Rainey observes, "The patterns you establish in your first few years of marriage tend to become permanent. Make sure they're patterns of biblical love, not cultural counterfeits."

The Child-Raising Season

For couples who have children, the parenting years bring tremendous joy but also significant stress on the marriage relationship. Time, energy, and financial resources are stretched thin. Many couples find their relationship taking a back seat to the demands of parenting.

During this season, focus on:

- Protecting time for your marriage amid parenting responsibilities
- Supporting each other through the challenges of raising children
- Maintaining physical and emotional intimacy despite fatigue
- Presenting a united front in parenting decisions
- Finding moments to enjoy each other amid the busyness

Gary Thomas reminds couples, "Your marriage is the foundation of your family. The best gift you can give your children is a strong, loving relationship with your spouse." When biblical love remains the priority, the entire family benefits.

The Middle Years

As careers advance and children grow more independent, couples enter what some call the "middle years" of marriage. This season often brings increased financial stability but can also include significant life transitions and questions about purpose and identity.

During this season, focus on:

- Rediscovering each other as individuals beyond your roles
- Supporting each other through career transitions or midlife questions
- Adapting to changing family dynamics as children become more independent
- Renewing romance and intimacy in your relationship
- Serving others together from the abundance of your experience

Timothy Keller notes, "The middle years of marriage are often when couples either grow significantly closer or begin to drift apart." Intentional investment in biblical love during this season yields rich dividends for the future.

The Later Years

The retirement years bring new opportunities and challenges. With children grown and careers completed, couples have more time together than ever before. Health concerns may arise, and the reality of aging becomes more apparent.

During this season, focus on:

- Caring for each other through health challenges
- Finding new shared purposes and activities
- Expressing appreciation for your history together
- Leaving a legacy for future generations
- Preparing for the reality that one of you will likely precede the other in death

Billy Graham, reflecting on his long marriage to Ruth, said, "A good marriage is the union of two forgivers." In the later years, couples often report that the accumulated experience of forgiving and being forgiven creates a deep, rich love, unlike any earlier season.

Conclusion: The Journey of Biblical Love

As we conclude this exploration of biblical love, remember that growing in love is a lifelong journey, not a destination you reach once and for all. Even the most mature Christians continue to develop in their capacity to love as God loves.

The good news is that God is committed to developing His love in you. Paul prayed for the Thessalonians, *"May the Lord make your love increase and overflow for each other and for everyone else"* (1 Thessalonians 3:12). This remains God's desire for every marriage—that love would continually grow and deepen.

As you prepare for marriage, commit yourself to this journey of biblical love. Reject cultural counterfeits that promise happiness without commitment. Embrace God's design for love that reflects His character and brings genuine fulfillment.

Remember that biblical love isn't primarily about feeling the right emotions but about making the right choices. It's about consistently acting for your spouse's highest good, even when it's difficult. As you practice this kind of love, the feelings often follow the actions.

Most importantly, stay connected to the source of love—God Himself. Jesus said, *"As the Father has loved me, so have I loved you. Now remain in my love"* (John 15:9). Your capacity to love your spouse flows directly from your experience of God's love for you in Christ.

May your marriage become a living testimony to the power and beauty of biblical love—a love that reflects God's character, blesses your spouse, and points others to the ultimate Lover of our souls, Jesus Christ.

Chapter 3

Biblical Foundations For Marriage

The Blueprint for Marriage

Every significant building project begins with a blueprint—a detailed plan that guides the construction process. Without this foundation, even the most beautiful structure will eventually fail. Marriage is no different. To build a marriage that will stand the test of time, we need to understand and follow God's blueprint.[1]

In our culture, marriage is often viewed as a human invention—a social contract that can be defined and redefined according to changing preferences. But Scripture presents a radically different perspective: marriage is a divine institution designed by God with specific purposes and parameters. As Wayne Grudem notes, "Marriage is not a human invention but a divine institution, established by God at the beginning of human history."[2]

In this chapter, we'll explore the biblical foundations for marriage—the essential truths that provide the framework for a God-honoring relationship. We'll examine marriage's origin in creation, its distortion through sin, its redemption through Christ, and its ultimate fulfillment in the new creation. Understanding these foundations will help you build a marriage that reflects God's design and brings glory to Him.

Marriage in Creation: The Original Design

To understand God's design for marriage, we must begin where marriage itself began—in the Garden of Eden. Genesis 1-2 provides our most fundamental teaching about marriage, establishing patterns that echo throughout Scripture.[3]

Created in God's Image

The creation account begins with a profound statement about human identity: *"So God created mankind in his own image, in the image of God he created them; male and female he created them"* (Genesis 1:27). This verse establishes several crucial truths about marriage.

First, both man and woman bear God's image equally. While they have different roles, they share equal value and dignity as image-bearers. As John Piper explains, "The Bible teaches that men and women are equal in value and dignity as image-bearers of God, but different in the roles God has designed for them."[4]

Second, God created humans as male and female—with physical, emotional, and psychological differences designed to complement each other. These differences aren't accidental or merely cultural; they're part of God's good design. Andreas Köstenberger observes, "The creation of humanity as male and female is not a cultural construct but a divine design that reflects God's wisdom and goodness."[5]

Third, the image of God is reflected not just in individuals but in the relationship between man and woman. Some theologians suggest that the plurality within the Godhead ("Let us make mankind in our image") finds expression in the plurality of human genders and their relationship. As Timothy Keller notes, "Marriage is a human reflection of the relationship within the Godhead, as well as the relationship between Christ and the church."[6]

The First Marriage

Genesis 2 provides a more detailed account of the first marriage, revealing God's purpose and pattern for this relationship. After creating Adam, God declared, *"It is not good for the man to be alone. I will make a helper suitable for him"* (Genesis 2:18). This statement is striking because it's the first time God pronounces something "not good" in creation.

Adam's aloneness wasn't good because humans are created for relationships. God designed us to live in community, and marriage represents the most intimate form of human community. As Gary Thomas observes, "God looked at perfect paradise, perfect weather, perfect food, perfect environment, and said, 'It is not good for the man to be alone.' Relationship is that important to God."[7]

God's solution to Adam's aloneness was to create "a helper suitable for him." The Hebrew word for "helper" (ezer) doesn't imply inferiority—in fact, it's often used in Scripture to describe God Himself as our helper. Rather, it indicates that Eve was created to complement Adam, providing strengths where he had weaknesses and working alongside him to fulfill God's purposes.

After creating Eve from Adam's side, God presented her to Adam, who responded with the first love poem in history: *"This is now bone of my bones and flesh of my flesh; she shall be called 'woman,' for she was taken out of man"* (Genesis 2:23). Adam recognized Eve as his perfect counterpart—like him yet different, equal in value yet uniquely feminine.[8]

The passage concludes with a foundational statement about marriage: *"That is why a man leaves his father and mother and is united to his wife, and they become one flesh"* (Genesis 2:24). This verse establishes several essential elements of marriage according to God's design:

1. **Leaving:** Marriage involves separating from parents to establish a new family unit. While honoring parents remains important, the primary loyalty shifts to one's spouse.

2. **Uniting:** The Hebrew word for "united" (dabaq) implies a strong bond—to cling to, to stick to, to be joined together. Marriage creates a covenant bond that supersedes all other human relationships.[9]

3. **One flesh:** This phrase encompasses the comprehensive union of marriage—physical, emotional, spiritual, and legal. It's not just about sexual union but about two lives becoming thoroughly intertwined.

Jesus later quoted this passage when teaching about marriage, adding, *"So they are no longer two, but one flesh. Therefore what God has joined together, let no one separate"* (Matthew 19:6). His commentary confirms that marriage according to God's design is:

- Between a man and a woman ("male and female")
- Exclusive ("a man... his wife")
- Permanent ("let no one separate")
- Divinely established ("what God has joined together")[10]

The Cultural Mandate

Immediately after creating humans as male and female, God gave them a mission: *"Be fruitful and increase in number; fill the earth and subdue it. Rule over the fish in the sea and the birds in the sky and over every living creature that moves on the ground"* (Genesis 1:28). This "cultural mandate" reveals another purpose for marriage: partnership in fulfilling God's purposes for humanity.[11]

Marriage provides the context for procreation—"be fruitful and increase in number." While not every couple can have biological children, and some may be called to childless service, the general pattern is that marriage creates the family units through which humanity continues, and children are nurtured.

Beyond procreation, the cultural mandate calls couples to "subdue" the earth and "rule over" creation as God's representatives. This involves developing culture, stewarding resources, and bringing order to God's world. Marriage partners are to work together in this mission, combining their unique strengths and perspectives.[12]

As Christopher Ash writes, "Marriage is not an end in itself but a means to enable men and women together to be fruitful in the widest sense: to develop godly culture, to steward the earth's resources, and to extend God's kingdom." This shared mission gives purpose and direction to the marriage relationship.

Naked and Unashamed

Genesis 2 concludes with a beautiful picture of the first marriage: *"Adam and his wife were both naked, and they felt no shame"* (Genesis 2:25). This statement goes far beyond physical nakedness to describe the complete openness, vulnerability, and acceptance that characterized their relationship.[13]

In this pre-fall state, Adam and Eve had nothing to hide from each other—no secrets, no masks, no defensive walls. They were fully known and fully accepted. This represents God's ideal for marriage: a relationship of complete transparency where couples can be their authentic selves without fear of rejection or judgment.

As Dan Allender and Tremper Longman explain, "Naked and unashamed is about far more than physical nudity. It's about being fully known—strengths and weaknesses, virtues and vices, successes and failures—and still being fully loved." This kind of intimacy is what many couples long for but struggle to achieve.

Marriage in the Fall: The Distortion of God's Design

The perfect marriage described in Genesis 2 didn't remain perfect for long. Genesis 3 recounts humanity's fall into sin, which profoundly damaged the marriage relationship. Understanding how sin distorts marriage helps us recognize unhealthy patterns and pursue healing and restoration.[14]

The Immediate Effects of Sin

After Adam and Eve sinned by disobeying God, several immediate changes affected their relationship:

1. **Shame replaced openness:** *"Then the eyes of both of them were opened, and they realized they were naked; so they sewed fig leaves together and made coverings for themselves"* (Genesis 3:7). Their first instinct was to hide from each other, covering their physical nakedness as a symbol of their new emotional and spiritual barriers.[15]

2. **Blame replaced responsibility:** When God confronted Adam, he immediately blamed Eve: *"The woman you put here with me—she gave me some fruit from the tree, and I ate it"* (Genesis 3:12). Notice how Adam implicitly blamed God as well ("the woman you put here with me"). Eve similarly deflected responsibility to the serpent. This blame-shifting pattern continues to damage marriages today.

3. **Fear replaced trust:** Adam explained his hiding from God by saying, *"I was afraid because I was naked"* (Genesis 3:10). This fear extended to his relationship with Eve. Where there had been complete trust, now there was suspicion and self-protection.

4. **Self-centeredness replaced selflessness:** Before the fall, Adam and Eve lived in harmony, each seeking the other's good. After sin entered, self-interest became the dominant motivation, creating competition instead of cooperation.[16]

The Curse of Marriage

As part of the consequences for sin, God pronounced specific judgments that would affect the marriage relationship:

To the woman, He said, *"I will make your pains in childbearing very severe; with painful labor, you will give birth to children. Your desire will be for your husband, and he will rule over you"* (Genesis 3:16).

To Adam, He said, *"Cursed is the ground because of you; through painful toil, you will eat food from it all the days of your life... By the sweat of your brow you will eat your food"* (Genesis 3:17-19).

These pronouncements weren't prescriptive (telling how marriage should be) but descriptive (telling how marriage would be affected by sin). They reveal two primary areas of conflict that would characterize fallen marriages:[17]

1. **Gender roles and authority:** The phrase "Your desire will be for your husband, and he will rule over you" indicates a distortion of the complementary relationship God designed. Many scholars interpret "your desire will be for your husband" as a desire to control or dominate him, while "he will rule over you" suggests harsh, self-serving leadership rather than loving headship.

Throughout history, this distortion has manifested in two opposite but equally harmful extremes: male domination (where men abuse their authority and treat women as inferior) and role reversal (where the created order is rejected altogether). Neither extreme reflects God's original design for marriage.[18]

1. **Work and provision:** Adam's punishment centered on his role as a provider, indicating that work would become difficult and frustrating. This creates pressure and stress that often spill over into marriage relationships. Many couples experience conflict around work-life balance, financial provision, and career decisions.

As Ray Ortlund observes, "The curse did not create new roles for men and women but rather distorted the existing roles." The fundamental design

72

of marriage remained, but sin twisted it in ways that continue to create conflict and pain.[19]

Common Distortions of Marriage

Throughout human history, various cultures have developed marriage practices that deviate from God's original design. These distortions reflect the brokenness of our fallen world:

1. **Polygamy:** While the Old Testament records instances of polygamy (multiple wives), it consistently shows the problems this practice created. God's original design was clearly monogamous—one man and one woman. Jesus reaffirmed this pattern when He quoted Genesis 2:24 in His teaching on marriage.[20]

2. **Divorce:** Moses permitted divorce because of *"hardness of heart"* (Matthew 19:8), but Jesus emphasized that this was a concession, not God's ideal. *"From the beginning, it was not so,"* He declared, pointing back to the creation design of permanent union.

3. **Same-sex relationships:** Throughout Scripture, marriage is consistently defined as a male-female union. This reflects the complementary design established in creation, where the differences between man and woman enable them to fulfill God's purposes together. As Kevin DeYoung notes, "The Bible's teaching on marriage doesn't merely assume a male-female component; it requires it."[21]

4. **Cohabitation:** Modern culture has largely separated marriage from formal commitment, with many couples living together without the covenant bond of marriage. This arrangement lacks the security, commitment, and legal/social recognition that God designed marriage to provide.

5. **Utilitarian marriage:** Many cultures have reduced marriage to a primarily economic or social arrangement, focused on practical benefits rather than a comprehensive union. While marriage certainly provides practical advantages, God designed it to be much more—a covenant relationship reflecting His character and purposes.[22]

Understanding these distortions helps us recognize how far our cultural practices often stray from God's blueprint. As Christians, we're called to align our understanding and practice of marriage with God's original design rather than conforming to cultural patterns.

Marriage in Redemption: The Restoration of God's Design

The good news of the gospel is that Christ came to redeem everything sin had damaged—including marriage. Through His life, death, and resurrection, Jesus made it possible for marriages to be restored to something closer to God's original design.[23]

Christ's Teaching on Marriage

Jesus addressed marriage directly in several Gospel passages, consistently pointing back to God's creation design. When the Pharisees asked about divorce, Jesus replied:

"Haven't you read that at the beginning, the Creator 'made them male and female,' and said, 'For this reason, a man will leave his father and mother and be united to his wife, and the two will become one flesh'? So they are no longer two but one flesh. Therefore what God has joined together, let no one separate" (Matthew 19:4-6).

This response reveals several important principles about Jesus' view of marriage:

1. He affirmed the creation account as authoritative, basing His teaching on Genesis 1:27 and 2:24.

2. He emphasized God's original design—one man and one woman united in a permanent covenant—rather than accommodating cultural distortions.

3. He elevated marriage as a divine institution ("what God has joined together"), not merely a human arrangement.[24]

In the same conversation, Jesus acknowledged that Moses permitted divorce because of *"hardness of heart"* but emphasized that *"from the beginning, it was not so"* (Matthew 19:8). He then limited legitimate grounds for divorce to sexual immorality (Matthew 19:9), upholding the sanctity and permanence of the marriage covenant.

Jesus also addressed the distortion of marriage through lust: *"Anyone who looks at a woman lustfully has already committed adultery with her in his heart"* (Matthew 5:28). This teaching shows that God's concern is not just with outward behavior but with the heart attitudes that undermine marital faithfulness.[25]

Marriage as a Picture of Christ and the Church

The most profound New Testament teaching on marriage appears in Ephesians 5:21-33, where Paul reveals that marriage was designed to picture the relationship between Christ and the church. This passage elevates marriage from a merely human institution to a living parable of the gospel.[26]

Paul begins with a call to mutual submission: *"Submit to one another out of reverence for Christ"* (Ephesians 5:21). This establishes the foundation for the specific instructions that follow—all Christian relationships should be characterized by humility, service, and putting others' needs first.

He then addresses wives: *"Wives, submit yourselves to your own husbands as you do to the Lord... Now as the church submits to Christ, so also wives should submit to their husbands in everything"* (Ephesians 5:22, 24). This submission isn't based on inferiority but on the wife's voluntary alignment with her husband's leadership, mirroring the church's relationship to Christ.[27]

To husbands, Paul gives an even more challenging command: *"Husbands, love your wives, just as Christ loved the church and gave himself up for her"* (Ephesians 5:25). The standard for a husband's love is nothing less than Christ's sacrificial, purifying, nurturing love for the church. This kind of love leaves no room for domination, selfishness, or abuse.[28]

Paul concludes by quoting Genesis 2:24 and adding, *"This is a profound mystery—but I am talking about Christ and the church"* (Ephesians 5:32). This reveals that marriage was designed from the beginning to reflect the relationship between Christ and His people. As Raymond Ortlund explains, "Marriage is not ultimately about us; it's about God. It was designed as a living picture of the gospel."[29]

This understanding transforms how we view marriage:

1. It gives cosmic significance to ordinary marriages. Your marriage isn't just about your happiness; it's about displaying God's redemptive love to a watching world.

2. It provides the pattern for marital roles. Husbands and wives can look to Christ and the church to understand how to live out their distinctive callings.

3. It offers hope for difficult marriages. Just as Christ doesn't abandon His imperfect church, spouses are called to persevere in love through challenges.

4. It establishes the ultimate purpose of marriage: to glorify God by reflecting the covenant relationship between Christ and His people.

As Timothy Keller observes, "When the Bible speaks of marriage, it uses the language of mystery, of profound spiritual significance. It is a human relationship, but it is so much more—a picture of the very heart of the gospel."[30]

The Power of the Gospel in Marriage

The gospel doesn't just give us a theological framework for understanding marriage; it provides practical power for living out God's design. Through Christ's redemptive work, couples can experience healing from sin's effects and grow toward the relationship God intended.[31]

Here are some ways the gospel transforms marriage:

1. **From shame to openness:** The gospel addresses our deepest shame by offering complete forgiveness and acceptance in Christ. As couples experience God's grace, they can risk being vulnerable with each other, moving toward the "naked and unashamed" relationship of Eden.

2. **From blame to responsibility:** The gospel confronts our tendency to blame others by showing that Christ took responsibility for sins He didn't commit. This empowers couples to own their contributions to conflict rather than pointing fingers.[32]

3. **From fear to trust:** Perfect love casts out fear (1 John 4:18). As couples ground their identity and security in Christ, they can risk trusting each other without the self-protection that characterizes fallen relationships.

4. **From self-centeredness to selflessness:** The gospel breaks the power of sin's self-focus by showing us Christ, who *"did not come to be served, but to serve, and to give his life as a ransom for many"* (Matthew 20:28). This enables the mutual self-giving love God designed for marriage.

5. **From power struggles to mutual submission:** The gospel subverts worldly power dynamics by showing that true greatness

comes through service (Mark 10:42-45). This frees couples from fighting for control and enables them to submit to one another out of reverence for Christ.

Paul David Tripp summarizes this transformative power: "The gospel doesn't just save your soul; it rescues your marriage from the self-centeredness that would otherwise destroy it. Only grace can give you the motivation and power to love your spouse the way God designed."[33]

Marriage in the New Creation: The Fulfillment of God's Design

To complete our understanding of the biblical foundations for marriage, we need to consider its place in God's future kingdom. Jesus' teaching about marriage in the resurrection provides an important perspective on its temporal nature and eternal significance.[34]

When the Sadducees tried to trap Jesus with a question about marriage in the resurrection, He replied:

"At the resurrection, people will neither marry nor be given in marriage; they will be like the angels in heaven" (Matthew 22:30).

Some have misinterpreted this to mean that marriage is unimportant or that marital relationships will be meaningless in eternity. But Jesus wasn't devaluing marriage; He was explaining that its current form will not continue in the new creation.

Marriage as we know it will end because it will have fulfilled its purpose. As a signpost pointing to the relationship between Christ and the church, marriage will be unnecessary when that relationship is consummated at the marriage supper of the Lamb (Revelation 19:7-9). The symbol gives way to the reality it symbolizes.[35]

This doesn't mean married couples will be strangers in heaven or that the love they developed will disappear. Rather, their relationship will be transformed and elevated within the perfect community of God's people. As C.S. Lewis suggested, "In heaven, all the things that made your marriage good—the love, the joy, the intimacy—will remain and be perfected, while all the things that made it difficult will fall away."[36]

Understanding marriage's temporal nature brings several important perspectives:

1. It prevents idolizing marriage. When we recognize that marriage is not an eternal institution, we're less likely to expect it to fulfill all our needs or define our ultimate identity.

2. It comforts those who never marry. Single believers can know that they're not missing an essential experience that will define them for eternity. In the resurrection, all believers will experience the perfect love and intimacy that marriage merely foreshadows.

3. It provides hope during marital struggles. The difficulties couples face are temporary, part of the "not yet" of God's kingdom. In eternity, all relationships will be perfected.

4. It reminds us of marriage's purpose. Marriage exists to point beyond itself to the ultimate marriage between Christ and His church. Its goal is not primarily our happiness but God's glory.

As John Piper explains, "The highest meaning and the most ultimate purpose of marriage is to put the covenant relationship of Christ and His church on display. That is why marriage exists. If you are married, that is why you are married. If you hope to be married, that should be your dream."[37]

Building on the Biblical Foundation

Now that we've explored the biblical foundations for marriage—its origin in creation, distortion through sin, redemption in Christ, and fulfillment in the new creation—let's consider how to build a marriage on this foundation.

1. Align Your Expectations with God's Design

Many marital problems stem from false expectations based on cultural myths rather than biblical truth. When couples understand God's purposes for marriage, they can adjust their expectations accordingly.[38]

For example, if you believe marriage exists primarily for your happiness and self-fulfillment, you'll likely become disillusioned when difficulties arise. But if you understand that marriage is designed to sanctify you, reflect Christ's relationship with the church, and bring glory to God, you'll approach challenges with a different perspective.

Gary Thomas asks a provocative question in his book *Sacred Marriage*: "What if God designed marriage to make us holy more than to make us happy?" This doesn't mean marriage won't bring happiness—it often does— but its primary purpose is spiritual formation and glorifying God.[39]

Take time to examine your expectations about marriage. Are they shaped more by romantic movies, social media, and cultural assumptions or by Scripture's teaching? Discuss these expectations with your fiancé or spouse, and work together to align them with God's design.

2. Embrace Your Distinct Roles

God created males and females with equal value but different and complementary roles. These differences aren't arbitrary or merely cultural but reflect God's wisdom and the relationship between Christ and the church.[40]

While Scripture doesn't provide exhaustive job descriptions for husbands and wives, it does establish general principles:

- Husbands are called to loving leadership, following Christ's example of sacrificial service, protection, and provision.

80

-Wives are called to respectful support, following the church's example of honoring Christ's leadership while contributing their strengths and perspectives.

These roles aren't about capability or worth but about reflecting the gospel story. As Wayne Grudem explains, "The different roles for men and women in marriage as outlined in Scripture do not stem from any supposed superiority of the husband or inferiority of the wife. Both are equal in value before God... The different roles are rather the way God has chosen for marriage to function best and to picture Christ and the church."[41]

In our culture, these distinct roles are often rejected as outdated or oppressive. But when lived out according to God's design—with mutual respect, love, and submission—they create a beautiful dance that honors both partners and reflects God's wisdom.

3. Practice Covenant Faithfulness

Unlike our culture's contract view of marriage (based on mutual benefit and terminable when benefits diminish), Scripture presents marriage as a covenant—a binding relationship established by solemn vows before God.

Covenant faithfulness means:

- Keeping your promises even when it's difficult
- Remaining committed through changing feelings and circumstances
- Seeking your spouse's good regardless of what you receive in return
- Reflecting God's faithful love toward His people

Malachi 2:14 describes the wife as *"your partner, the wife of your marriage covenant."* God takes these covenant vows seriously and calls us to do the same. As Michael Horton notes, "In a covenant, the relationship itself is the commitment, not just the benefits that flow from it."[42]

This covenant perspective transforms how we approach challenges in marriage. Instead of asking, "Am I getting what I want from this relationship?" we ask, "Am I being faithful to my covenant promises?" This shift from consumer thinking to covenant thinking provides stability when feelings fluctuate.

4. Pursue Intimacy in All Dimensions

God designed marriage as a comprehensive union—a "one flesh" relationship that encompasses every dimension of personhood. Building a strong marriage means developing intimacy in all these areas:

- **Spiritual intimacy:** Praying together, discussing Scripture, supporting each other's relationship with God, and sharing spiritual insights and struggles.
- **Emotional intimacy:** Sharing your feelings, dreams, fears, and hopes; listening deeply to understand each other's inner world.
- **Intellectual intimacy:** Discussing ideas, learning together, respecting each other's perspectives, and growing in knowledge as a couple.
- **Social intimacy:** Developing friendships together, navigating family relationships as a team, and presenting a united front to the world.
- **Physical intimacy:** Enjoying the gift of sexual union that God designed for pleasure, bonding, and procreation within marriage.[43]

These dimensions of intimacy are interconnected. Weakness in one area often affects others. For example, unresolved conflict (emotional dimension) frequently impacts physical intimacy. A holistic approach to marriage nurtures all aspects of the relationship.

Conclusion: The Foundation That Endures

Jesus concluded His Sermon on the Mount with the parable of two builders—one who built on rock and another on sand. When storms came, only the house with a solid foundation remained standing (Matthew 7:24-27). The same principle applies to marriage.

Marriages built on the shifting sands of cultural trends, romantic feelings, or self-fulfillment will eventually face challenges they cannot withstand. But marriages built on the solid rock of God's design—as revealed in creation, honored in redemption, and fulfilled in the new creation—have a foundation that endures.

This doesn't mean that marriages built on biblical foundations won't face difficulties. Every marriage experiences storms—health crises, financial pressures, parenting challenges, communication breakdowns, and more. But couples who have built on God's truth have the resources to weather these storms and even grow stronger through them.

As you prepare for marriage, invest time in understanding and applying these biblical foundations. Read Scripture together, discuss its implications for your relationship, and seek counsel from mature believers who have built their marriages on God's design. The effort you invest now in establishing this foundation will yield benefits throughout your marriage journey.

Remember that the ultimate purpose of marriage is not your personal happiness, though God often grants that as a byproduct. The ultimate purpose is to glorify God by reflecting the covenant love between Christ and His church. When this remains your focus, your marriage becomes not just a private relationship but a powerful testimony to God's faithfulness and love.

May your marriage be built so firmly on God's design that it stands as a witness to His wisdom and grace for generations to come? And may it point beyond itself to the ultimate marriage that awaits all believers—the wedding supper of the Lamb, where Christ and His bride will be united in perfect love forever.

Chapter 4

Communication

The Heart of Connection

"My dear brothers and sisters, take note of this: Everyone should be quick to listen, slow to speak, and slow to become angry." (James 1:19)

Communication lies at the heart of every successful marriage. It's the lifeline that connects two separate individuals, allowing them to share their thoughts, feelings, dreams, and concerns. When communication flows freely, marriages thrive; when it breaks down, even the strongest relationships can falter.[1]

In our increasingly distracted world, genuine communication has become more challenging than ever. Couples often live under the same roof while remaining emotionally distant, their connection hindered by busy schedules, digital distractions, and poor communication habits developed over time. As Gary Chapman observes, "Many couples are talking, but few are communicating. Words are spoken, but messages aren't received."[2]

This chapter explores the biblical foundations for healthy communication in marriage, common barriers that hinder connection, and practical skills for developing the kind of communication that builds intimacy and resolves conflict. Whether you're preparing for marriage or seeking to strengthen an existing relationship, these principles will help you develop the communication skills essential for a thriving marriage.

The Biblical Foundation for Communication

God is a communicating God. From the opening words of Scripture—*"God said, 'Let there be light'"*—to the closing invitation of Revelation—*"The Spirit and the bride say, 'Come!'"*—the Bible reveals a God who speaks, listens, and desires relationships. Created in His image, we, too, are designed for communication.[3]

In the Garden of Eden, Adam and Eve enjoyed perfect communication with God and with each other. Genesis 2:25 tells us they were "*both naked and felt no shame,*" a description that goes beyond physical nakedness to encompass complete transparency and vulnerability in their relationship. They had nothing to hide, nothing to fear, and no barriers to authentic communication.

The fall into sin damaged this perfect communication. When Adam and Eve sinned, their first instinct was to hide—from God and from each other. Fear, shame, and blame entered human relationships, creating barriers to the open communication God designed. Adam blamed Eve (and implicitly God) for his sin: "*The woman you put here with me—she gave me some fruit from the tree, and I ate it*" (Genesis 3:12). This blame-shifting pattern continues to damage marital communication today.[4]

Throughout Scripture, God calls His people back to honest, loving communication. The book of Proverbs particularly emphasizes the power of words: "*The tongue has the power of life and death*" (Proverbs 18:21). Our words can build up or tear down, heal or wound, strengthen or weaken our marriages. As Timothy Keller notes, "Words create worlds. The way we speak to each other literally creates the emotional environment in which our marriage will thrive or wither."[5]

The New Testament provides clear guidance for communication in all relationships, including marriage:

- "*Do not let any unwholesome talk come out of your mouths, but only what is helpful for building others up according to their needs, that it may benefit those who listen*" (Ephesians 4:29).
- "*My dear brothers and sisters, take note of this: Everyone should be quick to listen, slow to speak and slow to become angry*" (James 1:19).

87

- *"Speak the truth in love"* (Ephesians 4:15).

- *"Let your conversation be always full of grace, seasoned with salt"* (Colossians 4:6).[6]

These principles—building up rather than tearing down, listening before speaking, combining truth with love, and speaking with grace—form the foundation for godly communication in marriage. When couples apply these biblical principles, they create an environment where intimacy can flourish, and conflicts can be resolved constructively.

The Purpose of Communication in Marriage

Communication in marriage serves several vital purposes, each contributing to the overall health of the relationship:

1. Creating and Maintaining Intimacy

True intimacy—the deep knowing and being known that marriage is designed to provide—depends on effective communication. As Paul David Tripp explains, "Communication is the vehicle that carries two people into the experience of intimate marriage."[7]

Intimacy develops when couples regularly share their thoughts, feelings, hopes, fears, joys, and sorrows. This sharing goes beyond a surface-level conversation about schedules and tasks to reveal the inner life—what Gary Thomas calls "soul talk." He writes, "Soul talk happens when we move beyond discussing what we did today to sharing what we felt, what we feared, what we longed for."[8]

The Bible models this kind of intimate communication in the Song of Solomon, where the bride and groom freely express their admiration, desire, and delight in each other. Their transparent communication creates a deep bond that encompasses physical, emotional, and spiritual intimacy. As one commentator notes, "Their words to each other are as intimate as their physical embrace."

2. Resolving Conflict

Every marriage experiences conflict. Differences in personality, preferences, expectations, and backgrounds inevitably create tension. Communication provides the tools to address these conflicts constructively rather than allowing them to damage the relationship.

Proverbs 15:1 reminds us that *"a gentle answer turns away wrath, but a harsh word stirs up anger."* How we communicate during conflict largely determines whether the conflict will strengthen or weaken our marriage. As Emerson Eggerichs observes, "It's not the presence of conflict that destroys marriages; it's the absence of communication skills to deal with the conflict."[9]

Jesus provided clear guidance for addressing conflicts in Matthew 18:15-17, emphasizing the importance of direct, private conversation as the first step. While this passage specifically addresses church discipline, the principle applies to marriage as well: conflicts should be addressed directly and privately rather than involving others unnecessarily or letting resentment build.

3. Making Decisions Together

Marriage involves countless decisions—from daily choices about schedules and finances to major life decisions about careers, children, and living situations. Effective communication enables couples to make these decisions together in a way that honors both partners and strengthens the relationship.

The Bible presents a model of mutual submission in marriage: *"Submit to one another out of reverence for Christ"* (Ephesians 5:21). This mutual submission requires open communication where both spouses share their perspectives, listen to each other, and work toward consensus. As Timothy Keller explains, "Decision-making in marriage should not be a power struggle but a dance of mutual deference and wisdom-seeking."[10]

4. Supporting and Encouraging Each Other

God designed marriage as a partnership where spouses help each other grow and flourish. Communication is essential for this mutual support and encouragement. Hebrews 10:24-25 instructs believers to *"consider how we may spur one another on toward love and good deeds"* and to *"encourage one another."* This principle applies especially in marriage, where spouses have unique opportunities to build each other up through their words.[11]

Paul's instruction to *"encourage one another and build each other up"* (1 Thessalonians 5:11) takes on special significance in marriage. Through affirming words, active listening, and expressions of appreciation, spouses can strengthen each other to face life's challenges and pursue God's calling. As Gary Chapman notes, "Words of affirmation are powerful communicators of love. For many people, they are their primary love language."[12]

5. Spiritual Growth and Unity

For Christian couples, communication serves the ultimate purpose of growing together spiritually. Praying together, discussing Scripture, sharing spiritual insights, and processing questions of faith all contribute to spiritual intimacy and unity.

Amos 3:3 asks, *"Do two walk together unless they have agreed to do so?"* This principle applies to the spiritual journey of marriage. Couples who communicate openly about their faith experience greater unity and spiritual growth. As Dennis Rainey observes, "Spiritual intimacy in marriage is built through consistent, honest communication about what God is doing in your individual lives and in your relationship."[13]

Barriers to Effective Communication

Despite its importance, many couples struggle with communication. Understanding the common barriers can help couples identify and overcome the obstacles to connection in their own relationships.

1. Different Communication Styles

God created men and women with differences that extend to communication patterns. While individual personalities create variations, research consistently shows general differences in how men and women typically communicate. As Shaunti Feldhahn explains in her research-based book, "Men and women are often speaking different languages without realizing it."[14]

For example, many men tend to process internally before speaking, while many women process verbally by talking through their thoughts. Men often focus on facts and solutions, while women may emphasize feelings and connection. Neither approach is wrong—they're just different. Understanding and appreciating these differences can prevent frustration and misunderstanding.

Emerson Eggerichs, in his book Love and Respect, describes these differences as "pink and blue" communication: "She wants to connect through talking; he wants to connect through doing. She shares feelings to process them; he shares facts to solve problems." Recognizing these differences as complementary rather than competitive helps couples bridge the communication gap.[15]

2. Poor Listening Skills

James 1:19 instructs us to be *"quick to listen, slow to speak,"* yet many of us do the opposite. We focus more on formulating our response than on truly understanding what our spouse is saying. This barrier prevents the deep understanding that intimacy requires.

Active listening involves giving full attention, seeking to understand before being understood, and demonstrating that understanding through appropriate responses. As Stephen Covey famously said, "Most people do not listen with the intent to understand; they listen with the intent to reply." This tendency is particularly damaging in marriage.

Jesus modeled excellent listening skills. He asked thoughtful questions, gave people His full attention, and responded to the heart behind their words. When couples follow His example, they create space for genuine understanding and connection. As Paul David Tripp notes, "Listening is one of the most powerful ways we can communicate love to our spouse."[16]

3. Defensiveness

When we feel criticized or attacked, our natural response is to defend ourselves. This defensiveness creates a significant barrier to effective communication. Instead of seeking to understand our spouse's concern, we focus on protecting ourselves, often through counter-criticism, denial, or withdrawal.

The Bible addresses this tendency in Proverbs 18:13: *"To answer before listening—that is folly and shame."* Defensiveness prevents us from hearing the legitimate concerns our spouse may be expressing. As John Gottman's research has shown, defensiveness is one of the "Four Horsemen" that predict divorce when present in a relationship.[17]

Overcoming defensiveness requires humility—the willingness to consider that our spouse's perspective may have validity even if we don't initially agree. As James 1:19-20 reminds us, we should be *"slow to become angry, for man's anger does not bring about the righteous life that God desires."* When we respond with openness rather than defensiveness, we create space for productive conversation.

4. Fear and Insecurity

Fear often underlies communication problems in marriage. Spouses may fear rejection, criticism, conflict, or vulnerability. This fear leads to self-protective behaviors that hinder authentic communication. As John Powell writes, "We defend our dishonesty on the grounds that it may hurt another person, and then, having rationalized our phoniness into nobility, we settle for superficial relationships."[18]

The Bible repeatedly addresses fear with the assurance of God's love: *"Perfect love drives out fear"* (1 John 4:18). When couples create a safe environment where both partners know they are loved unconditionally, fear diminishes, and honest communication becomes possible. As Timothy Keller observes, "The gospel gives us both the humility and the confidence necessary for transparent communication."[19]

5. Digital Distractions

In our technology-saturated world, digital devices often compete for the attention that should be directed toward our spouse. Smartphones, tablets, computers, and televisions can create what researchers call "technoference"—technology-based interference in relationships.

While Scripture doesn't specifically address digital technology, the principle of giving full attention applies. Philippians 2:4 instructs us to *"look not only to your own interests but also to the interests of others."* When we're constantly checking our phones during conversations, we communicate that something else is more important than our spouse.[20]

Research by the Gottman Institute found that "phubbing" (phone snubbing) significantly decreases marital satisfaction. As Andy Crouch writes in The Tech-Wise Family, "Technology is in its proper place when it helps us bond with the real people we have been given to love. It's out of its proper place when we end up bonding with people at a distance rather than the people right in front of us."[21]

6. Unresolved Conflict

When conflicts remain unresolved, they create a backlog of hurt and resentment that hinders current communication. Ephesians 4:26-27 advises, *"Do not let the sun go down while you are still angry, and do not give the devil a foothold."* This doesn't mean every issue must be fully resolved before bedtime, but it does emphasize the importance of addressing conflicts promptly rather than allowing them to accumulate.[22]

Unresolved conflicts often lead to what John Gottman calls "negative sentiment override"—a state where spouses interpret even neutral or positive communications negatively because of accumulated negative feelings. Breaking this cycle requires intentionally addressing past hurts and establishing new patterns of communication. As Gary Chapman notes, "Unresolved conflicts are like unpaid bills—they accumulate interest over time."[23]

Building Effective Communication Skills

The good news is that communication skills can be learned and improved. With intentional effort and practice, couples can overcome barriers and develop patterns of communication that strengthen their relationship.

1. Create Time and Space for Communication

In our busy world, meaningful communication rarely happens spontaneously. Couples need to intentionally create time and space for connection. As William Doherty observes, "Couples who maintain strong communication have made talking together a priority, not something they hope will happen in the cracks of their busy lives."[24]

Many successful couples establish regular "couple time"—whether it's a weekly date night, a daily walk, or time to talk after the children are in bed. During these times, they minimize distractions and focus on connecting with each other. As Gary Thomas suggests, "Schedule time to talk as rigorously as you schedule other important commitments."

The content of these conversations matters as well. While discussing practical matters is necessary, the deeper connection comes through sharing thoughts, feelings, dreams, and spiritual insights. Gary Chapman recommends using conversation starters like "What made you feel loved this week?" or "What's something you're looking forward to?" to move beyond surface-level interaction.[25]

2. Develop Active Listening Skills

Active listening involves giving your full attention to understanding your spouse rather than formulating your response. James 1:19 instructs us to be *"quick to listen, slow to speak,"* a principle that transforms marital communication when applied consistently.

Practical steps for active listening include:

- Maintaining eye contact and an open posture
- Eliminating distractions (putting away phones, turning off the TV)
- Asking clarifying questions to ensure understanding
- Reflecting back on what you've heard ("What I hear you saying is...")
- Validating your spouse's feelings even if you don't share their perspective
- Resisting the urge to interrupt or immediately offer solutions[26]

As Les and Leslie Parrott note, "Listening well says to your spouse, 'You matter to me. What you think matters to me. What you feel matters to me.'" This message of valuing your spouse builds emotional intimacy and trust.

3. Practice Empathetic Understanding

Empathy goes beyond hearing words to understanding the emotions and needs behind them. Romans 12:15 instructs believers to *"rejoice with those who rejoice; mourn with those who mourn"*—a beautiful description of empathy in action.

Empathetic understanding requires temporarily setting aside your own perspective to enter your spouse's world. As John Gottman explains, "Empathy means listening without judgment and trying to understand your partner's perspective, even when you disagree with it." This doesn't mean you must agree with everything your spouse says, but it does mean making a genuine effort to understand their viewpoint.[27]

Phrases that communicate empathy include:

- "That sounds really difficult."
- "I can see why you'd feel that way."
- "Help me understand more about what you're experiencing."
- "I'm trying to put myself in your shoes."

When spouses feel understood, they're more likely to open up further, creating a positive cycle of deeper communication. As Timothy Keller observes, "Empathy is the prerequisite to both intimacy and wise counsel in marriage."[28]

4. Speak Truth with Love

Ephesians 4:15 instructs believers to *"speak the truth in love."* Both elements—truth and love—are essential for effective communication in marriage. Truth without love can be harsh and damaging; love without truth can enable unhealthy patterns.

Speaking truth means being honest about your thoughts, feelings, and concerns rather than hiding them to avoid conflict. As Proverbs 24:26 says, *"An honest answer is like a kiss on the lips"*—it's an act of intimacy and respect. Honesty builds trust, while dishonesty or omission erodes the foundation of the relationship.[29]

Speaking with love means considering how your words will impact your spouse and choosing to communicate in ways that show respect and care. This includes:

- Using "I" statements rather than accusatory "you" statements
- Addressing specific behaviors rather than attacking character
- Choosing appropriate timing for difficult conversations
- Speaking with a gentle tone and respectful language
- Focusing on current issues rather than bringing up past failures[30]

As Paul David Tripp explains, "Love is willing to speak difficult truths, but it always does so with grace, patience, and kindness." This balance of truth and love creates an environment where both spouses can grow, and the relationship can strengthen through honest communication.

5. Resolve Conflicts Constructively

Conflict is inevitable in marriage, but how couples handle conflict determines whether it will strengthen or damage their relationship. Scripture provides guidance for resolving conflicts in ways that honor God and each other.

Matthew 7:3-5 addresses the tendency to focus on our spouse's faults while ignoring our own: *"Why do you look at the speck of sawdust in your brother's eye and pay no attention to the plank in your own eye?"* Jesus instructs us to examine ourselves first, an approach that transforms conflict resolution in marriage. As Timothy Keller notes, "The gospel teaches us to approach conflict by first asking what we may have contributed to the problem."[31]

Practical steps for constructive conflict resolution include:

- Choosing an appropriate time and place for difficult conversations
- Starting with appreciation and affirmation
- Focusing on one issue at a time
- Using "I feel" statements rather than accusations
- Seeking to understand before being understood
- Working toward solutions that address both partners' concerns
- Apologizing specifically for your contributions to the problem
- Extending forgiveness when your spouse apologizes[32]

John Gottman's research has identified "repair attempts"—efforts to de-escalate tension during conflict—as a key factor in successful marriages. These might include humor, touch, taking a break, or explicitly asking to start over. Couples who recognize and respond positively to repair attempts can prevent conflicts from escalating into damaging interactions.

6. Express Appreciation and Affirmation

Positive communication is as important as addressing problems. Philippians 4:8 instructs believers to think about *"whatever is true, whatever is noble, whatever is right, whatever is pure, whatever is lovely, whatever is admirable."* When we focus on these positive qualities in our spouse and express our appreciation, we strengthen the relationship.[33]

Gary Chapman suggests that couples develop the habit of expressing at least one affirmation to their spouse each day. These might include:

- Appreciation for specific actions ("Thank you for taking care of the children while I was working.")

- Admiration for character qualities ("I really respect your integrity in that situation.")
- Affection ("I love you and enjoy being with you.")
- Acknowledgment of growth ("I've noticed how you've been working on being more patient.")[34]

Research by the Gottman Institute found that successful marriages maintain a 5:1 ratio of positive to negative interactions. This "magic ratio" creates an environment of appreciation and goodwill that helps couples navigate the inevitable challenges of marriage. As Shaunti Feldhahn's research revealed, "Highly happy couples tend to put a high priority on expressing appreciation to each other."[35]

7. Pray Together and About Your Communication

Prayer powerfully impacts marital communication in several ways. First, it invites God's wisdom and help into your relationship. James 1:5 promises, *"If any of you lacks wisdom, you should ask God, who gives generously to all without finding fault, and it will be given to you."* When couples pray together about communication challenges, they access divine resources beyond their own abilities.[36]

Second, prayer changes our hearts. As we bring our communication struggles before God, He often reveals our own contributions to the problem and gives us the humility to address them. As Dennis Rainey observes, "It's hard to stay angry at someone you're praying for regularly."

Third, praying together creates spiritual intimacy that enhances communication on all levels. Couples who pray together report greater overall intimacy and satisfaction in their marriages. As Gary Thomas notes, "Prayer together is one of the most intimate acts a couple can share."[37]

Practical suggestions for incorporating prayer into your communication include:

- Beginning difficult conversations with prayer for wisdom and understanding
- Praying together regularly about your relationship
- Asking God to reveal blind spots in your communication
- Thanking God together for growth and progress in your relationship
- Seeking God's help in specific communication challenges

Communication in Different Seasons of Marriage

Communication needs and challenges evolve throughout the seasons of marriage. Understanding these changes helps couples adapt their communication patterns to maintain a connection through life's transitions.

The Newlywed Season

In the early years of marriage, couples are establishing communication patterns that will shape their relationship for decades to come. This is a crucial time to develop healthy habits and address problematic patterns before they become entrenched.

Newlyweds often face the challenge of merging different family communication styles. As Ron Deal explains, "We all come into marriage with communication habits learned in our families of origin. Part of becoming 'one flesh' is developing a new communication style that works for your relationship."[38]

During this season, couples benefit from:

- Explicitly discussing expectations about communication
- Establishing regular times for meaningful conversation
- Learning each other's communication preferences and styles

- Creating healthy patterns for resolving conflicts
- Building the habit of praying together

The Parenting Years

When children enter the picture, couples often find their communication time and energy significantly reduced. The demands of parenting can push couple communication to the back burner, creating distance over time. As Gary Thomas warns, "Many couples make the mistake of putting their children at the center of their family rather than their marriage."[39]

During the parenting years, intentionality becomes even more important for maintaining connection. Successful couples:

- Protect time for adult conversation without children present
- Continue date nights or other couple time
- Develop efficient communication about parenting and logistics
- Support each other through the stresses of parenting
- Unite as a team in parenting decisions

The Middle Years

As careers advance and children become more independent, couples enter what some call the "middle years" of marriage. This season often brings new communication challenges as couples rediscover each other after years of focusing on parenting and building careers.

Some couples find they've grown apart and have little to talk about beyond practical matters. Others face midlife questions about purpose and identity that require deep conversation and mutual support. As Timothy Keller observes, "The middle years of marriage are often when couples either grow significantly closer or begin to drift apart."[40]

During this season, couples benefit from:

- Developing new shared interests and activities
- Having intentional conversations about dreams for the future
- Supporting each other through career transitions or midlife questions
- Discussing changing roles as children leave home
- Renewing romantic communication that may have diminished during busy parenting years

The Later Years

The retirement years bring both opportunities and challenges for marital communication. Couples often have more time together than ever before, which can either strengthen their connection or highlight communication problems that were previously masked by busy schedules.

Health concerns, changing roles, and end-of-life planning require sensitive, thoughtful communication. As Billy Graham reflected on his long marriage to Ruth, "A good marriage is the union of two good forgivers." This grace-filled approach to communication becomes especially important in navigating the challenges of aging together.[41]

During this season, couples benefit from:

- Discussing hopes and concerns about retirement
- Communicating clearly about health issues and care needs
- Sharing memories and life review
- Planning for end-of-life decisions and legacy
- Expressing appreciation for the journey shared together

Conclusion: The Lifelong Journey of Communication

Developing effective communication in marriage is not a destination but a lifelong journey. Even couples with strong communication skills continue to grow and adapt their communication throughout their relationship. As Paul wrote to the Philippians, *"Not that I have already obtained all this, or have already arrived at my goal, but I press on..."* (Philippians 3:12). This attitude of ongoing growth serves marriages well.[42]

The effort invested in improving communication yields rich dividends in marital satisfaction and intimacy. Research consistently shows that couples who communicate effectively report higher levels of happiness and stability in their marriages. More importantly, they experience the deep knowing and being known that God designed marriage to provide.

Remember that perfection is not the goal—progress is. Every couple faces communication challenges, but those who commit to working through these challenges rather than giving up grow stronger through the process. As Gary Thomas observes, "The goal isn't a perfect marriage but a growing marriage."

As you apply the principles in this chapter, be patient with yourself and your spouse. Change takes time, especially when it involves patterns developed over years. Celebrate small improvements, extend grace when you fall short, and keep pressing forward toward more effective, loving communication.

Above all, remember that God is for your marriage and your communication. He designed marriage for intimacy and provided guidance for achieving it. As you seek His help and apply His wisdom, your communication will grow in ways that strengthen your marriage and honor Him.

Chapter 5

Resolving Conflict

The Inevitable Reality of Conflict

"What causes quarrels and what causes fights among you? Is it not this, that your passions are at war within you?" (James 4:1)

Conflict is an inevitable part of every marriage. Two imperfect people living in close proximity, sharing resources, making joint decisions, and navigating life's challenges will inevitably experience disagreements and tensions. As Gary Thomas observes, "If you're married, you will have conflict. The issue isn't whether you'll experience conflict but how you'll handle it when it comes."[1]

Many couples enter marriage with unrealistic expectations about conflict. They believe that if they truly love each other, they shouldn't argue or disagree. When conflicts arise, they feel something is fundamentally wrong with their relationship. This misconception leads to disappointment, fear, and sometimes even the premature end of marriages that could have thrived with a healthier understanding of conflict.

The truth is that conflict itself isn't the problem—it's how we handle conflict that determines whether it will damage or strengthen our marriage. As Tim Keller notes, "The presence of conflict is not a sign that you have married the wrong person. It's a sign that you are human beings who need God's grace to grow in how you handle your differences."[2]

This chapter explores a biblical approach to resolving conflict in marriage. We'll examine the root causes of conflict, common patterns that escalate tensions, and practical skills for addressing disagreements in ways that lead to greater intimacy and growth. Whether you're preparing for marriage or seeking to strengthen an existing relationship, these principles will help you transform conflict from a threat to your marriage into an opportunity for deeper connection.

The Biblical Perspective on Conflict

Scripture doesn't shy away from the reality of conflict in human relationships. From Cain and Abel to Paul and Barnabas, the Bible honestly portrays the tensions that arise even between people of faith. Rather than pretending conflict doesn't exist, Scripture provides wisdom for understanding its roots and resolving it constructively.[3]

The Fall and Its Impact on Relationships

Genesis 3 recounts humanity's fall into sin, which profoundly damaged all relationships—including marriage. Before the fall, Adam and Eve enjoyed perfect harmony with God and each other. After sinning, they immediately began blaming and accusing: Adam blamed Eve (and implicitly God), while Eve blamed the serpent. This pattern of blame-shifting, defensiveness, and self-protection continues to fuel marital conflicts today.

The fall introduced several dynamics that create conflict in marriage:

1. **Self-centeredness:** Sin turned our focus inward, making our own desires, comfort, and preferences our primary concern. James 4:1-2 identifies this self-focus as the root of conflict: *"What causes quarrels and what causes fights among you? Is it not this that your passions are at war within you? You desire and do not have, so you fight and quarrel."*[4]

2. **Pride:** The desire to be right, to win arguments, and to avoid admitting fault stems from pride—the first sin that led to all others. Proverbs 13:10 observes, *"By pride comes nothing but strife, but with the well-advised is wisdom"* (NKJV). Pride makes us defensive when criticized and resistant to seeing our own contributions to problems.

3. **Fear:** After sinning, Adam and Eve hid from God and covered themselves, indicating the fear and shame that entered the human experience. In marriage, fear of rejection, abandonment, or failure often drives defensive behaviors that escalate conflict rather than resolve it.[5]

4. **Misunderstanding:** Sin clouded our perception and understanding, making it difficult to truly hear and comprehend others. This leads to misinterpreting motives, jumping to conclusions, and responding to what we think our spouse means rather than what they actually intended.

Understanding these fallen tendencies helps us recognize that conflict isn't just about the surface issues we argue about—it reveals our need for redemption at the heart level. As Paul David Tripp explains, "Most marriage problems are not really marriage problems. They're God's problems. They're a result of our failure to understand the gospel and apply it to our lives and our marriage."[6]

God's Redemptive Purpose in Conflict

While conflict results from the fall, God can use it redemptively in our marriages. Romans 8:28 reminds us that *"God causes all things to work together for good to those who love God, to those who are called according to His purpose"* (NASB). This includes the conflicts we experience in marriage.

When approached with humility and grace, conflict can:

1. Reveal areas where we need growth and sanctification
2. Deepen our dependence on God's grace
3. Teach us to love sacrificially rather than selfishly
4. Develop our character and spiritual maturity
5. Lead to greater intimacy as we work through difficulties together[7]

As Gary Thomas writes in Sacred Marriage, "What if God designed marriage to make us holy more than to make us happy?" This perspective transforms how we view marital conflict—not as an obstacle to happiness but as an opportunity for spiritual growth and character development.[8]

Biblical Principles for Resolving Conflict

Scripture provides clear guidance for addressing conflicts in ways that honor God and strengthen relationships. These principles apply to all relationships but have special relevance for marriage:

1. **Self-examination before confrontation:** Jesus taught, *"First take the log out of your own eye, and then you will see clearly to take the speck out of your brother's eye"* (Matthew 7:5). This principle calls us to examine our own contributions to a conflict before focusing on our spouse's faults. As Timothy Keller notes, "The gospel teaches us to approach conflict by first asking what we may have contributed to the problem."[9]

2. **Gentle restoration rather than harsh condemnation:** Paul instructs believers to *"restore"* those caught in sin *"in a spirit of gentleness"* while watching themselves lest they too be tempted (Galatians 6:1). This approach emphasizes the goal of restoration rather than punishment or winning.

3. **Speaking truth in love:** Ephesians 4:15 calls us to *"speak the truth in love."* Both elements—truth and love—are essential. Truth without love can be harsh and damaging; love without truth enables unhealthy patterns. As Paul David Tripp explains, "Love is willing to speak difficult truths, but it always does so with grace, patience, and kindness."[10]

4. **Quick resolution of anger:** Ephesians 4:26-27 advises, *"Do not let the sun go down on your anger, and give no opportunity to the devil."* While this doesn't mean every issue must be fully resolved before bedtime, it

emphasizes the importance of addressing conflicts promptly rather than allowing them to fester.[11]

5. **Forgiveness as Christ forgave us:** Colossians 3:13 instructs, *"Bear with each other and forgive one another if any of you has a grievance against someone. Forgive as the Lord forgave you."* This radical forgiveness—undeserved, complete, and costly—provides the model for forgiveness in marriage.[12]

6. **The pursuit of peace:** Romans 12:18 calls believers to *"live at peace with everyone"* as far as it depends on them. This doesn't mean avoiding necessary confrontation but approaching conflict with a genuine desire for reconciliation rather than victory.

These biblical principles provide the foundation for a redemptive approach to marital conflict—one that seeks growth, understanding, and stronger relationship rather than simply "winning" arguments or avoiding tension.

Common Sources of Conflict in Marriage

While every marriage is unique, research and counseling experience reveal several common areas of conflict that most couples face. Understanding these typical sources of tension can help couples anticipate challenges and develop strategies for addressing them constructively.[13]

1. Money and Financial Management

Financial issues consistently rank among the top sources of marital conflict. Couples often bring different attitudes, habits, and expectations about money into marriage, creating tension when these differences emerge. As Ron Blue observes, "Money problems in marriage are rarely about money. They're about values, goals, and communication."[14]

Common financial conflicts include:

- Different spending priorities
- Disagreements about saving versus spending
- Secrecy or dishonesty about purchases
- Imbalance in financial decision-making
- Stress over debt or financial insecurity
- Different attitudes toward risk

Scripture provides wisdom for financial management that can help couples navigate these challenges. Principles such as *avoiding debt* (Proverbs 22:7), *planning for the future* (Proverbs 21:5), *generosity* (2 Corinthians 9:6-7), and *contentment* (Hebrews 13:5) create a foundation for healthy financial decisions.

2. Division of Responsibilities

How couples divide household tasks, childcare, and other responsibilities often creates tension, especially when expectations differ or when one spouse feels the division is unfair. This area has become increasingly complex as more couples navigate dual careers while maintaining a home and raising children.

While Scripture doesn't provide a detailed "chore chart" for marriage, it does establish *principles of mutual service* (Galatians 5:13), *consideration of others' needs* (Philippians 2:4), and *working diligently in one's responsibilities* (Colossians 3:23). These principles guide couples toward arrangements that honor both partners' gifts, limitations, and circumstances.[15]

3. Sex and Physical Intimacy

Physical intimacy is designed by God as a beautiful gift for marriage, but it can become a source of conflict when couples have different expectations, desires, or approaches. As Kevin Leman notes, "Sex is a thermometer that reflects the health of the entire relationship. When there are problems in this area, they're usually symptoms of deeper issues."[16]

Common conflicts around physical intimacy include:

- Different levels of desire or frequency expectations
- Timing and initiation patterns
- Unresolved hurts or resentments affecting intimacy
- Communication difficulties about preferences and needs
- Past experiences or wounds influencing the present
- Physical or health challenges affecting sexual expression

Scripture addresses physical intimacy directly in 1 Corinthians 7:3-5, emphasizing mutual giving and receiving rather than one-sided demands or withholding. This passage establishes that physical intimacy involves mutual submission and consideration rather than self-focused gratification.[17]

4. In-laws and Extended Family

Navigating relationships with extended family—particularly parents and in-laws—creates challenges for many couples. Genesis 2:24 establishes that marriage involves "leaving" one's parents and "cleaving" to one's spouse, creating a new primary relationship. However, implementing this principle while maintaining healthy extended family connections requires wisdom and intentionality.[18]

Common conflicts in this area include:

- Different expectations about time spent with extended family
- Interference or unsolicited advice from parents or in-laws
- Divided loyalties during family disagreements
- Different family traditions and holiday expectations
- Boundary violations by extended family members
- Unresolved issues from the family of origin affecting the marriage

Jesus modeled both honors toward parents and appropriate boundaries. He remained subject to His parents as a child (Luke 2:51) but also established boundaries when His ministry required it (Mark 3:31-35). This balanced approach guides couples in developing healthy extended family relationships.

5. Parenting Approaches

For couples with children, differences in parenting philosophy, discipline methods, and child-rearing priorities often create significant tension. As James Dobson observes, "Few areas in marriage create more conflict than disagreements about how to raise and discipline children."[19]

Common parenting conflicts include:

- Different views on discipline methods and consistency
- Disagreements about appropriate boundaries and rules
- One parent being more permissive or strict than the other
- Different expectations about children's behavior or achievements
- Disagreements about education choices
- Different levels of involvement in childcare and parenting tasks

Scripture provides principles for parenting—such as training children in God's ways (Deuteronomy 6:6-7), not provoking them to anger (Ephesians 6:4), and providing both nurture and discipline (Proverbs 13:24, 22:6)—but allows flexibility in how these principles are applied in different families and with different children.

Destructive Conflict Patterns

How couples handle disagreements matters more than what they disagree about. Research by Dr. John Gottman has identified specific conflict patterns that predict relationship failure when they become habitual. He calls these "The Four Horsemen of the Apocalypse" because of their destructive power in relationships.[20]

1. Criticism

Criticism involves attacking your spouse's character or personality rather than addressing specific behaviors. It often includes generalizations like "you always" or "you never" and implies negative character traits rather than focusing on actions. For example, "You're so selfish. You never think about anyone but yourself" is criticism, while "I felt hurt when you made plans without checking with me first" addresses a specific behavior.

Criticism damages relationships by:

- Making the recipient feel attacked and defensive
- Creating an atmosphere of negativity and judgment
- Focusing on personality rather than changeable behaviors
- Implying permanent character flaws rather than temporary mistakes

The biblical alternative to criticism is described in Ephesians 4:29: *"Let no corrupting talk come out of your mouths, but only such as is good for building up, as fits the occasion, that it may give grace to those who hear."* This constructive communication addresses issues without attacking the person.[21]

2. Contempt

Contempt goes beyond criticism to express disgust, superiority, or disdain toward one's spouse. It includes sarcasm, eye-rolling, mockery, name-calling, and hostile humor. Gottman identifies contempt as the single greatest predictor of divorce because it communicates, "I'm better than you, and I don't respect you."[22]

Contempt violates the biblical command to honor others (Romans 12:10) and contradicts the marriage covenant, which involves promising to love and cherish one's spouse. As Timothy Keller observes, "Contempt is incompatible with the gospel, which reminds us that we are all sinners saved by grace, with no grounds for feeling superior to anyone."

The antidote to contempt is cultivating a culture of appreciation and respect in the marriage. This involves intentionally focusing on your spouse's positive qualities and expressing gratitude for their contributions, even amid disagreements. As Emerson Eggerichs emphasizes in Love and Respect, "Respect is as powerful for a husband as love is for a wife."[23]

3. Defensiveness

Defensiveness is a natural response to feeling attacked, but it escalates conflict rather than resolving it. Defensive responses include making excuses, counter-attacking, playing the victim, or denying responsibility. For example, "It's not my fault we're late. You always take forever to get ready" shifts blame rather than addressing the issue.

Defensiveness prevents genuine listening and problem-solving. As Proverbs 18:13 warns, *"If one gives an answer before he hears, it is his folly and shame."* When we're focused on defending ourselves, we cannot truly hear our spouse's concerns or take responsibility for our contributions to the problem.[24]

The biblical alternative to defensiveness is taking responsibility for our part in conflicts, even if it's just a small part. Jesus taught this principle in Matthew 7:3-5 when He instructed us to remove the log from our own eye before addressing the speck in another's eye. This humble self-examination creates space for genuine resolution.

4. Stonewalling

Stonewalling occurs when one partner withdraws from interaction, shuts down, or refuses to engage. It might look like silent treatment, physically leaving during an argument, or emotionally checking out. While sometimes presented as "just needing space," habitual stonewalling prevents resolution and creates emotional abandonment.[25]

Stonewalling often occurs when a person feels overwhelmed by negative emotions and doesn't know how to process them constructively. Physiologically, it may involve "flooding"—when heart rate increases, stress hormones surge, and the ability to think clearly and communicate effectively diminishes.

The biblical alternative to stonewalling is remaining engaged while managing emotions appropriately. Ephesians 4:26 instructs, *"Be angry and do not sin; do not let the sun go down on your anger."* This requires developing skills for emotional regulation and healthy time-outs rather than complete withdrawal.

Practical Skills for Resolving Conflict

While understanding biblical principles and recognizing destructive patterns is essential, couples also need practical skills for addressing conflicts constructively. These skills can be learned and developed with practice and intentionality.

1. Choose the Right Time and Place

Timing significantly impacts how conflicts unfold. Ecclesiastes 3:1 reminds us that *"there is a time for everything and a season for every activity under the heavens."* This wisdom applies to addressing marital conflicts as well.[26]

Effective conflict resolution typically requires:

- Privacy (not in front of children, family, or friends)
- Adequate time (not rushing to leave for work or before bed)
- Both partners being physically and emotionally available (not exhausted, hungry, or distracted)
- Relative calm (not in the heat of intense emotions)

2. Use "I" Statements Rather Than "You" Accusations

How we frame our concerns significantly impacts how they are received. "You" statements often sound accusatory and trigger defensiveness: "You never help around the house" or "You always interrupt me." In contrast, "I" statements express feelings and needs without attacking: "I feel overwhelmed when I'm handling all the household chores" or "I feel frustrated when I can't finish my thought."[27]

Effective "I" statements typically include three elements:

- A feeling ("I feel...")
- A specific behavior (not a character judgment)
- The impact of that behavior on you

For example, instead of "You're so inconsiderate with money," an "I" statement might be: "I feel anxious when large purchases are made without discussion because it affects our financial security."

This approach aligns with the biblical principle of speaking truth in love (Ephesians 4:15). It communicates honest concerns while minimizing blame and defensiveness, creating space for productive conversation rather than escalating conflict.

3. Practice Active Listening

James 1:19 instructs believers to be *"quick to listen, slow to speak, slow to become angry."* This principle is especially valuable during a conflict when our natural tendency is to focus on formulating our response rather than truly understanding our spouse.[28]

Active listening involves:

- Giving full attention (putting away phones, turning off the TV)
- Maintaining appropriate eye contact and open body language

- Asking clarifying questions to ensure understanding
- Reflecting back on what you've heard ("What I hear you saying is...")
- Validating emotions even if you don't share the perspective ("I can see why you'd feel that way")
- Resisting the urge to interrupt or immediately counter

4. Seek Win-Win Solutions

Once a couple understands each other's perspectives and the core issues involved, they can work together to find solutions that address both partners' concerns. Philippians 2:4 instructs believers to *"look not only to his own interests but also to the interests of others."* This principle guides couples toward solutions that honor both spouses rather than one person always sacrificing for the other.[29]

Developing win-win solutions involves:

- Brainstorming multiple options without immediately evaluating them
- Considering creative compromises that incorporate elements important to both spouses
- Focusing on shared goals and values
- Being willing to prioritize what matters most to each person
- Approaching the problem as a team rather than as opponents

5. Apologize Sincerely When Appropriate

Genuine apologies are powerful in resolving conflicts and healing relationships. James 5:16 instructs believers to *"confess your sins to one another and pray for one another, that you may be healed."* In marriage, this means taking responsibility for our contributions to conflicts and sincerely apologizing when we've caused hurt.[30]

Effective apologies include several elements:

- Specifically acknowledging what you did wrong
- Expressing genuine remorse
- Accepting responsibility without excuses
- Offering to make amends when possible
- Committing to change the behavior

6. Extend Forgiveness Freely

Forgiveness is at the heart of the gospel and essential for healthy marriages. Ephesians 4:32 instructs believers to *"be kind to one another, tenderhearted, forgiving one another, as God in Christ forgave you."* This radical forgiveness—undeserved, complete, and costly—provides the model for forgiveness in marriage.[31]

Biblical forgiveness involves:

- Choosing to release the offense rather than holding it against your spouse
- Committing not to bring up the forgiven offense as a weapon in future conflicts
- Extending grace rather than demanding penance
- Working toward the restoration of the relationship
- Trusting God with justice rather than seeking revenge

Conflict in Different Seasons of Marriage

Conflict patterns and challenges evolve throughout the seasons of marriage. Understanding these typical patterns helps couples anticipate and navigate conflicts appropriate to their stage of relationship.

The Newlywed Season

In the early years of marriage, couples often experience conflicts related to merging two lives and establishing new patterns together. Common areas of adjustment include:

- Establishing daily routines and habits
- Navigating differences in expectations about roles and responsibilities
- Learning each other's conflict styles
- Adjusting to each other's families and friends
- Managing finances together
- Developing healthy boundaries with others[32]

The Parenting Years

When children enter the picture, couples often experience new sources of conflict related to parenting responsibilities, reduced couple time, increased financial pressures, and fatigue. Research consistently shows that marital satisfaction typically decreases during the early parenting years unless couples are intentional about maintaining their relationship.[33]

The Middle Years

As careers advance and children become more independent, couples enter what some call the "middle years" of marriage. This season often brings conflicts related to:

- Reassessing life goals and priorities at midlife
- Navigating changing roles as children become more independent
- Addressing issues that were previously masked by busyness
- Caring for aging parents
- Adjusting to physical and hormonal changes

The Later Years

The retirement years bring both opportunities and challenges for conflict resolution. Couples often have more time together than ever before, which can either strengthen their connection or highlight unresolved issues. Health concerns, changing roles, and end-of-life planning require sensitive, thoughtful communication.[34]

When to Seek Help

While many conflicts can be resolved through the principles and skills discussed in this chapter, some situations require professional assistance. Seeking help is not a sign of failure but of commitment to the relationship. As Proverbs 12:15 reminds us, *"The way of a fool is right in his own eyes, but a wise man listens to advice."*[35]

Signs that professional help might be needed include:

1. Persistent negative patterns that don't improve despite your best efforts
2. Physical, emotional, verbal, or sexual abuse (which requires immediate intervention)
3. Addiction issues affecting the relationship
4. Infidelity or serious breaches of trust
5. Depression or other mental health issues complicating conflict resolution
6. Consideration of separation or divorce
7. Inability to discuss certain topics without extreme conflict

Conclusion: From Conflict to Connection

Conflict, while challenging, provides opportunities for growth that harmony never could. When handled with wisdom, grace, and skill, conflicts can lead to deeper understanding, stronger commitment, and more authentic intimacy. As Gary Thomas observes, "The couples who grow the most are often those who have faced significant challenges and worked through them together."[36]

The biblical approach to conflict resolution transforms marriage from a battlefield into a training ground for Christlike character. Through the daily practice of humility, forgiveness, patience, and love, spouses help sanctify each other and reflect God's redemptive work in their relationship.[37]

Remember that perfection is not the goal—progress is. Every couple faces conflicts, but those who commit to working through these challenges rather than avoiding them or giving up grow stronger through the process. As Paul wrote to the Philippians, *"Not that I have already obtained this or am already perfect, but I press on..."* (Philippians 3:12). This attitude of ongoing growth serves marriages well.

As you apply the principles in this chapter, be patient with yourself and your spouse. Change takes time, especially when it involves patterns developed over years. Celebrate small improvements, extend grace when you fall short, and keep pressing forward toward more constructive ways of handling conflict.[38]

Above all, remember that God is for your marriage. He designed this relationship and provided the wisdom and power to navigate its challenges. As you seek His help and apply His principles, your conflicts can become catalysts for deeper connection rather than causes of division.

Chapter 6

Intimacy In Marriage

The Sacred Union of Body, Heart, and Spirit

"Therefore a man shall leave his father and his mother and hold fast to his wife, and they shall become one flesh." (Genesis 2:24)

Intimacy represents one of God's greatest gifts to married couples—the opportunity to know and be known completely without shame or reservation. While our culture often reduces intimacy to merely physical connection, biblical intimacy encompasses a much richer, multidimensional relationship that includes emotional, intellectual, and spiritual dimensions alongside physical union.

This chapter explores God's design for marital intimacy in all its dimensions, addressing common challenges couples face and providing practical wisdom for building deeper connections. Whether you're preparing for marriage or have been married for decades, these insights will help you experience the profound intimacy God intended for husbands and wives.

The Biblical Foundation for Marital Intimacy

Scripture provides a rich theological framework for understanding intimacy in marriage. From Genesis to Revelation, we see God's affirmation of marital intimacy as a sacred gift designed for both procreation and profound union.[1]

Created for Intimate Connection

The creation account reveals that humans were designed for intimate relationships. Genesis 2:18 records God's declaration that *"it is not good that the man should be alone; I will make him a helper fit for him."* This statement establishes that solitude contradicts God's design for humanity—we were created for connection.

Timothy Keller observes that "marriage was created to address the fundamental human need for intimate companionship."[2] Unlike all other creatures, humans experience loneliness and require deep, personal relationships to flourish. Marriage provides the most comprehensive answer to this need, creating a relationship of unique closeness and vulnerability.

Genesis 2:24-25 describes the first marriage with profound simplicity: *"Therefore a man shall leave his father and his mother and hold fast to his wife, and they shall become one flesh. And the man and his wife were both naked and were not ashamed."* This passage establishes several foundational principles for marital intimacy:

1. **Exclusivity and priority:** "Leave father and mother" indicates that marriage creates a new primary relationship that takes precedence over all others.

2. **Permanent commitment:** "Hold fast" (the Hebrew term suggests being glued or welded together) establishes the permanence and strength of the marital bond.

3. **Complete union:** "Become one flesh" describes a comprehensive joining that includes physical union but extends to emotional, intellectual, and spiritual connection as well.

4. **Vulnerability without shame:** "Naked and not ashamed" indicates the freedom to be completely known and accepted without fear or hiding.

As Andreas Köstenberger notes, "The Genesis account establishes that intimate marital union reflects God's original design for humanity, not a concession to human weakness."[3] This theological foundation elevates marital intimacy from merely a physical act to a sacred experience that reflects God's intentions for human flourishing.

The Goodness of Physical Intimacy

While some religious traditions have viewed physical intimacy with suspicion or as a necessary evil for procreation, Scripture consistently affirms the goodness of physical union within marriage. The Song of Solomon celebrates the beauty and pleasure of physical intimacy between husband and wife with poetic appreciation rather than clinical detachment or embarrassment.

Ed Wheat observes that "the Bible's unabashed celebration of physical love in marriage provides a corrective to both prudish rejection and worldly distortion of sexuality."[4] This balanced perspective recognizes physical intimacy as a divine gift to be enjoyed within the protective boundaries of covenant commitment.

1 Corinthians 7:3-5 instructs married couples: *"The husband should give to his wife her conjugal rights, and likewise the wife to her husband. For the wife does not have authority over her own body, but the husband does. Likewise, the husband does not have authority over his own body, but the wife does. Do not deprive one another, except perhaps by agreement for a limited time, that you may devote yourselves to prayer; but then come together again, so that Satan may not tempt you because of your lack of self-control."*

This passage establishes several important principles:

- Physical intimacy represents a mutual obligation within marriage
- Spouses' bodies belong to each other in a unique way
- Regular physical intimacy provides protection against temptation
- Physical intimacy should only be postponed temporarily and by mutual agreement

Hebrews 13:4 further affirms, *"Let marriage be held in honor among all, and let the marriage bed be undefiled, for God will judge the sexually immoral and adulterous."*

This verse simultaneously elevates marital intimacy as honorable while establishing clear boundaries around its expression.

Intimacy as a Picture of Divine Relationship

Throughout Scripture, the intimate relationship between husband and wife serves as a metaphor for God's relationship with His people. The prophets frequently described God's covenant with Israel using marriage imagery (Isaiah 54:5, Jeremiah 3:14, Hosea 2:19-20), and the New Testament presents the church as the bride of Christ (Ephesians 5:25-32, Revelation 19:7-9).

Ray Ortlund notes that "the intimate union of marriage provides the most powerful earthly picture of the intimate spiritual union God desires with His people."[5] This theological connection infuses marital intimacy with profound spiritual significance, elevating it beyond mere physical pleasure or emotional connection to a living parable of divine love.

Ephesians 5:31-32 makes this connection explicit: *"'Therefore a man shall leave his father and mother and hold fast to his wife, and the two shall become one flesh.' This mystery is profound, and I am saying that it refers to Christ and the church."* The intimate union of husband and wife mysteriously reflects the union between Christ and His church—a relationship of sacrificial love, complete commitment, and profound intimacy.

This theological understanding transforms how couples view their intimate relationship. Rather than focusing primarily on personal satisfaction, they recognize their union as a sacred trust that can display the gospel to a watching world. As Gary Thomas observes, "Marital intimacy becomes a form of worship when we recognize its spiritual significance."[6]

The Multidimensional Nature of Intimacy

While physical union represents an important aspect of marital intimacy, Scripture presents a much richer, multidimensional understanding of intimate connection. True biblical intimacy encompasses physical, emotional, intellectual, and spiritual dimensions that work together to create a profound union.[7]

Physical Intimacy: The Union of Bodies

Physical intimacy—the sexual union of husband and wife—provides a unique form of connection that both expresses and deepens the marriage covenant. This dimension of intimacy involves not just the act of intercourse but the entire realm of physical affection, touch, and bodily connection.

Ed Wheat describes physical intimacy as "the natural culmination of the other forms of intimacy, not a separate or independent aspect of marriage."[8] When built upon emotional, intellectual, and spiritual connection, physical intimacy becomes a profound expression of complete knowing and being known.

Physical intimacy serves several important purposes in marriage:

1. **Procreation:** Genesis 1:28 establishes that one purpose of physical union is the creation of new life. This procreative potential infuses marital intimacy with profound significance as participation in God's creative work.
2. **Pleasure and delight:** The Song of Solomon celebrates the mutual pleasure and delight that physical intimacy brings to husband and wife. This pleasure represents a divine gift to be gratefully enjoyed.
3. **Comfort and reassurance:** Physical touch and sexual union provide powerful reassurance of acceptance and desire, meeting deep emotional needs for affirmation and security.

4. **Protection against temptation:** As 1 Corinthians 7:2-5 indicates, regular physical intimacy helps protect against sexual temptation outside the marriage covenant.

5. **Reconciliation after conflict:** Physical union often serves as a powerful means of reconciliation after conflict, helping restore emotional connection and reassurance of commitment.

As Kevin Leman notes, "God designed physical intimacy to be a multifaceted blessing in marriage, serving purposes far beyond mere physical release."[9] This rich understanding elevates sexual union from a merely physical act to a profound expression of covenant love.

Emotional Intimacy: The Union of Hearts

Emotional intimacy involves sharing feelings, desires, fears, and dreams with complete openness and vulnerability. This heart-to-heart connection creates a sense of being fully known and accepted that meets our deepest relational needs.

Gary Chapman observes that "emotional intimacy often proves more challenging than physical intimacy because it requires greater vulnerability and risk."[10] While the physical union can occur without emotional openness, true emotional intimacy requires the willingness to reveal one's inner world without pretense or protection.

Scripture provides numerous examples of emotional intimacy between spouses. In Genesis 24:67, we read that Isaac "loved" Rebekah, indicating emotional connection beyond mere arrangement or duty. The Song of Solomon repeatedly expresses the emotional vulnerability and affection between the lovers: *"My beloved is mine, and I am his"* (2:16).

Emotional intimacy develops through:

- Transparent sharing of feelings and experiences
- Empathetic listening without judgment or criticism
- Validation of each other's emotional reality
- Comfort and support during painful experiences
- Celebration of each other's joys and accomplishments

As Les and Leslie Parrott note, "Emotional intimacy creates the safety that allows other forms of intimacy to flourish."[11] When spouses feel emotionally secure with each other, they can be more vulnerable physically, intellectually, and spiritually.

Intellectual Intimacy: The Union of Minds

Intellectual intimacy involves sharing thoughts, ideas, opinions, and values with openness and respect. This meeting of minds creates connection through meaningful conversation, shared learning, and mutual understanding of how each person thinks and processes the world.

Timothy Keller observes that "intellectual intimacy often receives less attention than other forms but provides essential connection, especially during seasons when physical intimacy might be limited."[12] The ability to engage in stimulating conversation and share meaningful ideas creates bonds that can endure through many life changes.

Proverbs 27:17 states that *"iron sharpens iron, and one man sharpens another."* This principle applies powerfully in marriage, where intellectual engagement helps both spouses grow in wisdom, understanding, and perspective. Couples who maintain a curious interest in each other's thoughts and ideas often experience growing intellectual intimacy throughout their marriage.

Intellectual intimacy develops through:

- Meaningful conversations about ideas and beliefs
- Respectful discussion of differences in perspective
- Shared learning experiences and growth
- Curiosity about each other's thoughts and opinions
- Appreciation for each other's unique intellectual gifts

As Gary Thomas notes, "Intellectual intimacy creates a friendship dimension in marriage that sustains connection through changing seasons and circumstances."[13] Couples who enjoy talking with each other and learning together build resilience in their relationship.

Spiritual Intimacy: The Union of Souls

Spiritual intimacy involves sharing faith experiences, questions, insights, and practices. This soul-to-soul connection creates the deepest level of intimacy as couples encounter God together and support each other's spiritual growth.

Dennis Rainey describes spiritual intimacy as "the ultimate form of intimacy that sanctifies and enriches all other dimensions of marital connection."[14] When couples share authentic spiritual life together, they experience a transcendent dimension of intimacy that goes beyond human connection to include divine presence.

2 Corinthians 6:14 warns against being *"unequally yoked with unbelievers,"* recognizing that spiritual disconnection creates significant barriers to intimate marriage. Conversely, when couples share faith commitment, they can experience profound spiritual intimacy that strengthens their entire relationship.

Spiritual intimacy develops through:

- Praying together regularly

-Discussing Scripture and spiritual insights

-Worshiping together both publicly and privately

-Supporting each other through spiritual struggles

-Serving others together as an expression of faith

As Gary Chapman observes, "Spiritual intimacy doesn't require identical spiritual experiences but rather mutual respect and support for each other's faith journey."[15] Couples can experience deep spiritual connection even when they express their faith in somewhat different ways or are at different places in their spiritual development.

Common Barriers to Marital Intimacy

Despite God's design for profound intimacy in marriage, many couples struggle to experience the deep connection they desire. Understanding common barriers helps couples address these challenges intentionally.[16]

Unresolved Conflict and Resentment

Perhaps the most common barrier to intimacy is an unresolved conflict that creates emotional distance and resentment. When hurts accumulate without resolution, couples build emotional walls that prevent vulnerability and connection.

Emerson Eggerichs notes that "unresolved conflict affects all dimensions of intimacy but often impacts emotional and physical connection most immediately."[17] A spouse harboring resentment typically finds emotional openness difficult and may withdraw from physical intimacy as well.

Scripture addresses this reality in Ephesians 4:26-27: *"Do not let the sun go down on your anger, and give no opportunity to the devil."* This instruction recognizes that unresolved anger creates openings for damage to the relationship, including diminished intimacy.

Signs that conflict is hindering intimacy include:

- Emotional withdrawal or coldness
- Reduced physical affection and sexual connection
- Criticism or contempt in communication
- Avoidance of meaningful conversation
- Focusing on children or other relationships instead of marriage

Addressing this barrier requires a commitment to healthy conflict resolution—acknowledging hurts, extending forgiveness, making necessary changes, and rebuilding trust through consistent behavior. As Gary Chapman observes, "Intimacy cannot coexist with unresolved conflict; one will eventually eliminate the other."[18]

Mismatched Expectations and Desires

Differences in expectations and desires regarding intimacy—particularly its frequency, expression, and priority—create significant challenges for many couples. These differences can affect any dimension of intimacy but often emerge most visibly around physical connection.

Kevin Leman explains that "differences in desire for physical intimacy represent one of the most common sources of frustration in marriage."[19] When one spouse consistently desires more frequent sexual connection than the other, both partners can experience rejection, pressure, inadequacy, or resentment.

Similar mismatches can occur with other forms of intimacy:

- One spouse may desire deeper emotional conversations, while the other prefers more practical communication

131

- One may value intellectual discussion, while the other finds such conversation draining
- One may prioritize shared spiritual practices while the other prefers more individual expression of faith

1 Corinthians 7:3-5 addresses the importance of mutual consideration regarding physical intimacy, instructing spouses not to "deprive one another" but to make decisions about sexual intimacy by "agreement." This principle of mutual consideration applies to all dimensions of intimacy.

Addressing mismatched expectations requires honest communication, empathy for different needs, and willingness to find mutually satisfying approaches. As Les and Leslie Parrott note, "The goal isn't identical desires but rather loving accommodation of differences."[20]

Busyness and Distraction

The frenetic pace of contemporary life creates another common barrier to intimacy. Between work demands, parenting responsibilities, household management, technology distractions, and community involvement, many couples find little time or energy to nurture intimate connections.

Gary Thomas observes that "busyness doesn't merely limit time for intimacy but often depletes the emotional and physical energy intimacy requires."[21] Couples may technically have time together but lack the mental presence and emotional availability that intimate connection demands.

Scripture addresses this reality in various passages that emphasize the importance of rest, margin, and prioritizing what matters most. Mark 6:31 records Jesus telling his disciples, *"Come away by yourselves to a desolate place and rest a while,"* recognizing their need for respite from constant activity and demands.

Signs that busyness is hindering intimacy include:

- Consistently postponing a couple times for other activities
- Bringing work or other responsibilities into a couple times
- Falling asleep during conversation or physical intimacy
- Feeling too exhausted for meaningful connection
- Digital devices consuming potential times for intimacy

Addressing this barrier requires intentional choices about time and priorities. As Dennis Rainey notes, "Intimacy rarely happens spontaneously in our busy culture; it requires deliberate protection of time and energy."[22]

Past Wounds and Baggage

Many individuals bring wounds from previous relationships or childhood experiences into marriage. These past hurts can create significant barriers to intimacy, making vulnerability feel threatening rather than inviting.

H. Norman Wright explains that "past relational wounds often create protective patterns that limit intimacy, even when the current relationship is safe and loving."[23] Someone who experienced betrayal may struggle with trust; someone who experienced rejection may fear vulnerability; someone who experienced abuse may find aspects of physical intimacy triggering.

Scripture acknowledges the reality of woundedness while pointing toward healing. Isaiah 61:1 describes the Messiah's mission to *"bind up the brokenhearted,"* and 2 Corinthians 5:17 declares that *"if anyone is in Christ, he is a new creation."* These truths offer hope that past wounds need not permanently limit marital intimacy.

Common ways past wounds manifest in marriage include:

- Fear of abandonment leading to clingy behavior or emotional withdrawal
- Trust issues creating jealousy or constant questioning

133

- Shame about sexuality limiting physical intimacy
- Fear of conflict leading to people-pleasing or conflict avoidance
- Emotional numbness preventing deep connection

Addressing these barriers often requires professional help alongside spiritual resources. As Cloud and Townsend observe, "Healing from significant past wounds typically requires both divine grace and human assistance."[24]

Poor Communication Patterns

Ineffective communication creates significant barriers to all forms of intimacy. When couples cannot express needs, listen empathetically, or resolve differences constructively, the intimate connection becomes difficult or impossible.

Emerson Eggerichs notes that "communication problems often reflect deeper issues of respect and love that directly impact intimacy."[25] When communication patterns involve criticism, defensiveness, contempt, or stonewalling (what researcher John Gottman calls the "Four Horsemen" of relationship breakdown), intimacy inevitably suffers.

Ephesians 4:29 instructs believers to speak words *"that give grace to those who hear."* This principle applies powerfully to marriage, where grace-filled communication creates space for intimate connection while harsh or careless words create distance.

Common communication patterns that hinder intimacy include:

- Criticism that attacks character rather than addressing specific behaviors
- Defensiveness that rejects feedback instead of considering it thoughtfully
- Contempt that communicates disgust or superiority

- Stonewalling that withdraws from engagement rather than working through issues
- Mind-reading that assumes negative intentions without clarification

Addressing these patterns requires learning new communication skills and practicing them consistently. As Gary Chapman observes, "Communication skills aren't innate but learned, and most couples need intentional effort to develop healthy patterns."[26]

Cultivating Deeper Intimacy in Marriage

While barriers to intimacy are real, couples can develop practices that foster deeper connection in all dimensions of their relationship. These approaches help create the vulnerability, trust, and engagement that intimacy requires.[27]

Creating Space for Intimacy

Meaningful intimacy requires both time and appropriate space—physical, emotional, and mental room for connection to develop. In our busy, distracted culture, intentionally creating this space often represents the first step toward deeper intimacy.

Dennis Rainey emphasizes that "intimacy rarely happens accidentally but requires deliberate creation of space in our schedules and environments."[28] This intentionality demonstrates that intimate connection represents a genuine priority rather than merely a nice idea.

Practical approaches for creating space include:

1. **Schedule regular couple time:** Set aside specific times for connection without children, technology, or other distractions. This might include weekly date nights, daily check-in conversations, or weekend getaways.

2. **Create physical space for intimacy:** Ensure your bedroom provides a comfortable, appealing environment for physical and emotional connection. This might involve removing work materials, limiting technology, or enhancing comfort and aesthetics.

3. **Establish mental and emotional space:** Develop transition rituals that help you shift from work or parenting mode to couple mode. This might include changing clothes, taking a walk together, or sharing a cup of tea before engaging in deeper conversation.

4. **Protect boundaries around your marriage:** Learn to say no to activities or commitments that consistently infringe on couple time. This boundary-setting honors the priority of your marriage relationship.

5. **Limit digital distractions:** Establish technology-free zones or times that allow for undivided attention to each other. The constant presence of phones, tablets, and other devices often prevents the mental presence intimacy requires.

Song of Solomon 7:11-12 describes this intentional creation of space for intimacy: *"Come, my beloved, let us go out into the fields and lodge in the villages; let us go out early to the vineyards and see whether the vines have budded."* This invitation to a specific place and time for connection models the intentionality of an intimate relationship requires.

Building Emotional Intimacy

Emotional intimacy—the sharing of feelings, desires, fears, and dreams—creates a foundation for other forms of connection. Developing this heart-to-heart relationship requires specific skills and practices that many couples need to learn intentionally.

Gary Chapman observes that "emotional intimacy develops through consistent, small moments of connection rather than occasional grand gestures."[29] These everyday interactions gradually build the trust and understanding that allow deeper vulnerability.

Approaches for building emotional intimacy include:

1. **Practice empathetic listening:** Give full attention when your spouse shares feelings or experiences, seeking to understand their perspective without judgment or immediate problem-solving. This attentive presence communicates that their inner world matters to you.

2. **Share feelings with vulnerability:** Express your own emotions honestly but without accusation or blame. Using "I feel" statements rather than "you make me feel" statements takes responsibility for your emotions while still sharing them authentically.

3. **Validate each other's emotions:** Acknowledge the legitimacy of each other's feelings even when you don't share the same perspective or reaction. This validation communicates acceptance of your spouse's emotional reality.

4. **Ask meaningful questions:** Move beyond surface conversation with questions that invite deeper sharing. "What was that experience like for you?" or "What's been on your heart lately?" create openings for emotional connection.

5. **Respond to emotional bids:** Notice and respond positively when your spouse makes small overtures for connection—sharing an observation, expressing a concern, or seeking your opinion. These responses to "emotional bids" (as researcher John Gottman calls them) build connections over time.

Proverbs 20:5 observes that *"the purpose in a man's heart is like deep water, but a man of understanding will draw it out."* This imagery of drawing out what lies beneath the surface captures the patient, attentive approach that builds emotional intimacy.

Nurturing Physical Intimacy

Physical intimacy—from non-sexual affection to complete sexual union—provides a unique form of connection that both expresses and deepens the marriage covenant. Nurturing this dimension of intimacy requires understanding, communication, and intentionality.

Kevin Leman emphasizes that "satisfying physical intimacy develops from the broader relationship rather than existing independently from it."[30] When built upon emotional connection, mutual respect, and spiritual unity, physical intimacy becomes a natural expression of comprehensive intimacy rather than a disconnected physical act.

Approaches for nurturing physical intimacy include:

1. **Prioritize non-sexual affection:** Maintain regular physical connection through holding hands, embracing, kissing, and other forms of touch that communicate affection without sexual intent. This ongoing physical connection creates a foundation for sexual intimacy.

2. **Communicate about desires and needs:** Develop comfortable, respectful ways to express preferences, desires, and needs regarding physical intimacy. This communication prevents misunderstanding and helps create mutually satisfying experiences.

3. **Address physical barriers:** Proactively address health issues, fatigue, stress, or other physical factors that affect sexual intimacy. This might involve medical consultation, stress management, or adjusting schedules to ensure adequate energy.

4. **Create a romantic atmosphere:** Invest in setting the stage for intimate connection through attention to environment, timing, and preparation. This intentionality communicates that physical intimacy represents a priority worth planning for.

5. **Maintain physical well-being:** Recognize that general health significantly impacts sexual function and satisfaction. Regular exercise, adequate sleep, healthy nutrition, and limited alcohol contribute to physical intimacy.

The Song of Solomon portrays physical intimacy as both passionate and tender, with careful attention to atmosphere, appreciation of each other's bodies, and mutual pleasure. This biblical depiction provides a model of physical intimacy that is both exciting and emotionally connected.

Developing Intellectual Intimacy

Intellectual intimacy—the sharing of thoughts, ideas, opinions, and values—creates connection through meaningful conversation and mutual understanding of how each person thinks and processes the world. This meeting of minds provides essential connection, especially during seasons when physical intimacy might be limited.

Timothy Keller notes that "intellectual intimacy often grows rather than diminishes with age, providing a form of connection that can deepen throughout the marriage journey."[31] As physical energy may decrease in later years, the ability to engage in stimulating conversation and share meaningful ideas becomes increasingly valuable.

Approaches for developing intellectual intimacy include:

1. **Discuss ideas rather than just logistics:** Move beyond household management and scheduling to engage with each other's thoughts about more substantive topics. This might include current events, books, films, spiritual insights, or personal growth.
2. **Respect different thinking styles:** Recognize and appreciate different approaches to processing information and forming opinions. Some people think verbally while others process internally;

some focus on details while others see patterns; some make quick judgments while others consider multiple perspectives.

3. **Learn together intentionally:** Pursue shared learning experiences through reading the same book, taking a class together, watching documentaries, or attending lectures or conferences. These shared intellectual experiences create connections through common reference points.

4. **Ask thoughtful questions:** Express genuine curiosity about your spouse's perspective and thinking process. Questions like "What led you to that conclusion?" or "How do you see this situation?" invite intellectual sharing.

5. **Engage with differences respectfully:** When you disagree on ideas or perspectives, approach these differences with respect and genuine interest rather than dismissal or argument. These differences can enhance rather than threaten intellectual intimacy when handled well.

Proverbs 27:17 states that *"iron sharpens iron, and one man sharpens another."* This principle applies powerfully in marriage, where intellectual engagement helps both spouses grow in wisdom, understanding, and perspective.

Deepening Spiritual Intimacy

Spiritual intimacy—sharing faith experiences, questions, insights, and practices—creates the deepest level of connection as couples encounter God together and support each other's spiritual growth. This soul-to-soul connection provides a transcendent dimension to marriage that strengthens all other forms of intimacy.

Dennis Rainey describes spiritual intimacy as "the ultimate form of intimacy that sanctifies and enriches all other dimensions of marital connection."[32] When couples share an authentic spiritual life together, they experience a three-way relationship that includes God's presence and purpose.

Approaches for deepening spiritual intimacy include:

1. **Pray together regularly:** Develop comfortable patterns for shared prayer that fit your relationship style. This might range from formal prayers to conversational sharing with God to silent prayer holding hands. The specific approach matters less than the shared experience of approaching God together.

2. **Discuss Scripture and spiritual insights:** Share what you're learning through personal Bible reading, sermons, books, or life experiences. These conversations create spiritual connection through mutual growth and understanding.

3. **Worship together:** Participate in corporate worship regularly and find ways to worship in your home through music, Scripture reading, or other practices that acknowledge God's presence and character.

4. **Serve others together:** Find ministries or service opportunities that allow you to work together in expressing your faith through action. This shared service creates spiritual bonding through common purpose and experience.

5. **Share spiritual questions and struggles:** Create a safe space for authentic sharing about doubts, questions, or spiritual dry seasons. This vulnerability to spiritual struggles often creates a deeper connection than sharing only positive experiences.

Ecclesiastes 4:12 observes that *"a threefold cord is not quickly broken."* When God forms the third strand in the marriage relationship, the union gains strength and resilience beyond what two people alone could achieve.

Navigating Intimacy Challenges in Different Seasons

Intimacy needs, and challenges evolve throughout the marriage journey. Understanding these seasonal patterns helps couples adapt their approach to intimacy as circumstances change.[33]

The Newlywed Years: Establishing Patterns

The early years of marriage establish patterns of intimacy that often persist for decades. During this formative period, couples navigate differences in expectations, preferences, and backgrounds while building their unique approach to intimate connection.

H. Norman Wright notes that "patterns established in the first few years of marriage often determine the health of intimacy for decades to come."[34] This reality makes thoughtful navigation of early intimacy particularly important.

Key focuses during this season include:

1. **Learning each other's intimacy language:** Discovering how each person expresses and receives love and connection across all dimensions of intimacy. These patterns often reflect family background, personality, and previous relationship experiences.

2. **Establishing a comfortable sexual relationship:** Developing mutually satisfying physical intimacy that respects both partners' needs, preferences, and boundaries. This process often involves significant communication, patience, and adjustment.

3. **Creating intimacy rituals and habits:** Establishing regular practices that foster connection, such as evening check-in conversations, weekend activities, or morning prayer together. These rituals create a framework for ongoing intimacy.

4. **Navigating differences with respect:** Addressing differences in intimacy expectations or preferences with respect and compromise rather than criticism or pressure. These differences need not create conflict when approached with mutual consideration.

5. **Building privacy boundaries:** Determining what aspects of your relationship remain private between you and what can be appropriately shared with family, friends, or others. These boundaries protect the sacred space of your intimate relationship.

Song of Solomon 2:7 cautions, *"Do not stir up or awaken love until it pleases,"* suggesting the importance of allowing intimacy to develop naturally rather than forcing it according to external expectations or timelines. This patient approach allows genuine intimacy to flourish.

The Parenting Years: Maintaining Connection Amid Demands

The arrival of children transforms the marriage relationship, creating both new forms of intimacy and significant challenges to the couple's connection. The physical and emotional demands of parenting often leave little energy for nurturing marital intimacy.

Gary Chapman observes that "the parenting years often create the greatest challenge to marital intimacy due to divided attention, exhaustion, and changing roles."[35] Without intentional effort to maintain connection, many couples find themselves functioning more as co-parents than as intimate partners during this season.

Key focuses during this season include:

1. **Protecting couple time:** Establishing regular opportunities for connection without children present, whether through date nights, early morning conversations, or occasional getaways. This protected time communicates that the marriage relationship remains a priority even amid parenting responsibilities.

2. **Adapting intimacy to circumstances:** Finding creative approaches to intimacy that accommodate the realities of parenting, including limited time, energy, and privacy. This adaptation might involve shorter but more frequent connection points rather than extended time together.

3. **Maintaining physical connection:** Ensuring that physical affection and sexual intimacy continue despite fatigue and logistical challenges. This might require more intentional planning and communication than during pre-children years.

4. **Supporting each other's individual needs:** Recognizing and accommodating each other's needs for personal space, rest, and renewal. This mutual support prevents resentment and depletion that would hinder intimacy.

5. **Finding intimacy in shared parenting:** Discovering ways that parenting together can actually enhance intimacy through shared purpose, values, and experiences. These parenting connections complement rather than replace couple intimacy.

Malachi 2:15 connects marriage and parenting: *"Did he not make them one, with a portion of the Spirit in their union? And what was the one God seeking? Godly offspring."* This passage suggests that while parenting represents an important purpose of marriage, the oneness of the couple remains foundational.

The Middle Years: Rekindling and Deepening

As children become more independent and career demands often stabilize, the middle years of marriage provide opportunities for rekindling and deepening intimacy. This season allows couples to rediscover each other and invest in their relationship with renewed focus.

Dennis Rainey describes the middle years as "a season of potential renaissance in marital intimacy for couples who intentionally reconnect after the intense parenting period."[36] With more time, energy, and privacy available, couples can build on their history together while exploring new dimensions of intimacy.

Key focuses during this season include:

1. **Rediscovering each other:** Taking time to learn about each other's evolving interests, dreams, and perspectives rather than assuming you know your spouse completely. This curiosity prevents stagnation, and fosters continued growth together.

2. **Addressing accumulated issues:** Resolving lingering conflicts or disappointments that may have been set aside during busier seasons. This resolution clears barriers to deeper intimacy going forward.

3. **Renewing physical connection:** Investing in physical and sexual intimacy with fresh attention and creativity, recognizing that physical changes may require adaptation but need not diminish satisfaction. This renewal often involves both communication and experimentation.

4. **Developing shared interests:** Finding activities, causes, or pursuits that you enjoy together as a couple. These shared interests create new connection points and experiences.

5. **Planning for the future together:** Discussing and preparing for upcoming life stages, including retirement, potential health challenges, and desired legacy. These forward-looking conversations create a shared vision and purpose.

Psalm 92:14 promises that *"they still bear fruit in old age; they are ever full of sap and green."* This image of continued vitality and fruitfulness applies to marriage relationships that receive ongoing investment and care.

The Later Years: Intimacy Amid Change

The later years of marriage bring significant changes that affect all dimensions of intimacy, including retirement, health challenges, and the realities of aging bodies. These changes require adaptation but also offer unique opportunities for profound connection.

Billy Graham reflected that "the richest intimacy often develops in long marriages where couples have weathered life's challenges together and developed deep understanding of each other."[37] This seasoned intimacy has a depth and tenderness that younger couples have yet to experience.

Key focuses during this season include:

1. **Adapting to physical changes:** Adjusting approaches to physical intimacy to accommodate health conditions, reduced stamina, or other physical changes. These adaptations can maintain satisfying connection despite limitations.

2. **Expressing appreciation and affection:** Continuing to communicate love, desire, and appreciation verbally and physically. These expressions remain important regardless of age or circumstance.

3. **Supporting each other through losses:** Providing emotional and spiritual support through the losses that often accompany aging, including friends, family members, health, and certain activities. This mutual support deepens emotional and spiritual intimacy.

4. **Creating new memories:** Continuing to share new experiences and create fresh memories rather than only reminiscing about the past. These new experiences maintain vitality in the relationship.

5. **Discussing end-of-life matters:** Having honest conversations about preferences regarding medical care, living arrangements, and other end-of-life matters. While challenging, these discussions can

create profound intimacy through their significance and vulnerability.

Ecclesiastes 9:9 advises, *"Enjoy life with the wife whom you love, all the days of your vain life that he has given you under the sun."* This perspective recognizes both the preciousness of the marriage relationship and its temporal nature, encouraging grateful enjoyment of each season together.

Special Circumstances Affecting Marital Intimacy

Certain situations create unique intimacy challenges that require additional wisdom and support. Understanding these special circumstances helps couples navigate them with grace and clarity.[38]

Physical Illness or Disability

Chronic illness, injury, or disability can significantly impact all dimensions of intimacy, particularly physical connection. These health challenges require thoughtful adaptation to maintain intimate relationships despite limitations.

Joni Eareckson Tada, who became quadriplegic as a young woman and later married, observes that "physical limitations need not prevent profound intimacy when couples commit to creative adaptation and focus on the many expressions of intimacy still available."[39] This perspective emphasizes the multidimensional nature of intimate connection rather than reducing it to physical capacity.

Key considerations for couples facing health challenges include:

1. **Communicating openly about limitations and possibilities:** Discussing honestly how health conditions affect various aspects of intimacy and exploring creative alternatives together. This communication prevents misunderstanding and frustration.

2. **Focusing on available expressions of intimacy:** Emphasizing emotional, intellectual, and spiritual connection while adapting physical intimacy to accommodate limitations. This balanced approach prevents defining intimacy solely by physical capacity.

3. **Seeking appropriate medical advice:** Consulting healthcare providers about safe and comfortable approaches to physical intimacy given specific health conditions. Many physical limitations can be accommodated with proper guidance.

4. **Preventing caregiver/patient dynamics from dominating:** Maintaining husband-wife relationships alongside necessary caregiving roles. This distinction helps preserve the essential equality and mutuality of marriage.

5. **Finding support from others in similar situations:** Connecting with other couples navigating similar challenges for encouragement, practical suggestions, and perspective. This community reduces isolation and provides hope.

2 Corinthians 12:9 records God's promise that *"my grace is sufficient for you, for my power is made perfect in weakness."* This assurance applies powerfully to couples maintaining intimate connection despite physical limitations, as God's grace enables forms of intimacy that transcend physical capacity.

Sexual Difficulties and Dysfunctions

Many couples experience sexual difficulties at some point in their marriage, including low desire, pain with intercourse, erectile dysfunction, or inability to reach orgasm. These challenges can create significant stress and disconnection when not addressed with understanding and appropriate help.

Clifford and Joyce Penner, Christian sex therapists, note that "sexual difficulties are extremely common but rarely discussed openly, leaving many couples feeling isolated in their struggles."[40] This silence often prevents couples from seeking help that could resolve or significantly improve their situation.

Key considerations regarding sexual difficulties include:

1. **Ruling out medical causes:** Consulting healthcare providers to identify and address any physical factors contributing to sexual difficulties. Many sexual problems have medical components that respond well to appropriate treatment.

2. **Addressing psychological factors:** Recognizing how stress, anxiety, depression, past trauma, or relationship issues may contribute to sexual difficulties. These psychological factors often require professional help to resolve.

3. **Improving communication about sexual needs:** Developing comfortable, respectful ways to discuss preferences, concerns, and needs regarding sexual intimacy. This communication helps prevent misunderstanding and frustration.

4. **Expanding definition of sexual satisfaction:** Recognizing that satisfying sexual intimacy encompasses much more than specific physical acts or responses. This broader understanding reduces performance pressure and increases satisfaction.

5. **Seeking appropriate professional help:** Consulting sex therapists, counselors, or medical specialists with expertise in sexual health when difficulties persist. These professionals can provide specific guidance for your situation.

1 Corinthians 7:5 instructs couples not to *"deprive one another, except perhaps by agreement for a limited time,"* recognizing the importance of physical intimacy while allowing for temporary abstention when necessary. This balanced perspective acknowledges both the value of sexual connection and the reality that circumstances sometimes require adaptation.

149

Recovery from Infidelity

Infidelity creates profound damage to marital intimacy, shattering trust and security in the relationship. The journey toward healing and restored intimacy after betrayal requires significant time, effort, and often professional support.

Gary and Mona Shriver, who navigated recovery from infidelity in their own marriage, observe that "rebuilding intimacy after betrayal occurs gradually through consistent, trustworthy behavior, genuine repentance, and intentional reconnection."[41] This process cannot be rushed but can lead to eventual healing when both spouses commit to the difficult work involved.

Key elements in rebuilding intimacy after infidelity include:

1. **Establishing complete honesty:** Creating full disclosure about the infidelity and ongoing transparency that rebuilds trust gradually. This honesty provides the foundation for authentic reconnection.

2. **Working through stages of grief:** Acknowledging and processing the betrayed spouse's grief, anger, and other emotions without minimization or impatience. This emotional processing creates the capacity for eventual reconnection.

3. **Identifying and addressing contributing factors:** Examining relationship patterns, personal issues, and circumstances that created vulnerability to infidelity. This understanding helps prevent future betrayal while avoiding simplistic blame.

4. **Rebuilding trust through consistency:** Establishing patterns of reliability, transparency, and trustworthiness in daily interactions. This consistent behavior gradually rebuilds the security necessary for intimacy.

5. **Reconnecting intentionally in all dimensions:** Rebuilding emotional, intellectual, spiritual, and eventually physical intimacy

through gradual, patient steps. This reconnection often follows a natural progression from non-sexual forms of intimacy to eventual sexual reconnection.

Hosea 3:1 records God instructing the prophet to reconcile with his unfaithful wife: *"Go again, love a woman who is loved by another man and is an adulteress, even as the LORD loves the children of Israel, though they turn to other gods."* This divine example of reconciliation after betrayal offers hope for human marriages damaged by infidelity.

Pornography and Sexual Addiction

Pornography use and sexual addiction create significant barriers to genuine intimacy, affecting not just physical connection but emotional and spiritual dimensions as well. These issues have become increasingly common with the accessibility of explicit content through digital devices.

Mark Laaser, a Christian counselor specializing in sexual addiction, explains that "pornography creates counterfeit intimacy that damages capacity for authentic connection through objectification, unrealistic expectations, and neurochemical conditioning."[42] These effects can persist even after pornography use stops, requiring intentional healing and rewiring of the brain.

Key considerations regarding pornography and intimacy include:

1. **Acknowledging the damage to intimacy:** Recognizing how pornography use affects all dimensions of marital intimacy through comparison, objectification, shame, and trust issues. This acknowledgment motivates the difficult work of recovery.

2. **Establishing appropriate boundaries:** Creating clear boundaries around technology use, accountability, and situations that create vulnerability to relapse. These boundaries provide protection during the recovery process.

3. **Addressing underlying issues:** Identifying and healing the emotional, relational, or spiritual issues that contribute to pornography use or sexual addiction. This deeper healing prevents the cycle of relapse and shame.

4. **Rebuilding healthy sexuality:** Developing a biblical understanding of sexuality that values mutual pleasure, whole-person connection, and covenant commitment. This healthy perspective replaces distorted views created by pornography.

5. **Seeking appropriate help:** Utilizing resources designed for recovery from pornography and sexual addiction, including support groups, counseling, and specialized programs. These resources provide structure and guidance for the recovery process.

Matthew 5:27-28 records Jesus' teaching that *"everyone who looks at a woman with lustful intent has already committed adultery with her in his heart."* This statement establishes that sexual faithfulness involves not just physical behavior but also mental and emotional loyalty—a standard that excludes pornography use.

Conclusion: The Journey Toward Deeper Intimacy

Intimacy in marriage represents both one of God's greatest gifts and one of life's most significant challenges. The vulnerability required for true intimacy exposes our deepest insecurities and selfishness yet also creates the profound connection our hearts long for.

As you apply the insights from this chapter, remember these key principles:

1. True intimacy encompasses multiple dimensions—physical, emotional, intellectual, and spiritual—that work together to create profound connection.

2. Common barriers to intimacy can be identified and addressed through intentional effort, honest communication, and sometimes professional help.

3. Intimacy requires both vulnerability and safety—the courage to be fully known and the commitment to create an environment where such openness feels secure.

4. Different seasons of marriage bring unique intimacy challenges and opportunities that require adaptation and renewed commitment.

5. Special circumstances such as illness, sexual difficulties, or betrayal create additional challenges that can be navigated with wisdom, patience, and appropriate support.

The journey toward deeper intimacy continues throughout marriage, with each stage offering opportunities for growth and renewed connection. As Gary Thomas observes, "The pursuit of intimacy in marriage reflects our deeper longing for connection with God, who designed us for relationship with Himself and others."[43]

May your marriage become increasingly characterized by the beautiful vulnerability, acceptance, and connection God designed for husbands and wives—a relationship where you are fully known and fully loved.

Chapter 7

Premarital Counseling

Preparing for a Lifetime Covenant

"Unless the Lord builds the house, those who build it labor in vain." (Psalm 127:1)

Marriage is one of life's most significant commitments—a covenant relationship designed to last a lifetime. Yet many couples spend more time planning their wedding day than preparing for their marriage. As Dennis Rainey observes, "Most couples invest more effort in planning a one-day celebration than they do in preparing for a relationship meant to last fifty years or more."[1]

Premarital counseling provides an intentional process for couples to prepare for marriage by examining key relationship areas, developing essential skills, and establishing a solid foundation before saying "I do." This chapter explores the value of premarital counseling, the key topics couples should address before marriage, and practical ways to strengthen their relationship during the engagement period.

Whether you're currently engaged, considering marriage in the future, or mentoring couples preparing for marriage, these insights will help you build a relationship that honors God and withstands life's challenges. As Proverbs 24:3-4 reminds us, *"By wisdom a house is built, and through understanding it is established; through knowledge its rooms are filled with rare and beautiful treasures."*

The Value of Premarital Counseling

Many couples approach marriage with romantic idealism but limited preparation. They assume that love will naturally overcome any challenges they might face. However, research consistently shows that intentional preparation significantly increases a couple's chances of building a healthy, lasting marriage.[2]

Prevention Rather Than Intervention

It's far easier to prevent problems than to solve them after they've become entrenched patterns. Premarital counseling helps couples identify potential areas of conflict before they create serious damage. As Wayne Mack notes, "Premarital counseling is preventive maintenance rather than corrective repair."[3]

For example, a couple might discover during counseling that they have very different expectations about managing finances or relating to in-laws. Addressing these differences before marriage allows them to develop strategies and agreements rather than facing painful surprises after the wedding.

Establishing Realistic Expectations

Many couples enter marriage with unrealistic expectations shaped by romantic movies, social media, or their own wishful thinking. Premarital counseling helps them develop a more biblical and realistic understanding of marriage.

Paul Tripp warns against the danger of idealism: "Unrealistic expectations set you up for failure in marriage because they set a standard that no sinful human being could ever meet."[4] Good premarital counseling helps couples recognize that they're uniting two imperfect people who will need grace, forgiveness, and growth throughout their marriage.

Building Essential Skills

Marriage requires skills that don't come naturally to most people—effective communication, conflict resolution, financial management, and more. Premarital counseling provides couples with tools they'll need throughout their marriage journey.

Les and Leslie Parrott emphasize that "marriage skills aren't optional; they're essential. And they can be learned."[5] Through teaching, exercises, and guided practice, couples can develop habits that will serve them well for decades to come.

Establishing Biblical Foundations

Perhaps most importantly, premarital counseling helps couples build their marriage on the foundation of God's Word rather than cultural trends or personal preferences. As Jesus taught in Matthew 7:24-25, the wise person builds their house on the rock so that when storms come, the house stands firm.

Andreas Köstenberger notes that "in a culture that increasingly rejects biblical values, couples need a clear understanding of God's design for marriage more than ever."[6] Premarital counseling grounds couples in Scripture, helping them understand marriage as a covenant relationship that reflects Christ's relationship with the church.

Key Topics to Address Before Marriage

While every relationship has unique dynamics, certain core topics should be addressed by all couples preparing for marriage. These areas have consistently proven to be significant for marital success and satisfaction.[7]

Spiritual Foundation and Faith

For Christian couples, a shared faith provides the foundation for all other aspects of marriage. 2 Corinthians 6:14 warns against being *"unequally yoked with unbelievers,"* recognizing that spiritual dissonance creates significant challenges in marriage.

Even when both partners are believers, they may have different spiritual backgrounds, practices, or priorities that need to be discussed. Important questions to address include:

- What role will faith play in your marriage and family life?
- How will you nurture spiritual growth individually and as a couple?
- What church will you attend, and how involved will you be?
- How will you handle differences in theological understanding or spiritual practices?
- What spiritual disciplines do you want to establish in your home?

Gary Thomas emphasizes that "the spiritual dimension of marriage isn't optional for Christians—it's foundational. Couples who pray together and grow spiritually together develop a unique bond that strengthens all other aspects of their relationship."[8]

Family Background and Influences

We all bring patterns, expectations, and wounds from our families of origin into marriage. Understanding these influences helps couples recognize potential challenges and intentionally create healthy patterns for their own relationship.

John Trent and Gary Smalley note that "your family background affects virtually every aspect of your marriage—from how you communicate and resolve conflicts to how you view gender roles and express affection."[9] Important areas to explore include:

- What was your parents' marriage like, and how has it shaped your expectations?
- What family traditions or values do you want to carry forward?
- What patterns from your family do you want to avoid repeating?
- How were conflict, emotions, and affection handled in your family?
- What unresolved issues from your family might affect your marriage?

Understanding each other's family background creates empathy and helps couples intentionally choose the patterns they want to establish rather than unconsciously repeating unhealthy dynamics.

Communication Patterns

Communication forms the lifeblood of marriage. Couples who communicate effectively can navigate challenges, deepen intimacy, and build understanding. Those with poor communication patterns often experience frustration, distance, and unresolved conflicts.

Emerson Eggerichs observes that "men and women often communicate differently, creating unintentional misunderstandings."[10] Premarital counseling helps couples recognize these differences and develop effective communication skills. Key aspects to address include:

- How do you typically express thoughts, feelings, and needs?
- What communication patterns trigger defensiveness or shutdown?
- How do you handle disagreements or sensitive topics?

- What helps you feel heard and understood?
- How can you improve your listening skills and empathetic responses?

Learning effective communication before marriage establishes patterns that will serve couples well throughout their relationship. As Gary Chapman notes, "The ability to communicate effectively is the most important skill you can develop for marital success."[11]

Conflict Resolution

Every marriage experiences conflict. The difference between thriving and struggling marriages isn't the absence of conflict but how couples handle disagreements when they arise.

Ken Sande reminds us that "conflict provides opportunities to glorify God, serve others, and grow in Christlikeness."[12] Premarital counseling helps couples develop biblical approaches to conflict resolution. Important questions to address include:

- How did your families handle conflict, and how has that influenced you?
- What are your typical responses to conflict (fight, flight, freeze, appease)?
- What issues tend to create tension between you?
- How can you address disagreements in ways that strengthen rather than damage your relationship?
- What boundaries should you establish for healthy conflict (e.g., no name-calling, no bringing up past issues)?

Couples who develop effective conflict resolution skills before marriage are better equipped to handle the inevitable disagreements that will arise throughout their life together.

Financial Management

Money consistently ranks among the top sources of marital conflict. Couples often bring different attitudes, habits, and expectations about finances into marriage, creating tension when these differences emerge.

Ron Blue emphasizes that "money problems in marriage are rarely about money. They're about values, goals, and communication."[13] Important financial topics to discuss include:

- What are your attitudes toward saving, spending, debt, and giving?
- What financial goals do you have for the short and long term?
- How will you handle budgeting and financial decision-making?
- What debts do you each bring into marriage, and how will you address them?
- How will you balance individual freedom and mutual accountability in spending?

Developing a shared approach to financial management before marriage prevents many common conflicts and helps couples use their resources in ways that align with their values and goals.

Roles and Responsibilities

Expectations about roles and responsibilities in marriage have shifted dramatically in recent generations. Without clear discussion, couples often make assumptions based on their family backgrounds or personal preferences, leading to misunderstanding and disappointment.

Timothy Keller notes that "biblical teaching on marriage roles focuses more on mutual submission and service than on rigid divisions of labor."[14] Important questions to address include:

- What are your expectations about household responsibilities?
- How will you make decisions—jointly, separately, or some combination?
- What are your career goals, and how will they affect your marriage?
- If children enter the picture, how will parenting responsibilities be shared?
- How do you understand the biblical teaching on marriage roles?

Clarifying expectations about roles and responsibilities helps couples develop arrangements that honor both partners' gifts, limitations, and circumstances.

Sexual Relationship

God designed sexual intimacy as a beautiful gift for marriage, but many couples enter marriage with limited understanding, unrealistic expectations, or past wounds that affect this area of relationship.

Kevin Leman observes that "couples who can talk openly about sexual intimacy before marriage are better prepared for a fulfilling physical relationship after the wedding."[15] Important topics to address include:

- What are your expectations about the frequency and initiation of physical intimacy?
- How will you communicate preferences and needs in this sensitive area?
- What past experiences might influence your sexual relationship?
- How will you maintain physical intimacy amid life's demands and challenges?
- What boundaries are important to maintain before marriage?

While some aspects of sexual intimacy are best learned within marriage itself, establishing open communication and realistic expectations beforehand creates a foundation for a healthy physical relationship.

Children and Parenting

Whether and when to have children and how to raise them represents one of the most significant decisions couples make. Discussing these matters before marriage prevents painful surprises and conflicts later.

James Dobson notes that "few areas create more marital tension than disagreements about raising children."[16] Important questions to address include:

- Do you both want children? If so, how many and when?
- What are your views on adoption, fertility treatments, or remaining childless?
- What parenting approaches do you value (discipline, education, religious training)?
- How were you parented, and what patterns do you want to continue or change?
- How will you balance children's needs with maintaining your marriage relationship?

While perspectives on parenting often evolve over time, establishing general agreement on core values and approaches before marriage provides important alignment.

In-laws and Extended Family

Navigating relationships with extended family—particularly parents and in-laws—creates challenges for many couples. Genesis 2:24 establishes that marriage involves "leaving" one's parents and "cleaving" to one's spouse, creating a new primary relationship. However, implementing this principle while maintaining healthy extended family connections requires wisdom and intentionality.[17]

Important questions to address include:

- What role will parents and in-laws play in your marriage?
- How will you spend holidays and special occasions?
- What boundaries need to be established with extended family?
- How will you handle unsolicited advice or interference from family members?
- How will you honor your parents while prioritizing your marriage relationship?

Establishing clear expectations and boundaries with extended family before marriage prevents many common conflicts and helps couples navigate these important relationships with unity and wisdom.

Approaches to Premarital Counseling

Couples have several options for pursuing premarital counseling, each with distinct advantages. The most important factor isn't the specific approach but the commitment to intentional preparation.[18]

Pastoral Counseling

Many churches offer premarital counseling through pastors or ministry leaders. This approach typically emphasizes biblical foundations for marriage and may include both teaching and personalized guidance.

Advantages of pastoral counseling include:

- Integration of spiritual and practical aspects of marriage
- Often provided at no or low cost

- Connection to a faith community that can support the marriage
- Opportunity to build a relationship with a pastor who may perform the wedding

Timothy Keller suggests that "pastoral premarital counseling provides not just practical advice but a theological vision for marriage that grounds the relationship in something larger than the couple's happiness."[19]

Professional Counseling

Licensed marriage and family therapists or professional counselors offer another valuable option for premarital counseling. These professionals bring specialized training in relationship dynamics and often use research-based approaches.

Advantages of professional counseling include:

- Expertise in relationship dynamics and potential challenges
- Objective perspective from someone outside your immediate circle
- Structured assessment tools to identify strengths and growth areas
- Skills in facilitating difficult conversations about sensitive topics

When choosing a professional counselor, Christian couples should seek someone who respects their faith values and integrates them into the counseling process. As Leslie Vernick advises, "Find a counselor who understands that your faith isn't peripheral to your relationship but central to how you view marriage."[20]

Mentoring by Experienced Couples

Some churches and ministries offer mentoring programs where experienced married couples guide engaged couples through premarital preparation. This approach combines the wisdom of experience with personalized relationships.

Advantages of couple mentoring include:

- Learning from those who have successfully navigated marriage challenges
- Seeing a real-life example of a Christian marriage in action
- Building a supportive relationship that can continue after the wedding
- Often more relational and less clinical than other approaches

Organizations like Marriage Mentors and Prepare/Enrich provide training and resources for couples who serve as marriage mentors. As Dennis Rainey notes, "Mentoring allows engaged couples to learn not just from books but from the lived experience of those who have walked the marriage path before them."[21]

Group Programs

Many churches and community organizations offer group premarital programs where multiple engaged couples participate together. These programs typically combine teaching, discussion, and exercises over several sessions.

Advantages of group programs include:

- Learning from other couples' questions and insights
- Building relationships with others in a similar life stage
- Often more affordable than individual counseling
- Structured curriculum covering essential marriage topics

Popular group programs include *Preparing for Marriage* (Dennis Rainey), *Saving Your Marriage Before It Starts* (Les and Leslie Parrott), and *Marriage Preparation Course* (Nicky and Sila Lee). As Les Parrott observes, "Group programs create a community of couples who can support each other through engagement and early marriage."[22]

Self-Guided Preparation

For couples without access to formal premarital counseling, self-guided preparation using books, online courses, or workbooks provides another option. While this approach lacks the accountability and personalized guidance of other methods, it still offers valuable preparation when approached intentionally.

Advantages of self-guided preparation include:

- Flexibility in timing and pace
- Accessibility regardless of location
- Often more affordable than formal counseling
- Opportunity to focus on areas most relevant to your relationship

Quality resources for self-guided preparation include *Preparing for Marriage* (Dennis Rainey), *The Meaning of Marriage* (Timothy Keller), and *Before You Say "I Do"* (H. Norman Wright). As Norman Wright advises, "Self-guided preparation requires discipline and commitment, but couples who invest the effort gain valuable insights that strengthen their relationship."[23]

Making the Most of Premarital Counseling

Regardless of which approach you choose, certain attitudes and practices will help you gain maximum benefit from premarital preparation.[24]

Approach with Openness and Honesty

Premarital counseling provides value only to the extent that couples engage authentically. Hiding concerns, avoiding difficult topics, or presenting an idealized version of your relationship limits the effectiveness of preparation.

Paul Tripp emphasizes that "honesty about struggles and differences before marriage creates opportunity for growth; hiding them only postpones inevitable challenges."[25] While vulnerability can feel uncomfortable, it creates the possibility for genuine understanding and growth.

Focus on Understanding, Not Just Agreement

Many couples mistakenly believe that a successful relationship requires agreement on every issue. However, research consistently shows that how couples handle differences matters more than the differences themselves.

John Gottman's research demonstrates that "successful marriages aren't characterized by absence of conflict but by how couples manage inevitable disagreements."[26] Premarital counseling helps couples develop skills for understanding each other's perspectives and finding workable solutions even when complete agreement isn't possible.

Be Willing to Grow and Change

Effective premarital preparation often reveals areas where personal growth would benefit the relationship. Rather than becoming defensive or blaming your partner, view these insights as opportunities for positive change.

Gary Chapman notes that "the willingness to acknowledge weaknesses and grow is one of the strongest predictors of marital success."[27] This growth mindset creates a foundation for lifelong learning and development together.

Practice New Skills Consistently

Like any skill, relationship abilities improve with practice. Simply learning about communication or conflict resolution in counseling sessions won't transform your relationship unless you implement these principles consistently.

Les and Leslie Parrott emphasize that "knowledge without application doesn't change relationships. Couples must practice new skills until they become natural habits."[28] This practice might feel awkward initially, but becomes more comfortable with time and repetition.

Seek Additional Help for Significant Issues

Premarital counseling sometimes reveals issues that require more extensive attention—unresolved trauma, addiction, serious communication problems, or significant value conflicts. Addressing these concerns before marriage demonstrates wisdom and commitment to building a healthy relationship.

Timothy Clinton advises that "when significant issues emerge during premarital counseling, seeking additional help isn't a sign of relationship weakness but of courage and commitment."[29] Specialized counseling, support groups, or other resources can address specific challenges that exceed the scope of typical premarital preparation.

Practical Tools for Relationship Preparation

Beyond formal counseling, engaged couples can utilize various tools and practices to strengthen their relationship during the engagement period.[30]

Assessment Instruments

Several validated assessment tools help couples identify relationship strengths and growth areas. These instruments provide objective data that can guide preparation efforts.

Popular assessment tools include:

- **PREPARE/ENRICH:** Comprehensive assessment covering multiple relationship dimensions
- **RELATE:** Online assessment examining individual traits and relationship patterns
- **FOCCUS:** Facilitated assessment used by many Catholic and Protestant churches

As David Olson, creator of PREPARE/ENRICH, notes, "Assessment tools don't predict relationship success or failure but identify areas where intentional conversation and growth would benefit the couple."[31]

Relationship Education

Books, courses, podcasts, and other educational resources provide valuable information about marriage principles and practices. While these resources don't replace personalized guidance, they offer important knowledge that supports relationship development.

Quality relationship education resources include:

- *Sacred Marriage* (Gary Thomas)
- *The Meaning of Marriage* (Timothy Keller)
- *Love and Respect* (Emerson Eggerichs)
- *Boundaries in Marriage* (Henry Cloud and John Townsend)

As Gary Thomas observes, "Couples who read and discuss relationship books together develop shared language and concepts that facilitate ongoing growth."[32]

Practical Experiences

Certain shared experiences during engagement provide opportunities to develop relationship skills in practical contexts. These experiences often reveal patterns and dynamics that might not emerge in conversation alone.

Valuable shared experiences include:

- Financial planning and budgeting together
- Participating in premarital retreats or workshops
- Serving together in ministry or community service
- Meeting with mentor couples for discussion and guidance
- Visiting each other's extended families

As Dennis Rainey suggests, "Shared experiences during engagement provide windows into how you'll function together in marriage. Pay attention to what these experiences reveal about your relationship patterns."[33]

Spiritual Disciplines

For Christian couples, shared spiritual practices during engagement establish patterns that can continue throughout marriage. These practices nurture both individual spiritual growth and relationship development.

Important spiritual disciplines include:

- Praying together regularly
- Reading and discussing Scripture
- Participating in church community
- Serving others together

- Developing a shared vision for your marriage

As Gary Thomas emphasizes, "Couples who establish spiritual disciplines during engagement build a foundation that will sustain them through the challenges of married life."[34]

Intentional Conversations

Regular, focused conversations about important relationship topics help couples develop understanding and alignment before marriage. These discussions go beyond daily logistics to address values, expectations, and dreams.

Helpful conversation starters include:

- What did you learn about marriage from your parents?
- What are your top three expectations for our marriage?
- How do you envision our spiritual life together?
- What fears do you have about marriage?
- What traditions do you want to establish in our home?

As John Gottman's research shows, "Couples who regularly engage in meaningful conversation develop an emotional connection that strengthens their relationship foundation."[35]

Preparing for the Wedding Day and Beyond

While engagement naturally involves planning for the wedding celebration, wise couples maintain perspective about the event's place in the larger marriage journey.[36]

Keeping the Wedding in Perspective

The contemporary wedding industry often promotes unrealistic expectations about the "perfect day" that can create stress, financial strain, and distraction from relationship preparation. Maintaining proper perspective helps couples focus on what truly matters.

Paul Tripp advises, "Remember that your wedding is just one day, but your marriage is meant to last a lifetime. Invest your energy accordingly."[37] This perspective helps couples make wise decisions about time, money, and emotional investment during the engagement period.

Practical approaches include:

- Establishing a reasonable budget that doesn't create financial stress
- Involving family appropriately while maintaining boundaries
- Focusing on meaning and relationship rather than perfection
- Scheduling regular "wedding-free" times to nurture your relationship
- Remembering that the marriage, not the wedding, is the ultimate goal

Preparing for the Early Adjustment Period

The transition from engagement to marriage involves significant adjustments, even for couples who have dated for extended periods. Anticipating these changes helps couples navigate them more smoothly.

Common adjustment areas include:

- Living together and sharing space
- Managing finances as a unit
- Navigating family relationships in new ways
- Establishing routines and traditions
- Adjusting to married sexuality

As H. Norman Wright notes, "Couples who anticipate and discuss potential adjustment challenges before marriage navigate the early months more successfully."[38] This preparation doesn't eliminate all challenges but provides a framework for addressing them constructively.

Building a Support System

Marriage thrives with appropriate support from the community. Identifying and cultivating relationships that will encourage your marriage creates valuable resources for the journey ahead.

Important support relationships include:

- Mentor couples who model a healthy marriage
- Friends who respect your marriage boundaries
- A church community that values marriage
- Professional resources for specific challenges
- Family members who support your relationship

As Hebrews 10:24-25 encourages believers to *"consider how to stir up one another to love and good works"* and *"not neglect meeting together,"* couples benefit from a community that strengthens their commitment and provides wisdom for the journey.[39]

Conclusion: Investing in Your Future Together

Premarital counseling and preparation represent one of the most significant investments couples can make in their future happiness and relationship success. While no preparation can guarantee a perfect marriage, intentional preparation significantly increases the likelihood of building a relationship that honors God and brings joy to both partners.

Ron Blue suggests that "financial harmony in marriage isn't about equal control but about shared values and goals." When couples align around core financial values, they can develop systems that respect both partners' perspectives.

Kevin Leman emphasizes that "sexual intimacy in marriage involves ongoing communication, adjustment, and learning. Differences in desire or preference aren't necessarily problems but opportunities to grow in understanding and serving each other."

William Doherty observes that "couples who maintain strong connection have made their relationship a priority, not something they hope will happen in the cracks of their busy lives."

Remember that the goal of premarital preparation isn't a perfect wedding or even a perfect marriage but a relationship grounded in God's truth and grace. As Gary Thomas reminds couples, "A truly good marriage isn't something you find; it's something you make—and you make it by pursuing God together."

Chapter 8

Parenting

The Sacred Calling of Raising Children Together

"Children are a heritage from the Lord, offspring a reward from him." (Psalm 127:3)

Parenting represents one of life's most profound privileges and responsibilities. When God entrusts children to a married couple, He invites them to participate in His creative and redemptive work in a uniquely powerful way. As James Dobson observes, "No other task in life compares in importance to raising the next generation."[1]

For Christian couples, parenting isn't merely about raising healthy, successful individuals—it's about nurturing disciples who know, love, and serve God. This sacred calling requires intentionality, wisdom, and partnership between husband and wife. As Timothy Keller notes, "Christian parenting is essentially discipleship—helping children understand and live out the gospel in their daily lives."[2]

This chapter explores biblical principles for parenting within the context of marriage. We'll examine God's design for the family, practical approaches to raising children, and ways to maintain a strong marriage while navigating the challenges of parenthood. Whether you're preparing for children, currently raising them, or mentoring others in this journey, these insights will help you fulfill the high calling of Christian parenting.

The Biblical Foundation for Parenting

Scripture provides rich guidance for understanding God's design for the family and the parental role. From Genesis to Revelation, we find principles that shape a distinctly Christian approach to raising children.[3]

Created in God's Image

The biblical foundation for parenting begins with the creation account. Genesis 1:27-28 tells us that God created humans in His image and blessed them with the command to *"be fruitful and multiply."* This establishes procreation as part of God's original design—a means of filling the earth with image-bearers who would reflect His character and extend His kingdom.

As Andreas Köstenberger explains, "Having children isn't merely a biological function but a spiritual privilege—participating in God's creative work by bringing new image-bearers into the world."[4] This perspective elevates parenting from a merely natural process to a sacred calling with eternal significance.

The creation account also establishes that children are to be welcomed as blessings. Psalm 127:3-5 declares, *"Children are a heritage from the Lord, offspring a reward from him. Like arrows in the hands of a warrior, are children born in one's youth. Blessed is the man whose quiver is full of them."* This positive view of children contrasts sharply with cultural attitudes that often view children as burdens, inconveniences, or mere lifestyle choices.

The Fall and Its Impact on Parenting

While God designed parenting as a joyful privilege, the fall into sin introduced significant challenges to this calling. Genesis 3 describes how sin damaged all human relationships, including those between parents and children. The harmony of Eden gave way to struggle, pain, and conflict within families.

The effects of the fall on parenting include:

1. Pain in childbearing (Genesis 3:16), which extends beyond physical birth to the emotional struggles of raising children in a fallen world.

2. Distorted relationships between parents, affecting their ability to present a united front in child-rearing.

3. The inherent sinfulness of children, who are born with a natural bent toward rebellion rather than righteousness (Psalm 51:5).

4. Environmental challenges—economic hardship, disease, societal corruption—that complicate the parenting task.

As Paul Tripp observes, "The most significant parenting problem you face is not the misbehavior of your children but the sinfulness of your own heart."[5] Recognizing the reality of sin—both in ourselves and our children—shapes realistic expectations and drives us to depend on God's grace rather than our own abilities.

God's Redemptive Purpose for Families

Despite the challenges introduced by sin, God's redemptive purposes flow through families. Throughout Scripture, we see God working through imperfect parents to advance His kingdom and fulfill His promises.

In the Old Testament, God established His covenant with Abraham and his descendants, working through generations of flawed families to ultimately bring forth the Messiah. The genealogy of Jesus in Matthew 1 includes numerous examples of imperfect parents through whom God nevertheless accomplished His purposes.

The New Testament further develops this redemptive perspective on the family. Ephesians 6:4 instructs fathers to *"bring [children] up in the training and instruction of the Lord,"* indicating that Christian parenting participates in God's redemptive work by discipling the next generation. As Sally Clarkson notes, "God designed the family as the primary context for discipleship—where faith is caught as well as taught."[6]

This redemptive purpose gives meaning and direction to the parenting journey. Rather than merely raising successful individuals by worldly standards, Christian parents aim to nurture disciples who will carry forward God's kingdom purposes in their generation.

Parental Roles and Responsibilities

Scripture assigns specific responsibilities to parents while allowing flexibility in how these responsibilities are fulfilled within different family contexts.[7]

The Responsibility to Provide

Parents are called to provide for their children's physical needs. 1 Timothy 5:8 states plainly, *"Anyone who does not provide for their relatives, and especially for their own household, has denied the faith and is worse than an unbeliever."* This provision includes food, shelter, clothing, and other necessities.

While this responsibility has traditionally fallen primarily to fathers, Scripture doesn't mandate rigid divisions of labor. Proverbs 31 describes a wife who contributes significantly to her family's economic well-being through various enterprises. The essential principle is that parents together ensure their children's physical needs are met.

In today's context, couples may fulfill this responsibility through various arrangements—traditional breadwinner/homemaker models, dual-income approaches, or creative combinations based on each family's circumstances and convictions. As Dennis Rainey observes, "The biblical mandate is clear about what must be done, but allows freedom in how it's accomplished."[8]

The Responsibility to Protect

Parents are called to protect their children from physical, emotional, and spiritual harm. This protective role reflects God's character as the ultimate protector of His children (Psalm 91:4).

Protection includes:

- Physical safety and security

- Emotional nurture and stability

- Spiritual guidance and boundaries

- Age-appropriate limits and supervision

- Wisdom about external influences (media, peers, etc.)

As James Dobson notes, "Children need the security that comes from knowing their parents are actively protecting them from harm. This security forms the foundation for healthy development."[9]

The Responsibility to Train and Instruct

Deuteronomy 6:6-7 provides a foundational text for understanding the educational responsibility of parents:

"These commandments that I give you today are to be on your hearts. Impress them on your children. Talk about them when you sit at home and when you walk along the road when you lie down, and when you get up."

This passage establishes several important principles:

1. Parents must first internalize God's truth themselves ("on your hearts").
2. Instruction happens through intentional teaching ("impress them").
3. Education occurs in the context of daily life, not just formal lessons.
4. Training is an ongoing process, not a one-time event.

Proverbs reinforce this educational responsibility with numerous instructions about teaching children wisdom (Proverbs 22:6, 29:17). The New Testament continues this emphasis in passages like Ephesians 6:4, which instructs fathers to bring up children *"in the training and instruction of the Lord."*

As Voddie Baucham explains, "God has designed parents, not primarily the church or the school, to be the principal influencers and educators of their children."[10] This doesn't mean parents must personally deliver all instruction, but they remain responsible for overseeing their children's education and ensuring it aligns with biblical values.

The Responsibility to Discipline

Scripture clearly establishes parents' responsibility to provide loving discipline. Proverbs 13:24 states, *"Whoever spares the rod hates their children, but the one who loves their children is careful to discipline them."* Similarly, Hebrews 12:7-11 compares God's discipline of His children to a father's discipline, indicating that appropriate correction is an expression of love rather than its opposite.

Biblical discipline involves:

1. Clear boundaries and expectations
2. Consistent consequences for disobedience
3. Instruction that addresses heart attitudes, not just behavior
4. Correction motivated by love, not anger or frustration
5. Age-appropriate methods that respect the child's dignity

As Ted Tripp emphasizes in *Shepherding a Child's Heart*, "The goal of discipline is not merely behavior modification but heart transformation. We're not just trying to produce compliant children but to nurture God-honoring motivations and desires."[11]

While Scripture uses the metaphor of the "rod," Christian parents have diverse interpretations of how this principle applies to specific disciplinary methods. The essential point is that loving discipline—whatever its form—is necessary for children's spiritual and character development.

The Responsibility to Model Faith

Perhaps the most powerful parental responsibility is modeling authentic faith. Children learn more from what they observe in their parents than from what they're told. As Josh McDowell notes, "Rules without relationship lead to rebellion. Children need to see genuine faith lived out in their parents' lives."[12]

This modeling includes:

- Authentic relationship with God through prayer and Scripture
- Consistent attendance and participation in the church community
- Humble confession and repentance when parents fail
- Joyful obedience to God's commands
- Loving service to others
- Gracious responses to life's challenges

When children observe parents whose actions align with their professed beliefs, they're more likely to embrace faith themselves. As Deuteronomy 4:9 instructs, *"Only be careful, and watch yourselves closely so that you do not forget the things your eyes have seen or let them fade from your heart as long as you live. Teach them to your children and to their children after them."*

Parenting Approaches and Styles

While Scripture provides clear principles for parenting, it allows flexibility in how these principles are applied. Christian parents have developed various approaches based on biblical wisdom and practical experience.[13]

Authoritative Parenting

Research consistently identifies authoritative parenting—which balances loving warmth with appropriate boundaries—as the most effective for children's development. This approach aligns well with biblical principles, combining the nurture emphasized in passages like 1 Thessalonians 2:7-8 with the guidance and discipline emphasized in Proverbs.

Characteristics of authoritative parenting include:

- High expectations coupled with high support
- Clear boundaries with reasonable flexibility
- Open communication that values children's perspectives
- Discipline that teaches rather than merely punishes
- Respect for children's developmental stages and individuality

As Kevin Leman explains, "Authoritative parents provide both roots and wings—the security of clear boundaries and the freedom to develop independence within those boundaries."[14]

This approach contrasts with less effective styles:

- Authoritarian parenting (high control with low warmth)
- Permissive parenting (high warmth with minimal boundaries)
- Neglectful parenting (low involvement in both nurture and guidance)

Grace-Based Parenting

Tim Kimmel's "grace-based parenting" approach applies gospel principles to the parent-child relationship. This perspective emphasizes that just as God relates to us through grace rather than legalism, parents should extend grace to their children while maintaining appropriate boundaries.

Key elements of grace-based parenting include:

1. **Acceptance:** Communicating unconditional love regardless of performance

2. **Authority:** Providing clear boundaries motivated by love rather than control

3. **Affirmation:** Actively building up children's sense of worth and capability

4. **Accountability:** Teaching responsibility within a context of forgiveness

As Kimmel explains, "Grace-based parenting mirrors how God relates to us—with unconditional love, clear boundaries, and restorative discipline rather than punitive control."[15]

This approach recognizes that rules without relationships foster rebellion, while relationship without rules fails to provide necessary guidance. The balance of grace and truth reflects Jesus' character as described in John 1:14.

Shepherding a Child's Heart

Ted Tripp's influential approach focuses on addressing children's heart attitudes rather than merely managing behavior. Based on Proverbs 4:23 (*"Above all else, guard your heart, for everything you do flows from it"*), this perspective recognizes that external compliance without internal transformation doesn't produce lasting character.

Key principles of this approach include:

- Identifying heart issues behind behavior problems
- Using discipline as an opportunity for instruction, not just correction
- Pointing children to their need for God's grace
- Addressing motivations, not just actions
- Applying Scripture to daily situations

As Tripp explains, "The goal isn't to raise children who simply follow rules but to nurture hearts that desire to honor God. Behavior modification may produce temporary compliance, but heart transformation produces lasting character."[16]

Discipleship Parenting

This approach views parenting primarily through the lens of discipleship—intentionally nurturing children as followers of Jesus. Based on the Great Commission (Matthew 28:19-20) and Deuteronomy 6:6-7, discipleship parenting focuses on passing faith to the next generation.

Key elements include:

1. Intentional spiritual training through Bible study and discussion
2. Regular family worship and prayer
3. Service opportunities that apply faith practically
4. Mentoring relationships with other believers
5. Integration of faith into all aspects of family life

As Voddie Baucham notes, "Christian parenting is fundamentally about making disciples. Everything else—education, discipline, life skills—flows from this primary purpose."[17]

This approach recognizes that faith formation happens most effectively through relationships and experiences, not just formal instruction. As Deuteronomy 6 indicates, discipleship occurs in the context of daily life— "when you sit at home and when you walk along the road, when you lie down and when you get up."

Developmental Awareness in Parenting

Effective parenting requires understanding children's developmental stages and adapting approaches accordingly. While Scripture doesn't provide detailed developmental psychology, it does recognize that children have different needs at different stages (1 Corinthians 13:11, Hebrews 5:12-14).

Early Childhood (0-5 years)

During these formative years, children develop basic trust, security, and attachment. Parenting focuses on:

- Consistent, loving care that builds secure attachment
- Simple, clear boundaries with gentle guidance
- Introduction to faith through stories, songs, and simple prayers
- Establishing family rhythms and routines

As Gary Ezzo and Robert Bucknam note in their work on early childhood, "These early years establish the foundation for a child's understanding of love, trust, and authority—concepts that will later transfer to their understanding of God."[18]

Middle Childhood (6-12 years)

During this stage, children develop competence, industry, and a sense of identity within the family and peer group. Parenting focuses on:

- Expanding responsibilities and privileges
- More detailed moral and spiritual instruction
- Developing work habits and character qualities
- Guiding peer relationships and outside influences

James Dobson emphasizes the importance of this stage: "The elementary years provide a crucial window for character formation before the turbulence of adolescence. During this period, children are generally receptive to parental guidance and eager to please."[19]

Adolescence (13-18 years)

During these transitional years, teens develop independence, identity, and deeper faith ownership. Parenting shifts toward:

- Coaching rather than controlling

- Deeper discussions about faith, values, and life choices
- Gradually increasing freedom with continued guidance
- Preparing for adult responsibilities and decisions

As Walt Mueller observes in Understanding Today's Youth Culture, "Adolescence requires a delicate balance—maintaining influence while allowing increasing independence. Parents must transition from controlling to coaching, all while maintaining strong relationship."[20]

Young Adulthood (18+ years)

As children transition to adulthood, parenting shifts to an advisory role characterized by:

- Respect for adult children's autonomy
- Available wisdom without unsolicited advice
- Supportive encouragement of independent faith
- Evolving relationship toward adult friendship

Dennis Rainey notes, "The goal of parenting isn't to raise children but to raise adults. Success is measured not by continued dependence but by launching children who can function as responsible, faithful adults."[21]

Understanding these developmental stages helps parents avoid common pitfalls—expecting too much from young children, micromanaging adolescents, or failing to give young adults appropriate independence. As 1 Corinthians 13:11 reminds us, *"When I was a child, I talked like a child, I thought like a child, I reasoned like a child. When I became a man, I put the ways of childhood behind me."*

Key Challenges in Christian Parenting

While parenting brings tremendous joy, it also presents significant challenges. Understanding common difficulties helps couples navigate them with wisdom and grace.[22]

Balancing Marriage and Parenting

One of the greatest challenges for parents is maintaining a strong marriage while meeting children's needs. When children arrive, many couples focus so intensely on parenting that their marital relationship suffers. As Gary Thomas observes, "One of the best gifts you can give your children is a strong marriage. They draw security from your relationship even more than from your parenting."[23]

Practical approaches for balancing marriage and parenting include:

1. Maintaining regular couple time through date nights or intentional connection at home
2. Presenting a united front in parenting decisions
3. Supporting each other's parenting efforts rather than criticizing
4. Remembering that the marriage relationship precedes and will outlast the active parenting years
5. Modeling healthy marriage as part of children's education about relationships

As Kevin Leman emphasizes, "Your marriage is the hub of the family wheel. When it's strong, everything else works better. When it's weak, the whole family feels the wobble."[24]

Navigating Different Parenting Styles

Even couples who agree on basic values often discover they have different parenting styles or approaches. These differences can create tension if not addressed constructively.

Common differences include:

- One parent more strict, the other more lenient
- Different comfort levels with children's independence
- Varying approaches to discipline
- Different communication styles with children
- Distinct priorities in child development (academics, character, social skills, etc.)

Emerson Eggerichs suggests that these differences often reflect complementary strengths: "Mothers typically bring nurture and sensitivity to children's emotional needs, while fathers often bring challenge and preparation for the outside world. Children need both perspectives."[25]

Navigating these differences requires:

- Appreciating the value in different approaches rather than assuming one is right
- Discussing significant parenting decisions privately before presenting them to children
- Supporting each other's authority even when approaches differ
- Finding a compromise that incorporates both parents' wisdom
- Focusing on shared values and goals rather than specific methods

Cultural Challenges to Biblical Parenting

Today's parents face unprecedented cultural challenges that previous generations didn't encounter. As Josh McDowell notes, "Parents today aren't just competing with peer influence but with sophisticated media and technology that shapes children's values and worldview."[26]

Significant cultural challenges include:

1. Digital technology and social media, which can consume attention, expose children to inappropriate content, and create unhealthy comparison
2. Secular educational environments that may undermine Christian values
3. Shifting sexual ethics that contradict biblical teaching
4. Materialistic values that emphasize consumption over character
5. Busy schedules that fragment family life and diminish spiritual formation
6. Relativistic worldviews that reject absolute truth

Addressing these challenges requires:

- Creating a strong family culture rooted in biblical values
- Maintaining open communication about cultural issues
- Providing age-appropriate guidance about media and technology
- Intentionally counter-cultural practices (Sabbath rest, service, simplicity)
- Connecting with like-minded families for support and encouragement

As Andy Crouch advises in *The Tech-Wise Family*, "The goal isn't isolation from culture but wisdom within it—creating family practices that put technology and other cultural influences in their proper place."[27]

Special Parenting Situations

Many families face unique challenges that require additional wisdom, support, and resources.[28]

Single Parenting

Single parents face the challenge of fulfilling roles typically shared by two people. Whether through death, divorce, or other circumstances, parenting alone brings both special challenges and opportunities.

Biblical encouragement for single parents includes:

- God's special concern for single parents and their children (Psalm 68:5)
- The sufficiency of God's grace for challenging circumstances (2 Corinthians 12:9)
- The availability of community support within the church (Galatians 6:2)

Practical wisdom for single parents includes:

- Building a support network of extended family, church, and friends
- Finding healthy role models of the opposite gender for children
- Establishing sustainable routines and expectations
- Practicing self-care to maintain emotional and spiritual health
- Connecting with other single parents for encouragement

As Robert Lewis notes in *Raising a Modern-Day Knight*, "Single parents may need to be more intentional about finding additional mentors and role models, but they can absolutely raise healthy, faithful children with God's help and community support."[29]

Blended Families

Blended families formed through remarriage face unique challenges in establishing new relationships, navigating complex dynamics, and creating family unity.

Wisdom for blended families includes:

- Realistic expectations about the time needed to build relationships
- Patience with children's adjustment to new family structures
- Clear but flexible boundaries and household expectations
- Respect for different parenting histories and approaches
- Intentional creation of new family traditions alongside respect for previous ones

Ron Deal, in *The Smart Stepfamily*, emphasizes that "blended families aren't instant families but crockpot families—they need low heat and plenty of time to blend well. Patience and grace are essential ingredients."[30]

Adoptive and Foster Parenting

Adoption and foster care reflect God's heart for the vulnerable and His own adoption of believers into His family (Ephesians 1:5). These special callings bring both unique joys and challenges.

Important considerations include:

- Understanding the impact of early trauma or attachment disruption
- Navigating cultural or racial differences in transracial adoption
- Addressing questions about identity and birth family
- Accessing appropriate support services when needed
- Balancing openness about adoption with privacy and discretion

Moore, in *Adopted for Life*, notes that "adoption isn't second-best but a beautiful reflection of God's redemptive work. Adoptive parents aren't just providing a home but participating in God's reclaiming of broken situations for His glory."[31]

Parenting Children with Special Needs

Parents of children with disabilities, chronic illness, or other special needs often face intensified demands and unique challenges. These situations require additional support, resources, and spiritual perspective.

Biblical wisdom includes:

- Recognizing each child's inherent value as created in God's image
- Understanding that disability doesn't diminish purpose or worth
- Seeing challenging circumstances as opportunities for God's work to be displayed (John 9:3)
- Finding God's sufficient grace for daily challenges (2 Corinthians 12:9)

Practical approaches include:

- Connecting with support groups and resources specific to your child's needs
- Advocating effectively within educational and medical systems
- Maintaining realistic expectations while encouraging growth
- Attending to the needs of siblings and the marital relationship
- Practicing sustainable self-care to prevent burnout

As Emily Colson writes in Dancing with Max, "Parenting a child with special needs isn't just about managing challenges but discovering unique gifts and perspectives that enrich the entire family and community."[32]

Practical Principles for Effective Parenting

While parenting approaches may vary based on children's personalities, developmental stages, and family circumstances, certain principles consistently contribute to effective Christian parenting.[33]

Consistency and Unity

Children thrive with consistent expectations and united parental authority. When parents present a unified front and maintain consistent boundaries, children develop security and a clear understanding of expectations.

Practical applications include:

- Discussing parenting approaches privately to resolve differences
- Supporting each other's decisions in front of children
- Maintaining consistent consequences for behavior
- Establishing clear family rules and expectations
- Following through on both promises and consequences

As James Dobson observes, "Inconsistency and disunity create confusion and insecurity for children. They need to know that the boundaries are firm and that parents stand together."[34]

Relationship Before Rules

While boundaries and discipline are essential, they must be established within the context of a loving relationship. Rules without connection often produce either rebellion or mere external compliance without a heart change.

Practical applications include:

- Investing in quality time and meaningful conversation
- Listening to understand children's perspectives and feelings
- Expressing affection and appreciation regularly
- Connecting before correcting when addressing behavior issues
- Building relationship deposits that sustain through disciplinary withdrawals

As Gordon Neufeld explains in *Hold On to Your Kids*, "Children are naturally inclined to follow the guidance of those to whom they are attached. Relationship provides the context in which influence can occur."[35]

Individualized Approach

Each child is uniquely created with distinct personalities, gifts, challenges, and learning styles. Effective parenting recognizes and respects these differences rather than applying identical approaches to every child.

Proverbs 22:6 instructs parents to *"train up a child in the way he should go,"* which many scholars interpret as referring to the child's bent or natural inclinations. This suggests adapting approaches to each child's unique design.

Practical applications include:

- Observing and understanding each child's temperament
- Adjusting communication styles to different personalities
- Recognizing diverse gifts and interests
- Tailoring discipline approaches to what effectively reaches each child
- Avoiding comparisons between siblings

As Cynthia Tobias notes in *You Can't Make Me (But I Can Be Persuaded)*, "Different children require different parenting approaches. What motivates one child may completely discourage another."[36]

Age-Appropriate Expectations

Effective parenting requires understanding developmental stages and setting expectations accordingly. Expecting too much or too little can frustrate children and hinder their growth.

Practical applications include:

- Learning about normal development at each age
- Gradually increasing responsibilities and privileges

- Adjusting discipline approaches as children mature
- Providing appropriate challenges that stretch without overwhelming
- Recognizing that spiritual understanding deepens with cognitive development

As Gary Chapman and Ross Campbell explain in *The 5 Love Languages of Children*, "Children at different developmental stages need different expressions of love and guidance. What works for a five-year-old won't necessarily work for a fifteen-year-old."[37]

Balancing Protection and Preparation

Parents face the ongoing tension between protecting children from harm and preparing them for life's challenges. Too much protection leaves children unprepared for reality, while insufficient boundaries expose them to unnecessary risks.

Practical applications include:

- Gradually expanding freedom as children demonstrate responsibility
- Teaching discernment rather than just imposing rules
- Allowing natural consequences when it is safe to do so
- Discussing rather than sheltering from cultural challenges
- Providing guided exposure to age-appropriate challenges

As Tim Kimmel notes in *Raising Kids Who Turn Out Right*, "Our job isn't to raise safe kids but strong kids—children who can navigate challenges with wisdom, courage, and faith."[38]

Nurturing Faith in Children

For Christian parents, nurturing children's faith represents the highest priority. While parents cannot guarantee their children's spiritual choices, they can create an environment where faith can flourish.[39]

Family Discipleship Practices

Deuteronomy 6:6-9 provides a model for family discipleship that integrates faith into daily life:

"These commandments that I give you today are to be on your hearts. Impress them on your children. Talk about them when you sit at home and when you walk along the road, when you lie down, and when you get up. Tie them as symbols on your hands and bind them on your foreheads. Write them on the doorframes of your houses and on your gates."

This passage suggests several key practices:

1. **Family Bible engagement:** Reading and discussing Scripture together in age-appropriate ways
2. **Prayer:** Regular family prayer times and modeling personal prayer
3. **Faith conversations:** Discussing God's truth in the context of daily life and current events
4. **Visual reminders:** Creating environments that reinforce faith through art, Scripture displays, etc.
5. **Celebration of Christian holidays and milestones:** Using special occasions to reinforce spiritual truths

As Rob Rienow emphasizes in Visionary Parenting, "Family discipleship isn't primarily about formal devotions but about intentionally connecting faith to everyday life and conversations."[40]

Church Partnership

While parents bear primary responsibility for children's spiritual formation, the church provides essential partnership in this process. Psalm 78:4-7 describes how faith is passed down through both family and community:

"We will not hide them from their descendants; we will tell the next generation the praiseworthy deeds of the Lord, his power, and the wonders he has done... so the next generation would know them, even the children yet to be born, and they, in turn, would tell their children. Then they would put their trust in God and would not forget his deeds but would keep his commands."

Effective church partnerships include:

- Regular participation in corporate worship
- Age-appropriate children's and youth ministries
- Intergenerational relationships within the church community
- Parental reinforcement of church teaching at home
- Church support and resources for parents

As Reggie Joiner notes in Think Orange, "When church and family combine their influence, the impact on children's faith formation is multiplied. Neither should attempt to function independently of the other."[41]

Allowing Questions and Doubts

Nurturing authentic faith requires creating space for children to ask questions, express doubts, and wrestle with difficult issues. When parents respond to questions with respect and thoughtfulness rather than defensiveness, they create an environment where faith can develop genuine roots.

Practical approaches include:

- Welcoming questions rather than shutting them down
- Admitting when you don't have all the answers
- Exploring difficult questions together through research and discussion
- Distinguishing between core doctrines and secondary issues

198

- Modeling intellectual engagement with faith

As Kara Powell and Chap Clark explain in Sticky Faith, "Teenagers who feel free to express doubts and questions are more likely to develop lasting faith than those who feel they must suppress uncertainties."[42]

Conclusion: The Joy and Challenge of Parenting

Parenting represents both one of life's greatest challenges and one of its most profound privileges. As Christians navigate this journey, they can take comfort in several important truths:

1. God's grace is sufficient. No parent is perfect, but God's grace covers our failures and weaknesses. As Paul David Tripp reminds us, "God knew exactly the parents your children needed, and in His sovereignty, He chose you—not despite your weaknesses but often because of how He works through them."

2. Faithfulness matters more than perfection. God doesn't call parents to raise perfect children or to parent flawlessly. He calls us to faithful obedience, trusting Him with the results. As Deuteronomy 6 indicates, the primary requirement is that God's commands be on our own hearts as we seek to impress them on our children.

3. Parenting is a sanctifying journey. Through the challenges of raising children, God shapes parents' own character and faith. The patience, selflessness, and trust required in parenting become instruments of spiritual growth. As Gary Thomas observes, "God often uses our children to change us even as He uses us to raise them."

4. The goal is God's glory, not parental success. When parents focus on raising children who bring glory to God rather than reflect well on themselves, they find freedom from performance pressure and comparison. As Tedd Tripp notes, "The ultimate goal isn't raising

successful children by worldly standards but nurturing disciples who love and serve God."

As you navigate the joys and challenges of parenting within marriage, remember that you're participating in God's redemptive work in the next generation. By God's grace, the seeds of faith, character, and wisdom you plant will bear fruit—sometimes quickly, sometimes after many years, but always according to God's faithful purposes.

Chapter 9

Spiritual Growth

Growing Together in Faith

"As for me and my house, we will serve the LORD." (Joshua 24:15)

Marriage provides a unique context for spiritual growth—a relationship where two believers can encourage, challenge, and support each other in their journey with God. When couples intentionally nurture spiritual growth together, they experience not only a deeper connection with each other but also a stronger foundation for navigating life's challenges.

This chapter explores how couples can grow spiritually together, addressing common barriers to shared faith and providing practical approaches for building a marriage that honors God and nurtures spiritual vitality. Whether you're just beginning your marriage journey or have been married for decades, these insights will help you experience the profound blessing of growing together in faith.

The Biblical Foundation for Spiritual Growth in Marriage

Scripture provides a rich theological framework for understanding how marriage can foster spiritual growth. From Genesis to Revelation, we see God's design for marriage as a relationship that reflects His character and purposes.[1]

Created for Relationship with God and Each Other

The creation account reveals that humans were designed for relationships—both with God and with each other. Genesis 1:27 states that *"God created man in his own image, in the image of God he created him; male and female he created them."* This passage establishes that both husband and wife bear God's image and are created for a relationship with Him.

Timothy Keller observes that "marriage was designed to reflect the relationship between God and His people, making it inherently spiritual in nature."[2] This theological foundation means that spiritual growth isn't merely an optional add-on to marriage but central to its purpose and design.

Genesis 2:18 records God's declaration that *"it is not good that the man should be alone; I will make him a helper fit for him."* The Hebrew term for "helper" (ezer) is significant—the same word used elsewhere in Scripture to describe God Himself as Israel's helper. This connection suggests that spouses are meant to help each other in all dimensions of life, including spiritual development.

As Andreas Köstenberger notes, "The helper role involves spiritual support and encouragement, not merely practical assistance."[3] This understanding elevates the spiritual dimension of marriage to a central rather than peripheral aspect of the relationship.

Marriage as a Sanctifying Relationship

Scripture presents marriage as a relationship that God uses to shape and sanctify us. The daily interactions, challenges, and joys of marriage provide countless opportunities for spiritual growth as couples learn to love sacrificially, forgive generously, and serve humbly.

Gary Thomas observes that "God designed marriage to make us holy more than to make us happy."[4] While this perspective might initially sound discouraging, it actually infuses marriage with profound purpose—our relationship becomes a context for becoming more like Christ rather than merely meeting our emotional needs.

Ephesians 5:25-27 instructs husbands to *"love your wives, as Christ loved the church and gave himself up for her, that he might sanctify her, having cleansed her by the washing of water with the word, so that he might present the church to himself in splendor, without spot or wrinkle or any such thing, that she might be holy and without blemish."* This passage connects Christ's sanctifying work for the church with the husband's role in marriage, suggesting that marriage provides a context for mutual spiritual growth and development.

1 Peter 3:7 instructs husbands to live with their wives *"in an understanding way, showing honor to the woman as the weaker vessel, since they are heirs with you of the grace of life, so that your prayers may not be hindered."* This connection between how spouses treat each other and their prayer life establishes that marital relationship directly impacts spiritual vitality.

As Francis Chan notes, "Marriage provides daily opportunities to practice the spiritual disciplines of forgiveness, patience, selflessness, and grace—often more intensively than any other relationship."[5] These opportunities for spiritual formation make marriage a powerful context for growth in Christlikeness.

Marriage as a Picture of Christ and the Church

Throughout Scripture, the relationship between husband and wife serves as a metaphor for God's relationship with His people. The prophets frequently described God's covenant with Israel using marriage imagery (Isaiah 54:5, Jeremiah 3:14, Hosea 2:19-20), and the New Testament presents the church as the bride of Christ (Ephesians 5:25-32, Revelation 19:7-9).

Ray Ortlund explains that "the intimate union of marriage provides the most powerful earthly picture of the intimate spiritual union God desires with His people."[6] This theological connection infuses marriage with profound spiritual significance, elevating it beyond mere human arrangement to a living parable of divine love.

Ephesians 5:31-32 makes this connection explicit: *"'Therefore a man shall leave his father and mother and hold fast to his wife, and the two shall become one flesh.' This mystery is profound, and I am saying that it refers to Christ and the church."* The intimate union of husband and wife mysteriously reflects the union between Christ and His church—a relationship of sacrificial love, complete commitment, and profound intimacy.

This theological understanding transforms how couples view their relationship. Rather than focusing primarily on personal happiness, they recognize their marriage as a sacred trust that can display the gospel to a watching world. As Gary Thomas observes, "A spiritually vibrant marriage becomes a powerful testimony to God's faithfulness and love."[7]

The Unique Spiritual Opportunities in Marriage

Marriage provides unique opportunities for spiritual growth that differ from other relationships. Understanding these distinctive opportunities helps couples intentionally nurture their faith together.[8]

Intimate Knowledge and Accountability

Marriage creates a relationship of unique intimacy where spouses observe each other's daily behavior, attitudes, and choices. This intimate knowledge provides natural accountability that can foster spiritual growth.

Dennis Rainey notes that "spouses witness the gap between public persona and private reality, creating natural accountability that can be either resented or embraced for growth."[9] When approached with humility and grace, this accountability becomes a powerful catalyst for spiritual development.

Proverbs 27:17 states that *"iron sharpens iron, and one man sharpens another."* This principle applies powerfully in marriage, where the close relationship allows spouses to "sharpen" each other through honest feedback, loving confrontation, and mutual encouragement.

Ecclesiastes 4:9-10 observes that *"two are better than one because they have a good reward for their toil. For if they fall, one will lift up his fellow. But woe to him who is alone when he falls and has not another to lift him up."* This passage highlights the practical spiritual support marriage provides—a partner who notices when we stumble and helps us regain our footing.

The intimate knowledge marriage provides creates opportunities for:

- Gentle confrontation when attitudes or behaviors contradict stated values
- Encouragement to maintain spiritual discipline during busy or difficult seasons
- Recognition and celebration of spiritual growth that might go unnoticed by others
- Support during times of doubt, discouragement, or spiritual dryness

As Gary Chapman observes, "No one else has the opportunity to provide the kind of loving accountability that a spouse can offer."[10] This unique position creates powerful opportunities for spiritual growth when approached with grace rather than criticism.

Shared Spiritual Experiences

Marriage allows couples to share spiritual experiences that create common reference points and memories. These shared experiences—from worship services to answered prayers to ministry involvement—build a reservoir of faith that sustains the relationship through challenges.

H. Norman Wright explains that "shared spiritual experiences create a unique bond that strengthens both the marriage relationship and individual faith."[11] When couples worship, pray, serve, or study Scripture together, they build a spiritual connection that enriches their relationship.

Acts 2:42 describes the early church as *"devoted to the apostles' teaching and the fellowship, to the breaking of bread and the prayers."* This pattern of shared spiritual practices applies powerfully to marriage, where couples can create similar rhythms of learning, fellowship, communion, and prayer together.

Shared spiritual experiences might include:

- Worshiping together in corporate gatherings
- Praying together about family needs and decisions
- Studying Scripture or devotional materials together
- Serving in ministry or missions together
- Discussing sermons or spiritual insights
- Celebrating God's faithfulness in answered prayer

As Dennis Rainey notes, "These shared experiences create a spiritual history together that strengthens faith and marriage simultaneously."[12] This spiritual history becomes particularly valuable during challenging seasons when couples can remind each other of God's past faithfulness.

Spiritual Nurture and Support

Marriage provides a context for ongoing spiritual nurture and support as spouses encourage each other's faith development. This mutual nurture creates a greenhouse effect where faith can flourish with consistent care and attention.

Gary Thomas observes that "spouses have unique insight into each other's spiritual strengths, weaknesses, and needs, allowing for customized encouragement and support."[13] This personalized spiritual nurture differs from the more generalized support available through other relationships.

1 Thessalonians 5:11 instructs believers to *"encourage one another and build one another up,"* a command that applies powerfully in marriage. Spouses have daily opportunities to speak words of encouragement, offer perspective during struggles, and celebrate growth in each other's lives.

Hebrews 10:24-25 urges Christians to *"consider how to stir up one another to love and good works, not neglecting to meet together, as is the habit of some, but encouraging one another, and all the more as you see the Day drawing near."* This mutual stirring up to love and good works happens naturally in marriage when couples intentionally support each other's spiritual development.

Spiritual nurture in marriage might include:

- Encouraging consistent engagement with spiritual disciplines
- Providing perspective during times of doubt or discouragement
- Recommending resources that address specific spiritual needs
- Creating space for spiritual reflection and renewal
- Celebrating evidence of spiritual growth and maturity

As Francis Chan notes, "The daily interaction of marriage provides countless opportunities for spiritual encouragement that no other relationship can match."[14] This consistent nurture creates an environment where faith can flourish.

Unified Spiritual Leadership

Marriage creates the opportunity for unified spiritual leadership in the home, particularly as couples raise children or influence extended families. This shared spiritual leadership allows couples to multiply their impact and create a legacy of faith.

Joshua's declaration in Joshua 24:15—*"As for me and my house, we will serve the LORD"*—exemplifies this unified spiritual leadership. When couples make joint commitments to follow God and lead their household spiritually, they create a powerful testimony and influence.

Deuteronomy 6:6-7 instructs parents to keep God's commands in their hearts and *"teach them diligently to your children, and shall talk of them when you sit in your house, and when you walk by the way, and when you lie down, and when you rise."* This spiritual leadership responsibility becomes a shared mission in marriage, uniting couples around a common purpose.

Unified spiritual leadership involves:

- Making decisions that reflect shared spiritual values
- Creating family rhythms and traditions that nurture faith
- Modeling authentic relationship with God
- Teaching and discussing spiritual truth
- Addressing challenges from a biblical perspective

As Dennis Rainey observes, "When couples lead together spiritually, they create a powerful synergy that impacts not just their children but their broader community."[15] This unified influence extends the impact of their individual faith commitments.

Common Barriers to Spiritual Growth in Marriage

Despite God's design for marriage as a context for spiritual growth, many couples struggle to experience this dimension of their relationship. Understanding common barriers helps couples address these challenges intentionally.[16]

Different Spiritual Backgrounds or Maturity Levels

Many couples enter marriage with different spiritual backgrounds, denominational traditions, or levels of spiritual maturity. These differences can create challenges for growing together spiritually when not addressed with understanding and respect.

H. Norman Wright notes that "differences in spiritual background or maturity often create tension around spiritual practices, priorities, and leadership."[17] When one spouse values daily Scripture reading while the other finds it tedious, or when one prioritizes church involvement while the other sees it as optional, conflict and disconnection can result.

2 Corinthians 6:14 warns against being *"unequally yoked with unbelievers,"* recognizing that fundamental spiritual disconnection creates significant barriers to intimate marriage. Even among believers, however, differences in spiritual maturity or expression can create challenges for growing together.

Signs that differences are creating barriers include:

- Conflict over church attendance or involvement
- Disagreement about spiritual priorities or practices
- Criticism of each other's spiritual expression
- Withdrawal from shared spiritual activities
- Parallel rather than shared spiritual lives

Addressing these differences requires mutual respect, patience, and willingness to learn from each other. As Gary Thomas observes, "Differences in spiritual background or maturity need not prevent growth together when approached with humility rather than judgment."[18]

Busyness and Distraction

The frenetic pace of contemporary life creates another common barrier to spiritual growth in marriage. Between work demands, parenting responsibilities, household management, technology distractions, and community involvement, many couples find little time or energy for nurturing spiritual connection.

Kevin DeYoung observes that "busyness has become one of the most effective tools of the enemy in preventing spiritual growth in modern marriages."[19] When couples consistently prioritize activity over reflection, productivity over presence, and achievement over relationship, spiritual growth inevitably suffers.

Luke 10:38-42 records Jesus' gentle correction of Martha, who was *"distracted with much serving"* while her sister Mary sat at Jesus' feet. *"Martha, Martha,"* Jesus said, *"you are anxious and troubled about many things, but one thing is necessary. Mary has chosen the good portion, which will not be taken away from her."* This passage highlights how even good activities can distract from the "necessary thing" of being present with Jesus.

Signs that busyness is hindering spiritual growth include:

- Consistently postponing couple prayer or devotional time
- Rushing through spiritual conversations or activities
- Feeling too exhausted for meaningful spiritual engagement
- Digital devices consuming potential time for spiritual connection
- Prioritizing productivity over spiritual reflection

Addressing this barrier requires intentional choices about time and priorities. As Dennis Rainey notes, "Spiritual growth rarely happens spontaneously in our busy culture; it requires deliberate protection of time and energy."[20]

Unresolved Conflict or Relational Distance

Unresolved conflict creates significant barriers to spiritual growth in marriage. When hurt, resentment, or emotional distance characterizes the relationship, couples find it difficult to connect spiritually.

Emerson Eggerichs explains that "unresolved conflict affects all dimensions of marriage but often impacts spiritual connection most immediately."[21] A spouse harboring resentment typically finds spiritual intimacy difficult or impossible, as the emotional barriers prevent authentic spiritual connection.

Matthew 5:23-24 addresses this reality: *"So if you are offering your gift at the altar and there remember that your brother has something against you, leave your gift there before the altar and go. First, be reconciled to your brother, and then come and offer your gift."* This instruction recognizes that relational reconciliation must precede spiritual worship.

1 Peter 3:7 connects how husbands treat their wives with the effectiveness of their prayers, stating that husbands should honor their wives *"so that your prayers may not be hindered."* This passage establishes a direct link between marital relationships and spiritual vitality.

Signs that relational issues are hindering spiritual growth include:

- Reluctance to pray together during conflict
- Superficial spiritual conversations that avoid vulnerability
- Using spirituality as a weapon in conflict
- Withdrawal from shared spiritual activities
- Parallel rather than shared spiritual lives

Addressing this barrier requires a commitment to healthy conflict resolution—acknowledging hurts, extending forgiveness, making necessary changes, and rebuilding trust through consistent behavior. As Gary Chapman observes, "Spiritual intimacy cannot coexist with unresolved conflict; one will eventually eliminate the other."[22]

Misunderstanding of Spiritual Leadership

Confusion or disagreement about spiritual leadership creates another common barrier to growth in marriage. When couples have different understandings of how spiritual leadership should function, tension and disconnection often result.

Dennis Rainey notes that "misunderstanding of biblical teaching about spiritual leadership frequently creates either domination or disengagement rather than mutual growth."[23] When spiritual leadership is viewed as the husband making unilateral decisions or exclusively leading spiritual activities, wives often feel marginalized rather than partnered in spiritual growth.

Ephesians 5:21 establishes mutual submission as the context for marriage relationships: *"submitting to one another out of reverence for Christ."* This foundation of mutual submission shapes how spiritual leadership functions in marriage—as service rather than domination and as a partnership rather than hierarchy.

Ephesians 5:25-27 instructs husbands to love their wives *"as Christ loved the church and gave himself up for her."* This sacrificial, serving love characterizes biblical leadership rather than authoritarian control or passivity.

Signs that misunderstanding of spiritual leadership is creating barriers include:

- One spouse dominating all spiritual decisions or activities
- One spouse disengaging from spiritual leadership responsibilities
- Conflict over who should initiate or lead spiritual practices
- Resentment about spiritual leadership patterns
- Criticism of each other's spiritual leadership style

Addressing this barrier requires developing a biblical understanding of mutual submission and servant leadership. As Timothy Keller observes, "Biblical spiritual leadership involves taking initiative to serve, not exercising control or making unilateral decisions."[24]

Lack of Spiritual Disciplines or Skills

Many couples desire spiritual growth together but lack the practical skills or disciplines to nurture this dimension of their relationship. Without specific approaches for praying, studying Scripture, or discussing spiritual matters together, couples often find their intentions for spiritual growth remain unfulfilled.

Donald Whitney explains that "spiritual disciplines provide the structure and practices through which spiritual growth occurs, yet many couples have never learned these disciplines individually or together."[25] Without these practical skills, couples may feel awkward or uncertain about how to nurture spiritual growth in their marriage.

2 Timothy 3:16-17 states that Scripture is *"profitable for teaching, for reproof, for correction, and for training in righteousness, that the man of God may be complete, equipped for every good work."* This passage highlights the importance of biblical engagement for spiritual growth, yet many couples lack practical approaches to studying Scripture together.

Signs that the lack of spiritual discipline is creating barriers include:

- Uncertainty about how to pray together
- Awkwardness when attempting spiritual conversations
- Starting and stopping various spiritual practices
- Frustration with failed attempts at spiritual activities
- Confusion about what spiritual growth should look like

Addressing this barrier requires learning specific spiritual disciplines and adapting them to fit your relationship. As Richard Foster notes, "Spiritual disciplines are not rigid requirements but flexible practices that can be adapted to different personalities and circumstances."[26]

Cultivating Spiritual Growth in Marriage

Despite the barriers that exist, couples can develop practices that foster spiritual growth together. These approaches help create the conditions where faith can flourish in the context of marriage.[27]

Developing Individual Spiritual Vitality

While shared spiritual growth is important, it builds upon the foundation of individual spiritual vitality. Each spouse's personal relationship with God provides the resources and strength for nurturing faith together.

Gary Thomas emphasizes that "the most important thing you can do for your marriage is to pursue God individually with passion and consistency."[28] This individual spiritual vitality brings life and authenticity to shared spiritual practices rather than creating dependence on the other person for spiritual nourishment.

Mark 12:30 records Jesus' instruction to *"love the Lord your God with all your heart and with all your soul and with all your mind and with all your strength."* This wholehearted love for God begins as an individual commitment that then enriches the marriage relationship.

Approaches for developing individual spiritual vitality include:

1. **Establish a consistent time for personal prayer and Scripture reading:** Create a sustainable rhythm for connecting with God individually through prayer and engagement with His Word. This personal connection provides the foundation for a shared spiritual life.

2. **Pursue spiritual growth through various resources:** Engage with books, podcasts, sermons, or other resources that nurture your faith and understanding. These individual inputs create material for meaningful spiritual conversation together.

3. **Participate in same-gender discipleship relationships:** Develop friendships with same-gender believers who can provide specific encouragement and accountability for your spiritual growth. These relationships complement rather than compete with marriage.

4. **Practice spiritual disciplines that fit your personality:** Discover and develop spiritual practices that align with your unique personality and circumstances. These might include journaling, silence, fasting, worship, service, or other disciplines.

5. **Share individual spiritual insights with your spouse:** Create regular opportunities to share what God is teaching you individually. This sharing connects your individual spiritual journeys without creating dependence.

As Francis Chan observes, "The healthiest spiritual growth in marriage occurs when both spouses are pursuing God passionately as individuals and then sharing that journey together."[29] This individual vitality prevents unhealthy spiritual dependence while enriching shared spiritual life.

Praying Together Regularly

Prayer together represents one of the most powerful practices for spiritual growth in marriage. This shared communication with God creates a spiritual connection while addressing needs, expressing gratitude, and seeking guidance together.

Dennis Rainey describes couple prayer as "the single most important spiritual practice for marriage, creating both vertical connection with God and horizontal connection with each other."[30] When couples pray together regularly, they experience God's presence and power in their relationship in unique ways.

Matthew 18:19-20 records Jesus' promise: *"If two of you agree on earth about anything they ask, it will be done for them by my Father in heaven. For where two or three*

216

are gathered in my name, there am I among them." This assurance applies powerfully to husband and wife praying together, inviting Christ's presence into their relationship.

Approaches for developing meaningful prayer together include:

1. **Start with brief, simple prayers:** Begin with short, comfortable prayers rather than feeling pressure to pray at length. This approach reduces awkwardness and builds confidence for deeper prayer over time.

2. **Use written prayers when helpful:** Utilize prayer books, Scripture prayers, or other written resources when spontaneous prayer feels difficult. These structured prayers can provide language and direction that make shared prayer more comfortable.

3. **Develop regular prayer rhythms:** Establish consistent times for prayer together, whether in the morning, evening, mealtime, or other natural points in your day. These rhythms help prayer become a natural part of your relationship.

4. **Create a prayer list together:** Maintain a shared list of prayer concerns, whether written or digital. This list helps focus your prayers and allows you to track God's faithfulness in answering over time.

5. **Pray about your relationship specifically:** Include your marriage, parenting, and family life in your prayers together. This specific focus invites God's wisdom and strength into your relationship directly.

As Gary Chapman notes, "Couples who pray together regularly report significantly higher marital satisfaction and spiritual connection than those who don't."[31] This powerful practice creates both spiritual and relational benefits.

Studying Scripture Together

Engaging with Scripture together provides another foundational practice for spiritual growth in marriage. This shared exploration of God's Word creates common understanding, values, and language that strengthen both faith and relationship.

Timothy Keller explains that "couples who regularly engage with Scripture together develop a shared spiritual vocabulary and framework that shapes their entire relationship."[32] This common biblical foundation influences decision-making, conflict resolution, parenting, and every other aspect of marriage.

Psalm 119:105 describes Scripture as *"a lamp to my feet and a light to my path."* When couples study the Bible together, they receive shared guidance for their journey rather than following separate lights.

Approaches for meaningful Scripture study together include:

1. **Read through a book of the Bible together:** Select a biblical book and read through it systematically, discussing insights and applications. This approach provides context and continuity rather than isolated verses.

2. **Use a couple's devotional resource:** Utilize devotional materials designed specifically for couples, which typically include Scripture passages, brief commentary, and discussion questions. These resources provide a helpful structure for beginning the practice.

3. **Discuss sermon applications:** After attending worship services, discuss how the teaching applies specifically to your marriage and family. This conversation connects corporate worship with your relationship.

4. **Memorize key verses together:** Select Scripture passages particularly relevant to marriage and commit them to memory

together. This shared memorization creates common reference points during challenges.

5. **Apply Scripture to specific situations:** When facing decisions or challenges, intentionally seek biblical wisdom together. This application connects Scripture directly to your lived experience.

Hebrews 4:12 describes God's Word as *"living and active, sharper than any two-edged sword, piercing to the division of soul and of spirit, of joints and of marrow, and discerning the thoughts and intentions of the heart."* This transformative power works powerfully when couples engage with Scripture together.

Worshiping Together

Shared worship—both in corporate gatherings and private settings—creates a powerful spiritual connection in marriage. This joint expression of praise, gratitude, and submission to God aligns couples around their ultimate purpose and identity.

Gary Thomas observes that "worship reorients marriage around its true center—God Himself—preventing the relationship from becoming self-focused or idolatrous."[33] This God-centered perspective strengthens marriage by placing it within its proper context as a relationship that reflects and honors God.

Psalm 34:3 invites, *"Oh, magnify the LORD with me, and let us exalt his name together!"* This call to shared worship applies beautifully to marriage, where spouses can magnify God together in unique and powerful ways.

Approaches for meaningful worship together include:

1. **Participate in corporate worship regularly:** Attend worship services together consistently, engaging fully rather than merely being present. This shared experience creates common spiritual reference points and community connections.

2. **Discuss worship experiences afterward:** Take time to share what spoke to you during worship services—whether music, teaching, communion, or other elements. This conversation extends the impact of corporate worship.

3. **Create simple worship moments at home:** Incorporate worship music, Scripture reading, or expressions of gratitude into your home routines. These moments acknowledge God's presence in your daily life together.

4. **Develop family worship practices:** If you have children, establish age-appropriate family worship rhythms that you lead together. These practices create a spiritual legacy while strengthening your shared spiritual leadership.

5. **Express worship in nature or beauty:** Experience God's creation together through outdoor activities, art, or music that inspire worship. These experiences often create natural opportunities for spiritual conversation.

Colossians 3:16 instructs believers to *"let the word of Christ dwell in you richly, teaching and admonishing one another in all wisdom, singing psalms and hymns and spiritual songs, with thankfulness in your hearts to God."* This rich worship life applies powerfully to marriage relationships.

Serving Others Together

Serving others together creates unique opportunities for spiritual growth in marriage. This shared outward focus prevents self-absorption while allowing couples to exercise their gifts in complementary ways.

Francis Chan explains that "serving together often reveals aspects of your spouse's character and gifting that might remain hidden in other contexts."[34] These revelations deepen appreciation and understanding while creating a shared purpose beyond the marriage itself.

1 Peter 4:10 instructs believers to *"use whatever gift you have received to serve others, as faithful stewards of God's grace in its various forms."* When couples serve together, they steward both their individual gifts and the unique synergy of their relationship.

Approaches for meaningful service together include:

1. **Identify complementary spiritual gifts:** Recognize how your different spiritual gifts can work together effectively in service. This complementary function often creates a greater impact than serving separately.

2. **Choose service opportunities aligned with shared passions:** Select ministries or causes that both spouses feel genuinely passionate about. This shared enthusiasm creates sustainable commitment and joy in service.

3. **Include children in age-appropriate service:** If you have children, involve them in service activities when appropriate. This inclusion models spiritual values while creating a family identity around serving others.

4. **Reflect on service experiences together:** After serving, discuss what you observed, learned, or experienced. These conversations connect service activities with spiritual growth and relationship development.

5. **Balance service with rest and relationship nurture:** Ensure that service commitments don't consistently deplete your marriage relationship. This balance prevents burnout while maintaining healthy boundaries.

Galatians 6:9-10 encourages believers, *"Let us not become weary in doing good, for at the proper time we will reap a harvest if we do not give up. Therefore, as we have opportunity, let us do good to all people, especially to those who belong to the family of believers."* This commitment to persistent good works applies powerfully to couples serving together.

Creating a Spiritually Nurturing Home

The home environment significantly influences spiritual growth in marriage. Creating a space that reflects and reinforces spiritual values provides constant support for faith development.

Dennis Rainey describes the home as "a greenhouse for spiritual growth, where the environment itself nurtures faith development for both the couple and any children in the home."[35] This intentionally created atmosphere communicates values and priorities without words.

Deuteronomy 6:6-9 instructs believers to keep God's commands *"on your hearts"* and to *"impress them on your children. Talk about them when you sit at home and when you walk along the road, when you lie down, and when you get up. Tie them as symbols on your hands and bind them on your foreheads. Write them on the doorframes of your houses and on your gates."* This passage emphasizes creating an environment saturated with spiritual truth.

Approaches for creating a spiritually nurturing home include:

1. **Establish technology boundaries that protect relationships:** Create limits around digital devices and media that prevent distraction from relationships and spiritual priorities. These boundaries might include tech-free zones, times, or activities.

2. **Incorporate visual reminders of faith:** Include artwork, Scripture displays, or other visual elements that reflect your spiritual values and provide reminders of God's truth. These visual cues reinforce spiritual focus.

3. **Practice hospitality together:** Welcome others into your home regularly, creating a place of belonging and blessing for friends,

family, neighbors, or those in need. This shared hospitality extends your spiritual influence.

4. **Create space for spiritual practices:** Designate physical spaces in your home that support prayer, Scripture reading, or other spiritual disciplines. These dedicated spaces encourage consistent spiritual practices.

5. **Establish rhythms that honor Sabbath principles:** Develop patterns of work and rest that reflect God's design, including regular times for renewal, worship, and relationship. These rhythms counteract cultural patterns of constant productivity.

Joshua 24:15 declares, *"As for me and my house, we will serve the LORD."* This commitment to creating a God-honoring household applies powerfully to couples seeking to nurture spiritual growth in their marriage and family.

Spiritual Growth in Different Seasons of Marriage

Spiritual growth takes different forms throughout the marriage journey. Understanding these seasonal patterns helps couples adapt their approach to spiritual development as circumstances change.[36]

The Early Years: Establishing Spiritual Foundations

The early years of marriage establish patterns for spiritual growth that often persist for decades. During this formative period, couples navigate differences in spiritual background, expectations, and practices while building their unique approach to faith development.

H. Norman Wright notes that "patterns established in the first few years of marriage often determine the trajectory of spiritual growth for decades to come."[37] This reality makes thoughtful navigation of early spiritual development particularly important.

Key focuses during this season include:

1. **Discussing spiritual backgrounds and expectations:** Explore each other's spiritual history, traditions, and expectations for spiritual life in marriage. These conversations create understanding and prevent misunderstanding.

2. **Establishing spiritual practices that fit your relationship:** Develop approaches to prayer, Scripture, worship, and service that align with your unique relationship rather than imposing external expectations. These personalized practices create sustainability.

3. **Building relationships with other couples of faith:** Connect with couples who share your commitment to spiritual growth in marriage. These relationships provide encouragement, modeling, and accountability.

4. **Creating spiritual rhythms and habits:** Establish regular practices that foster spiritual growth, such as evening prayer, weekend worship, or seasonal retreats. These rhythms create a framework for ongoing development.

5. **Learning to navigate spiritual differences with respect:** Address differences in spiritual expression, maturity, or priorities with mutual respect rather than criticism or pressure. This respectful approach prevents spiritual growth from becoming a source of conflict.

Proverbs 24:3-4 observes that *"by wisdom, a house is built, and through understanding, it is established; through knowledge, its rooms are filled with rare and beautiful treasures."* This passage highlights the importance of intentionally building a spiritual foundation in the early years.

The Parenting Years: Spiritual Leadership and Growth

The arrival of children transforms the spiritual dimension of marriage, creating both new opportunities and significant challenges. The responsibility of spiritual leadership for children often catalyzes growth while simultaneously creating time and energy constraints.

Gary Thomas observes that "the parenting years often prompt significant spiritual growth as couples recognize their need for wisdom beyond themselves."[38] This awareness of inadequacy frequently drives deeper dependence on God and more intentional spiritual development.

Key focuses during this season include:

1. **Modeling authentic faith:** Demonstrate a genuine relationship with God rather than religious performance. This authentic modeling provides children with a compelling picture of lived faith.

2. **Developing family spiritual practices:** Create age-appropriate family worship, prayer, service, and discussion that nurture faith development for the entire family. These shared practices build a spiritual legacy.

3. **Maintaining a couple's spiritual connection:** Protect time for spiritual connection as a couple apart from children. This continued investment prevents spiritual growth from becoming exclusively child-focused.

4. **Addressing children's spiritual questions together:** Develop unified approaches to children's faith questions and challenges. This unity provides security and clarity for children's spiritual development.

5. **Supporting each other through parenting challenges:** Offer spiritual perspective and encouragement during the inevitable challenges of parenting. This mutual support prevents parenting stress from derailing spiritual growth.

Psalm 78:4 instructs believers to *"tell the coming generation the glorious deeds of the LORD, and his might, and the wonders that he has done."* This responsibility to transmit faith to the next generation shapes spiritual growth during the parenting years.

The Middle Years: Deepening Spiritual Maturity

As children become more independent and career demands often stabilize, the middle years of marriage provide an opportunity for deepened spiritual maturity. This season allows couples to invest more intentionally in their spiritual growth together.

Dennis Rainey describes the middle years as "a season of potential spiritual deepening as couples have more time and perspective for reflection and ministry."[39] With life experience and potentially more margin, couples can build on their spiritual foundation in significant ways.

Key focuses during this season include:

1. **Reflecting on God's faithfulness over time:** Take time to recognize and celebrate how God has worked in your marriage and family throughout previous seasons. This reflection builds faith for current and future challenges.

2. **Deepening spiritual practices:** Move beyond basic spiritual disciplines to more contemplative or challenging practices that foster continued growth. This deepening prevents spiritual stagnation.

3. **Expanding ministry involvement together:** Invest more significantly in ministry or service opportunities that utilize your experience and gifts. This expanded influence extends your spiritual impact.

4. **Mentoring younger couples:** Share wisdom and encouragement with couples in earlier stages of marriage. This mentoring relationship benefits both the mentors and those mentored.

5. **Addressing accumulated spiritual issues:** Resolve lingering spiritual questions, doubts, or areas of disobedience that may have

been set aside during busier seasons. This resolution creates freedom for continued growth.

Isaiah 40:31 promises that *"they who wait for the LORD shall renew their strength; they shall mount up with wings like eagles; they shall run and not be weary; they shall walk and not faint."* This renewal of strength applies to couples who continue investing in spiritual growth during the middle years.

The Later Years: Legacy and Continued Growth

The later years of marriage bring both unique challenges and significant opportunities for spiritual growth. Health limitations, retirement, and awareness of mortality often prompt deeper spiritual reflection and intentionality.

Billy Graham reflected that "the richest spiritual growth often occurs in long marriages where couples have weathered life's challenges together and developed eternal perspective."[40] This seasoned faith has a depth and authenticity that younger couples have yet to experience.

Key focuses during this season include:

1. **Creating a spiritual legacy:** Intentionally transmit spiritual values, stories, and wisdom to children, grandchildren, and others. This legacy-building extends your spiritual influence beyond your lifetime.

2. **Adapting spiritual practices to changing circumstances:** Modify approaches to spiritual disciplines to accommodate health limitations or other changes. These adaptations maintain spiritual vitality despite limitations.

3. **Preparing for eternity together:** Discuss heaven, legacy, and end-of-life matters from a spiritual perspective. These conversations, while challenging, create profound spiritual intimacy.

4. **Maintaining spiritual vitality amid physical decline:** Focus on the renewal of the inner person even as the outer person weakens. This focus prevents discouragement as physical abilities change.

5. **Ministering from accumulated wisdom:** Utilize your spiritual maturity and life experience to encourage and support others. This ministry prevents self-absorption while creating purpose.

2 Corinthians 4:16-18 encourages believers that *"though our outer self is wasting away, our inner self is being renewed day by day. For this light momentary affliction is preparing for us an eternal weight of glory beyond all comparison, as we look not to the things that are seen but to the things that are unseen."* This eternal perspective provides powerful motivation for continued spiritual growth in the later years.

Special Circumstances Affecting Spiritual Growth

Certain situations create unique challenges for spiritual growth in marriage. Understanding these special circumstances helps couples navigate them with wisdom and grace.[41]

When One Spouse Is More Spiritually Engaged

Many marriages experience seasons or ongoing patterns where one spouse demonstrates greater spiritual interest or engagement than the other. This imbalance can create tension, disappointment, or resentment when not handled with understanding and respect.

Gary Thomas advises that "the more spiritually engaged spouse often needs guidance to avoid pressuring, judging, or withdrawing from the less engaged spouse."[42] These negative responses typically widen rather than narrow the spiritual gap between spouses.

Key considerations for navigating this circumstance include:

1. **Avoid spiritual comparison or criticism:** Refrain from comparing your spouse's spiritual engagement to your own or to others. This comparison creates shame and resistance rather than motivation.

2. **Pray for rather than preach at your spouse:** Commit to regular, faithful prayer for your spouse's spiritual growth rather than lecturing or pressuring. This prayer acknowledges God's role in spiritual development.

3. **Invite rather than demand participation:** Extend warm invitations to spiritual activities without manipulation or guilt. This invitational approach respects freedom while creating opportunity.

4. **Appreciate different spiritual expressions:** Recognize that spiritual engagement may look different based on personality, background, and gifting. This appreciation prevents narrow definitions of spiritual growth.

5. **Continue your own spiritual development:** Maintain your spiritual vitality without making it contingent on your spouse's engagement. This consistent example provides the most compelling invitation.

1 Peter 3:1-2 instructs believing wives married to unbelieving husbands to win them *"without words by the conduct of their wives when they see your respectful and pure conduct."* While this passage addresses an unequally yoked situation, the principle of influence through example rather than pressure applies to any spiritual imbalance.

Spiritual Dryness or Crisis

Most marriages experience seasons where one or both spouses encounter spiritual dryness, doubt, or crisis. These challenging periods test faith while potentially creating deeper authenticity and dependence on God.

Timothy Keller notes that "spiritual dryness or doubt, while painful, often precedes significant spiritual growth when navigated with honesty and perseverance."[43] These desert experiences, while difficult, can ultimately strengthen rather than weaken faith.

Key considerations for navigating this circumstance include:

1. **Create a safe space for honest spiritual expression:** Allow genuine sharing of doubts, questions, or spiritual struggles without judgment or quick fixes. This safety prevents isolation during spiritual challenges.

2. **Maintain spiritual routines even during dryness:** Continue basic spiritual practices even when they feel mechanical or empty. This consistency provides structure during disorienting seasons.

3. **Seek appropriate spiritual counsel:** Connect with pastors, counselors, or mature believers who can provide perspective and guidance during a spiritual crisis. This outside support complements spousal encouragement.

4. **Explore resources addressing spiritual struggles:** Engage with books, podcasts, or other materials specifically addressing doubt, spiritual dryness, or faith crisis. These resources normalize the experience while providing direction.

5. **Adjust expectations for this season:** Recognize that spiritual growth looks different during desert seasons—often more about endurance and honesty than emotional experience. This adjusted expectation prevents unnecessary discouragement.

Psalm 42:1-3 expresses the pain of spiritual dryness: *"As a deer pants for flowing streams, so pants my soul for you, O God. My soul thirsts for God, for the living God. When shall I come and appear before God? My tears have been my food day and night while they say to me all the day long, 'Where is your God?'"* This honest lament demonstrates that spiritual struggle has been part of faith throughout history.

Significant Life Transitions

Major life transitions—career changes, relocations, health crises, empty nest, retirement—significantly impact spiritual growth in marriage. These transitions disrupt established patterns while creating opportunities for renewed spiritual focus and development.

H. Norman Wright observes that "major transitions often function as spiritual crucibles, revealing the true foundation of a couple's faith while creating opportunity for deeper dependence on God."[44] These challenging seasons test spiritual resources while potentially strengthening them.

Key considerations for navigating this circumstance include:

1. **Acknowledge the spiritual impact of transitions:** Recognize how changes affect your spiritual practices, community connections, and emotional capacity for spiritual engagement. This acknowledgment creates realistic expectations.

2. **Maintain core spiritual practices during change:** Identify and protect essential spiritual disciplines that can continue despite transition. These consistent practices provide stability amid change.

3. **Process transitions from a spiritual perspective:** Discuss how current changes connect to God's purposes and character. This perspective-taking creates meaning within challenging circumstances.

4. **Seek new spiritual community when needed:** Intentionally build new spiritual relationships after relocations or other transitions that affect community connections. These relationships provide essential support for continued growth.

5. **Allow transition to prompt spiritual reassessment:** Use major life changes as opportunities to evaluate and potentially adjust

spiritual priorities and practices. This reassessment prevents stagnation.

Isaiah 43:19 records God's promise: *"Behold, I am doing a new thing; now it springs forth, do you not perceive it? I will make a way in the wilderness and rivers in the desert."* This assurance of God's continued work, even in wilderness seasons, provides hope during significant transitions.

Conclusion: The Journey Toward Deeper Spiritual Connection

Spiritual growth in marriage represents both one of God's greatest gifts and one of life's most significant challenges. The vulnerability required for authentic spiritual connection exposes our deepest insecurities and selfishness yet also creates the profound unity our hearts long for.

As you apply the insights from this chapter, remember these key principles:

1. Spiritual growth in marriage builds upon individual spiritual vitality while creating unique opportunities for shared faith development.

2. Common barriers to spiritual growth can be identified and addressed through intentional effort, honest communication, and sometimes professional help.

3. Specific practices—prayer, Scripture study, worship, service, and creating a spiritually nurturing home—foster spiritual growth in practical, sustainable ways.

4. Different seasons of marriage bring unique spiritual challenges and opportunities that require adaptation and renewed commitment.

5. Special circumstances such as spiritual imbalance, dryness, or major transitions create additional challenges that can be navigated with wisdom and grace.

The journey toward deeper spiritual connection continues throughout marriage, with each stage offering opportunities for growth and renewed commitment. As Gary Thomas observes, "The pursuit of spiritual growth in marriage reflects our deeper longing for connection with God, who designed us for relationship with Himself and others."[45]

May your marriage become increasingly characterized by the beautiful spiritual intimacy God designed for husbands and wives—a relationship where you grow together in faith, hope, and love.

Chapter 10

Dealing With Extended Family

Navigating Family Relationships Beyond the Marriage

"Therefore a man shall leave his father and his mother and hold fast to his wife, and they shall become one flesh." (Genesis 2:24)

One of the most significant challenges for many marriages involves navigating relationships with extended family—parents, siblings, in-laws, and other relatives. These relationships can be sources of tremendous blessing and support, but they can also create significant stress and conflict when boundaries are unclear, or expectations differ.

This chapter explores biblical principles for relating to extended family, common challenges couples face, and practical approaches for building healthy relationships that support rather than undermine your marriage. Whether you're just beginning your marriage journey or have been married for years, these insights will help you navigate extended family relationships with wisdom, grace, and unity.

The Biblical Foundation for Extended Family Relationships

Scripture provides clear principles for how married couples should relate to their families of origin. These principles establish a foundation for healthy extended family relationships while protecting the primary marriage bond.[1]

The Principle of Leaving and Cleaving

The most fundamental biblical principle regarding marriage and extended family appears in Genesis 2:24: *"Therefore a man shall leave his father and his mother and hold fast to his wife, and they shall become one flesh."* This passage establishes that marriage creates a new primary relationship that takes precedence over the relationship with parents.

Andreas Köstenberger explains that "the Hebrew terms for 'leave' and 'hold fast' indicate a decisive shift in primary allegiance and loyalty from parents to spouse."[2] This shift doesn't sever the relationship with parents but fundamentally changes its nature and priority.

Jesus reaffirmed this principle in Matthew 19:4-6: *"Have you not read that he who created them from the beginning made them male and female, and said, 'Therefore a man shall leave his father and his mother and hold fast to his wife, and the two shall become one flesh'? So they are no longer two but one flesh. What therefore God has joined together, let not man separate."* This reaffirmation emphasizes the divine design for marriage as the formation of a new family unit.

The "leaving" aspect of this principle involves:

- Emotional independence from parents
- Financial self-sufficiency when possible
- Independent decision-making as a couple
- Establishing separate living arrangements
- Shifting primary loyalty from parents to spouse

The "cleaving" or "holding fast" aspect involves:

- Forming a strong marital bond
- Developing unity in decisions and direction
- Creating new family traditions and patterns
- Building a shared life together
- Protecting the marriage relationship

As Timothy Keller observes, "The leaving and cleaving principle doesn't eliminate relationships with parents but transforms them from relationships of dependence to relationships of honor and respect between adults."[3] This transformation creates the foundation for healthy extended family relationships.

The Command to Honor Parents

While establishing the primacy of the marriage relationship, Scripture also commands adult children to honor their parents. This ongoing responsibility creates a tension that married couples must navigate with wisdom and discernment.

Exodus 20:12 commands, *"Honor your father and your mother, that your days may be long in the land that the LORD your God is giving you."* This commandment, part of the Ten Commandments, carries lifelong application rather than ending at adulthood or marriage.

Ephesians 6:2-3 reaffirms this command in the New Testament: *"Honor your father and mother (which is the first commandment with a promise), that it may go well with you and that you may live long in the land."* This passage confirms the continuing relevance of this command for Christians.

The biblical concept of honor includes:

- Showing respect in words and actions
- Expressing gratitude for parental contributions
- Maintaining appropriate relationship
- Providing care when needed
- Speaking respectfully about parents to others

Dennis Rainey notes that "honoring parents after marriage requires finding the balance between appropriate independence and continued respect and care."[4] This balance looks different in various cultural contexts and family situations, requiring couples to apply biblical principles with wisdom.

1 Timothy 5:4 instructs believers to *"show godliness to their own household and to make some return to their parents, for this is pleasing in the sight of God."* This passage establishes that adult children have ongoing responsibilities toward parents, particularly in times of need.

As Gary Chapman observes, "The biblical commands to leave parents and to honor parents create a healthy tension that must be navigated with wisdom rather than resolved with simplistic formulas."[5] This tension requires ongoing communication, prayer, and discernment.

The Pattern of Healthy Family Blessing

Beyond the specific commands regarding parents, Scripture presents a pattern where extended family relationships provide blessing and support rather than interference or control. This pattern offers a positive vision for extended family relationships.

Ruth 4:11-12 records the blessing pronounced on Boaz and Ruth at their marriage: *"May the LORD make the woman, who is coming into your house, like Rachel and Leah, who together built up the house of Israel. May you act worthily in Ephrathah and be renowned in Bethlehem, and may your house be like the house of Perez, whom Tamar bore to Judah because of the offspring that the LORD will give you by this young woman."* This blessing from the community exemplifies the supportive role extended family and community should play.

Proverbs 17:6 observes that *"grandchildren are the crown of the aged, and the glory of children is their fathers."* This passage highlights the mutual blessing that can flow between generations when relationships are healthy.

The book of Ruth portrays the beautiful relationship between Ruth and her mother-in-law, Naomi, demonstrating how in-law relationships can be characterized by loyalty, love, and mutual support rather than tension or conflict.

Timothy Keller notes that "Scripture presents extended family as a source of blessing, support, and generational continuity rather than control or interference."[6] This positive vision guides couples toward building healthy extended family relationships.

Examples of healthy family blessings include:

- Practical support without control
- Wisdom shared without manipulation
- Resources offered without strings attached
- Traditions passed down without rigidity
- Relationships maintained without enmeshment

As Dennis Rainey observes, "The biblical pattern shows extended family providing a supportive context for the marriage relationship rather than competing with or undermining it."[7] This supportive role allows the marriage to flourish while maintaining meaningful extended family connections.

Common Challenges with Extended Family

Despite God's design for extended family as a blessing, many couples experience significant challenges in these relationships. Understanding common difficulties helps couples address them proactively and wisely.[8]

Different Family Cultures and Expectations

One of the most fundamental challenges couples face involves navigating the different family cultures and expectations they bring into marriage. These differences can create confusion, conflict, and stress when not addressed with understanding and flexibility.

H. Norman Wright explains that "each spouse enters marriage with unwritten rules and expectations about family relationships absorbed from their family of origin."[9] These unwritten rules often remain unconscious until violated, creating confusion and conflict.

Differences in family culture might include:

1. **Communication patterns:** One family may communicate directly and explicitly, while another uses indirect hints or non-verbal cues. These differences can create misunderstandings about what extended family members expect or need.

2. **Boundary expectations:** Families differ significantly in their expectations about privacy, spontaneous visits, sharing of information, and involvement in decision-making. These differences often create tension when extended family members violate boundaries that seem obvious to one spouse but foreign to the other.

3. **Holiday and celebration traditions:** Families develop strong traditions around holidays, birthdays, and other celebrations. These traditions carry emotional significance that can create conflict when couples must choose between competing family expectations.

4. **Expressions of care and support:** Families demonstrate care in different ways—some through practical help, others through gifts, and others through quality time. These differences can lead to misinterpretation of motives or intentions.

5. **Conflict resolution approaches:** Some families address conflict directly, while others avoid confrontation entirely. These differences affect how couples navigate disagreements with extended family members.

Gary Chapman notes that "recognizing and discussing these differences before they create conflict helps couples develop unified approaches to extended family relationships."[10] This proactive conversation prevents unnecessary tension and misunderstanding.

Boundary Violations and Interference

Many couples experience challenges with extended family members who violate appropriate boundaries or interfere in the marriage relationship. These boundary violations can range from subtle to blatant but consistently undermine the primary marriage bond.

Emerson Eggerichs observes that "boundary violations often occur because parents struggle to transition from their role as primary influencers to supportive extended family."[11] This transition difficulty can manifest in various forms of interference.

Common boundary violations include:

1. **Uninvited visits or expectations of unlimited access:** Extended family members who arrive without invitation or expect to be welcomed at any time violate the couple's right to privacy and independent family life.

2. **Unsolicited advice or criticism:** Parents or in-laws who regularly offer unsolicited advice about parenting, finances, career, or other personal matters violate the couple's autonomy in decision-making.

3. **Triangulation in conflict:** Extended family members who take sides in marital disagreements or attempt to mediate conflicts undermine the couple's responsibility to resolve their own issues.

4. **Financial manipulation:** Parents who use financial support as leverage to influence decisions or extract compliance violate the couple's independence and authority.

5. **Excessive contact or emotional dependence:** Parents who expect daily contact or demonstrate excessive emotional dependence on adult children violate the primary marital relationship.

Henry Cloud and John Townsend explain that "healthy boundaries with extended family protect the marriage relationship while still allowing meaningful connection."[12] These boundaries require clear communication, consistency, and sometimes difficult conversations.

Proverbs 25:17 wisely advises, *"Let your foot be seldom in your neighbor's house, lest he have his fill of you and hate you."* This principle of respecting others' space and privacy applies to extended family relationships as well, suggesting that even close family members should respect boundaries.

Divided Loyalties and Triangulation

Many couples experience the challenge of divided loyalties when extended family members create pressure to prioritize family of origin over the marriage relationship. This pressure creates internal conflict and marital tension.

Dennis Rainey notes that "divided loyalty situations force spouses to choose between pleasing their parents or supporting their spouse, creating no-win scenarios that damage relationships."[13] These situations violate the biblical principle of leaving and cleaving.

Common divided loyalty scenarios include:

1. Parents expecting adult children to maintain family traditions that conflict with the couple's preferences or values
2. Extended family scheduling events without consulting the couple and expecting attendance regardless of other commitments
3. Parents or siblings making demands during holidays that compete with the couple's plans or other family obligations
4. Family members expecting the adult child to keep secrets from their spouse or withhold information
5. Extended family criticizing the spouse and expecting the adult child to agree or remain silent

Triangulation—where a third party becomes inappropriately involved in a relationship between two others—frequently occurs in extended family relationships. This unhealthy pattern damages both the marriage and the extended family relationship.

Gary Chapman observes that "triangulation prevents direct communication and resolution of issues, creating ongoing tension and resentment."[14] Breaking these triangulation patterns requires a commitment to direct communication and appropriate boundaries.

Matthew 18:15 instructs believers, *"If your brother sins against you, go and tell him his fault, between you and him alone."* This principle of direct communication applies to extended family relationships, discouraging triangulation and promoting healthy conflict resolution.

In-Law Relationship Tensions

The relationship between spouses and their in-laws often creates unique challenges. These relationships lack the foundation of shared history and unconditional love that typically characterizes parent-child relationships, making them more vulnerable to misunderstanding and conflict.

H. Norman Wright explains that "in-law relationships begin without the years of bonding and understanding that parent-child relationships enjoy, creating potential for misinterpretation and tension."[15] This relationship begins in adulthood rather than developing gradually from birth.

Common in-law tensions include:

1. **Different expectations about the in-law relationship:** One person may expect a close, parent-like relationship, while the other prefers more distance and formality.

2. **Perceived criticism or rejection:** In-laws may interpret differences in values, practices, or preferences as implicit criticism or rejection rather than normal variation.

3. **Competition for influence or time:** Parents and in-laws may compete for influence over the couple or time with them, creating tension and forcing the couple to navigate competing demands.

4. **Difficulty accepting the spouse's family culture:** Adjusting to different communication styles, traditions, or relationship patterns can create discomfort and resistance.

5. **Loyalty conflicts:** Spouses may feel caught between loyalty to their family of origin and support for their spouse in tensions with in-laws.

The biblical story of Ruth and Naomi provides a positive model for in-law relationships characterized by loyalty, respect, and mutual support. Ruth's declaration to Naomi—*"Where you go I will go, and where you stay I will stay. Your people will be my people and your God my God"* (Ruth 1:16)—demonstrates commitment to her husband's family even after his death.

Gary Thomas notes that "healthy in-law relationships develop gradually through mutual respect, appropriate boundaries, and intentional relationship building."[16] These relationships require patience and grace from all parties.

Financial Entanglements and Expectations

Financial relationships with extended family create another common challenge for married couples. Whether receiving financial support, providing assistance to aging parents, or navigating inheritance issues, money matters often complicate extended family relationships.

Dave Ramsey observes that "financial entanglements with extended family frequently create tension, resentment, and boundary confusion in marriages."[17] These entanglements can undermine the couple's financial independence and decision-making authority.

Common financial challenges include:

1. **Ongoing financial dependence on parents:** Continuing to rely on parental financial support after marriage can prevent full "leaving" and create unhealthy power dynamics.

2. **Financial support with strings attached:** Parents providing financial assistance while expecting control or influence over decisions violates the couple's autonomy.

3. **Unequal financial treatment of adult children:** Parents who provide significantly different levels of support to adult children and their families can create resentment and comparison.

4. **Disagreement about financial support for aging parents:** Couples may have different expectations or capacities for providing financial assistance to aging parents.

5. **Inheritance issues creating family tension:** Anticipated inheritance or disagreements about estate planning can create unhealthy dynamics in extended family relationships.

Proverbs 22:7 warns that *"the borrower is slave to the lender."* This principle applies to family loans as well, highlighting how financial dependence creates power imbalance in relationships.

1 Timothy 5:8 establishes responsibility to provide for family members: *"But if anyone does not provide for his relatives, and especially for members of his household, he has denied the faith and is worse than an unbeliever."* This passage confirms the obligation to care for family members in need while requiring wisdom about how this care is provided.

As Dave Ramsey advises, "Clear communication, written agreements, and appropriate boundaries help prevent financial entanglements from damaging family relationships."[18] These practices protect both the marriage and the extended family relationship.

Geographic Distance and Proximity Challenges

The geographic distance between couples and their extended families creates unique challenges that require intentional navigation. Whether living very close to family or at great distance, couples face different but significant issues.

Dennis Rainey notes that "both extreme proximity and significant distance from extended family create distinct challenges that couples must address proactively."[19] These challenges affect communication, boundaries, and relationship development.

Challenges with geographic proximity include:

1. Boundary violations through unexpected visits or excessive involvement
2. Difficulty establishing independent family identity and traditions
3. Extended family expecting priority in time and attention
4. Pressure to participate in all family events and activities
5. Interference in parenting or other personal decisions

Challenges with geographic distance include:

1. Limited opportunity for relationship building, especially between in-laws
2. Difficulty providing support for aging or ill parents
3. Expensive and logistically challenging visits, especially with children
4. Unequal distance from respective families creating imbalance in visits
5. Children having limited relationships with grandparents and extended family

Proverbs 27:10 advises, *"Do not forsake your friend or a friend of your family, and do not go to your relative's house when disaster strikes you—better a neighbor nearby than a relative far away."* This passage acknowledges the practical limitations of geographic distance while encouraging development of local supportive relationships.

As Gary Chapman observes, "Technology provides new opportunities for maintaining connection despite geographic distance, though these connections differ qualitatively from in-person relationship."[20] Video calls, social media, and other technologies help bridge distance while requiring intentional effort.

Building Healthy Extended Family Relationships

Despite the challenges, couples can build healthy relationships with extended family that support rather than undermine their marriage. These approaches help navigate common difficulties while fostering meaningful connection.[21]

Establishing Clear Boundaries

Establishing and maintaining clear boundaries with extended family provides the foundation for healthy relationships. These boundaries protect the marriage while allowing appropriate connection with parents and other relatives.

Henry Cloud and John Townsend define boundaries as "property lines that define where you end and someone else begins."[22] In extended family relationships, these boundaries clarify expectations, responsibilities, and appropriate involvement.

Key boundaries to establish include:

1. **Time boundaries:** Clarify expectations about frequency of visits, phone calls, and other contact. Establish that invitations will be issued rather than assuming open access.

2. **Privacy boundaries:** Determine what information about your marriage and family will be shared with extended family and what remains private. Establish that personal disagreements will be resolved without involving parents.

3. **Decision-making boundaries:** Clarify that decisions about parenting, finances, career, and other personal matters will be made by the couple, with input from others welcomed when requested.

4. **Holiday and celebration boundaries:** Develop clear approaches to holidays and special occasions that balance time with different extended family groups while protecting time for your immediate family.

5. **Physical space boundaries:** Establish expectations regarding home access, including whether extended family members have keys, how visits are arranged, and guest room policies.

Galatians 6:5 states that *"each one should carry their own load."* This principle supports appropriate boundaries, distinguishing between normal responsibilities individuals should carry themselves and legitimate burdens that require family support.

As Henry Cloud notes, "Healthy boundaries are not walls but gates, allowing selective access rather than either complete openness or total restriction."[23] These boundaries require clear communication, consistency, and sometimes difficult conversations.

Prioritizing the Marriage Relationship

Consistently prioritizing the marriage relationship above extended family relationships helps couples navigate challenges with unity and clarity. This prioritization follows the biblical principle of leaving and cleaving while preventing divided loyalties.

Timothy Keller emphasizes that "the marriage relationship must take precedence over extended family relationships for both spouses, creating a united front in family interactions."[24] This unity prevents triangulation and manipulation.

Practical ways to prioritize marriage include:

1. **Discussing extended family issues privately before responding:** Take time to process requests, invitations, or issues together rather than making individual commitments or responses.

2. **Presenting a united front to extended family:** Communicate decisions as coming from both of you rather than attributing unpopular decisions to one spouse.

3. **Speaking positively about your spouse to family members:** Avoid criticizing your spouse to your family, which creates triangulation and undermines respect.

4. **Supporting your spouse's boundaries with their family:** Each spouse should take primary responsibility for communicating boundaries to their own family of origin.

5. **Checking with your spouse before making commitments:** Consult your spouse before accepting invitations or making promises that affect your shared time or resources.

Genesis 2:24 establishes that in marriage, the two become *"one flesh."* This unity applies to extended family relationships, where couples function as a unit rather than as separate individuals with competing loyalties.

As Gary Chapman observes, "When extended family members recognize that you consistently prioritize your marriage, they typically adjust their expectations accordingly."[25] This consistency helps establish healthy patterns over time.

Developing Effective Communication Strategies

Effective communication with extended family helps prevent misunderstanding, address issues before they escalate, and build positive relationships. These communication strategies apply biblical principles of honesty, respect, and peacemaking.

H. Norman Wright notes that "communication problems with extended family often reflect unclear expectations or assumptions rather than intentional conflict."[26] Addressing these unclear expectations directly can prevent many common difficulties.

Effective communication strategies include:

1. **Using "I" statements rather than accusations:** Express your needs and feelings without attacking or blaming. "I feel overwhelmed when we have unexpected visitors" communicates more effectively than "You always show up without warning."

2. **Expressing appreciation before addressing concerns:** Begin difficult conversations by affirming the relationship and expressing gratitude for positive aspects before addressing problems.

3. **Choosing appropriate timing and privacy:** Address sensitive issues in private rather than in group settings, and select times when everyone is calm rather than already stressed.

4. **Listening to understand before responding:** Take time to understand extended family members' perspectives and concerns before formulating your response.

5. **Being direct rather than hinting:** Clearly state expectations, boundaries, and requests rather than dropping hints or expecting others to read between the lines.

Ephesians 4:15 instructs believers to speak *"the truth in love."* This balanced approach avoids both harsh confrontation and conflict avoidance, addressing issues directly while maintaining respect and care.

Proverbs 15:1 advises that *"a gentle answer turns away wrath, but a harsh word stirs up anger."* This wisdom applies particularly to extended family communication, where emotional history can quickly escalate conflicts.

As Dennis Rainey observes, "Most extended family conflicts can be resolved through direct, respectful communication that addresses issues before resentment builds."[27] This proactive approach prevents small issues from becoming major conflicts.

Creating New Family Traditions

Developing unique traditions and patterns as a couple helps establish your identity as a new family unit while honoring elements of your family of origin. These new traditions support the biblical principle of "leaving and cleaving" while creating meaningful family experiences.

Gary Thomas notes that "creating new family traditions allows couples to establish their unique identity while selectively incorporating elements from their families of origin."[28] This selective incorporation honors heritage without being bound by it.

Approaches to creating new traditions include:

1. **Discussing which traditions from each family of origin you want to continue:** Evaluate traditions from both families, selecting those that align with your values and preferences.

2. **Developing entirely new traditions that reflect your unique family:** Create traditions that express your specific values, interests, and circumstances rather than simply adopting existing patterns.

3. **Adapting existing traditions to fit your family:** Modify traditions from either family to better fit your circumstances, preferences, or values.

4. **Creating space for both connection and independence:** Develop traditions that include extended family at appropriate times while preserving space for your immediate family.

5. **Remaining flexible as circumstances change:** Allow traditions to evolve as your family grows, and circumstances change rather than rigidly maintaining patterns that no longer serve your family well.

Joshua 24:15 declares, *"As for me and my house, we will serve the LORD."* This passage affirms each family's right and responsibility to establish their own spiritual priorities and practices.

As Timothy Keller observes, "New family traditions communicate that while you value your heritage, you are establishing a new family with its own identity and practices."[29] This balance honors parents while establishing appropriate independence.

Navigating Holidays and Special Occasions

Holidays and special occasions often create particular stress in extended family relationships. Developing clear approaches to these events helps prevent conflict while creating meaningful celebrations.

Dennis Rainey explains that "holidays concentrate extended family expectations and emotions, requiring particularly thoughtful navigation."[30] These high-stakes occasions benefit from proactive planning and clear communication.

Strategies for navigating holidays include:

1. **Discussing expectations and preferences as a couple first:** Before making commitments to extended family, clarify what each of you values and needs during holidays.

2. **Communicating plans early and clearly:** Provide extended family with clear information about your holiday plans well in advance to prevent last-minute pressure or disappointment.

3. **Creating rotation systems when appropriate:** For some families, alternating holidays between different extended family groups work well (e.g., Thanksgiving with one family, Christmas with another).

4. **Hosting celebrations at your home when possible:** Inviting extended family to your home for celebrations allows you to maintain some control over timing and activities.

5. **Establishing some celebrations for your immediate family only:** Reserve certain days or portions of holidays for just your immediate family to build your own traditions and memories.

Ecclesiastes 3:1 reminds us that *"there is a time for everything and a season for every activity under the heavens."* This principle applies to holiday celebrations, where different seasons of life may require different approaches to extended family involvement.

As Gary Chapman advises, "Approach holidays with flexibility and generosity while maintaining appropriate boundaries for your immediate family's needs."[31] This balanced approach prevents holidays from becoming sources of ongoing tension.

Building Healthy In-Law Relationships

The relationship between spouses and their in-laws requires particular attention and intentional development. These relationships lack the foundation of shared history that characterizes parent-child relationships, requiring extra effort and understanding.

H. Norman Wright observes that "healthy in-law relationships develop gradually through mutual respect, appropriate boundaries, and intentional relationship building."[32] These relationships benefit from realistic expectations and patient investment.

Strategies for building healthy in-law relationships include:

1. **Approaching the relationship with realistic expectations:** Recognize that close relationships with in-laws typically develop gradually rather than instantly and may never exactly mirror parent-child relationships.

2. **Finding common interests or activities:** Identify shared interests, hobbies, or activities that provide natural connection points and positive shared experiences.

3. **Expressing appreciation for specific actions or qualities:** Notice and verbalize appreciation for positive qualities or actions, building goodwill and positive interaction.

4. **Respecting differences in background, preferences, and style:** Acknowledge that differences in approach or preference don't necessarily indicate criticism or rejection.

5. **Supporting your spouse's relationship with their parents:** Encourage appropriate connection between your spouse and their parents without jealousy or competition.

The biblical example of Ruth and Naomi demonstrates the potential for beautiful in-law relationships characterized by loyalty, respect, and mutual support. Ruth's declaration to Naomi—*"Your people will be my people and your God my God"* (Ruth 1:16)—shows her commitment to embracing her husband's family even after his death.

As Gary Thomas notes, "The most important factor in in-law relationships is the attitude you bring—choosing to see them as family you're gaining rather than competition you're managing."[33] This positive perspective creates foundation for healthy relationship.

Managing Financial Relationships Wisely

Financial relationships with extended family require particular wisdom and clear boundaries. Whether receiving support, providing assistance, or navigating inheritance matters, financial clarity prevents many common problems.

Dave Ramsey emphasizes that "financial entanglements with family members require even clearer communication and boundaries than financial relationships with non-family."[34] The emotional connection in family relationships complicates financial interactions.

Principles for managing financial relationships include:

1. **Moving toward financial independence from parents:** Work toward complete financial independence from parents as quickly as possible after marriage, even if it requires lifestyle adjustments.

2. **Treating financial assistance as business arrangements:** When financial help is necessary, create clear written agreements about whether money is a gift or loan, repayment terms, and any conditions.

3. **Avoiding financial comparisons between siblings:** Recognize that parents may provide different types or levels of support to adult children based on varying needs and circumstances.

4. **Planning proactively for aging parent support:** Discuss expectations and capacity for supporting aging parents before crises occur, including siblings in these conversations when possible.

5. **Maintaining appropriate privacy about financial matters:** Establish boundaries around what financial information is shared with extended family, preventing unnecessary advice or judgment.

Proverbs 22:7 warns that *"the borrower is slave to the lender."* This principle applies to family loans as well, highlighting how financial dependence creates power imbalance in relationships.

As Dave Ramsey advises, "The best financial help often comes in forms other than direct money transfer—such as education, training, or temporary housing—which support independence rather than creating dependence."[35] These approaches provide assistance while maintaining appropriate boundaries.

Addressing Cultural and Religious Differences

Many couples navigate significant cultural or religious differences between their families of origin. These differences require particular sensitivity, clear communication, and thoughtful boundary-setting.

Timothy Keller notes that "cultural and religious differences between families of origin often create the most deeply felt tensions, as they touch core values and identity."[36] These differences affect holiday celebrations, child-raising approaches, and many other aspects of family life.

Approaches for navigating these differences include:

1. **Educating each family about the other's traditions:** Help each extended family understand and appreciate elements of the other's cultural or religious background.
2. **Selecting which elements of each tradition to incorporate:** Thoughtfully choose which aspects of each cultural or religious tradition you will maintain in your family.

3. **Creating clear boundaries around religious instruction for children:** Establish clear agreements about religious teaching and practice, particularly when extended family members have different beliefs.

4. **Finding opportunities to honor both traditions when possible:** Look for ways to acknowledge and respect both cultural backgrounds without compromising your own values.

5. **Preparing for and addressing insensitive comments:** Develop strategies for responding to culturally insensitive or religiously inappropriate comments from extended family members.

Acts 10 records Peter's growing understanding that God shows no partiality between people of different cultural backgrounds. This biblical principle supports respecting diverse cultural expressions while maintaining core spiritual commitments.

As H. Norman Wright observes, "Cultural and religious differences need not divide families when approached with mutual respect, clear communication, and appropriate boundaries."[37] This balanced approach allows for diversity within unity.

Caring for Aging Parents

Caring for aging parents presents one of the most significant extended family challenges many couples face. This responsibility requires balancing honor for parents with appropriate boundaries and marriage priorities.

Dennis Rainey explains that "caring for aging parents tests the leaving and cleaving principle as couples navigate competing responsibilities and limited resources."[38] This challenge typically emerges just as couples are also managing career demands and raising children.

Principles for caring for aging parents include:

1. **Discussing expectations and capacity before crises:** Talk openly as a couple about your values, capacity, and limitations regarding parent care before urgent situations arise.

2. **Involving siblings and other family members:** Engage all available family members in parent care rather than assuming primary responsibility automatically falls to one child.

3. **Considering various care options objectively:** Evaluate different care approaches—from in-home support to assisted living to moving parents into your home—based on parents' needs, your capacity, and available resources.

4. **Maintaining appropriate boundaries even in caregiving:** Establish clear parameters around financial support, time commitment, and decision-making authority even while providing necessary care.

5. **Protecting your marriage relationship amid caregiving demands:** Ensure that parent care doesn't consistently take precedence over marriage relationship and immediate family needs.

1 Timothy 5:4 instructs believers to *"show godliness to their own household and to make some return to their parents, for this is pleasing in the sight of God."* This passage establishes the responsibility to care for aging parents while requiring wisdom about how this care is provided.

As Gary Thomas advises, "The biblical command to honor parents in their aging years requires thoughtful application rather than formulaic responses, considering the needs of all involved."[39] This balanced approach prevents either neglect of parents or sacrifice of the marriage relationship.

Navigating Extended Family Challenges in Different Seasons

Extended family relationships evolve throughout the marriage journey. Understanding these seasonal changes helps couples adapt their approach appropriately as circumstances change.[40]

The Newlywed Years: Establishing Patterns

The early years of marriage establish patterns for extended family relationships that often persist for decades. During this formative period, couples navigate differences in family background while building their unique approach to extended family relationships.

H. Norman Wright notes that "patterns established in the first few years of marriage often determine the trajectory of extended family relationships for decades to come."[41] This reality makes thoughtful navigation of early extended family dynamics particularly important.

Key focuses during this season include:

1. Discussing family of origin differences explicitly: Explore each other's family background, traditions, and expectations regarding extended family involvement. These conversations create understanding and prevent misunderstanding.
2. Establishing clear boundaries from the beginning: Set appropriate boundaries with both families early in marriage rather than attempting to change established patterns later.
3. Creating your own holiday and celebration traditions: Develop your unique approach to holidays and special occasions rather than simply adopting patterns from either family of origin.
4. Building relationships with in-laws intentionally: Invest in developing positive relationships with your spouse's family without expecting instant closeness or understanding.

5. Presenting a united front from the beginning: Establish patterns of unity and mutual support in extended family interactions rather than allowing triangulation or divided loyalties.

Proverbs 24:3-4 observes that *"by wisdom, a house is built, and through understanding, it is established; through knowledge, its rooms are filled with rare and beautiful treasures."* This passage highlights the importance of intentionally building family relationships with wisdom from the beginning.

The Parenting Years: Grandparent Relationships

The arrival of children transforms extended family relationships, particularly as parents become grandparents. This transition creates both new opportunities and potential challenges that require thoughtful navigation.

Gary Thomas observes that "grandparent relationships often intensify extended family dynamics, creating both deeper connection and potential boundary challenges."[42] The emotional investment grandparents have in grandchildren can either strengthen or complicate family relationships.

Key focuses during this season include:

1. Establishing clear boundaries around parenting decisions: Clarify that while grandparent input may be welcomed, parenting decisions remain the parents' responsibility.
2. Creating opportunities for grandparent-grandchild relationships: Facilitate appropriate connection between grandparents and grandchildren through visits, video calls, and other interactions.
3. Addressing differences in parenting philosophy respectfully: Develop approaches for managing differences between your parenting approach and your parents' expectations or advice.
4. Balancing time between different sets of grandparents: Create systems for dividing holiday and special occasion time fairly between different grandparents.

5. Addressing inappropriate grandparent behavior directly: Develop strategies for addressing overstepping, undermining, or other problematic grandparent behaviors.

Psalm 78:4 instructs believers to *"tell the coming generation the glorious deeds of the LORD, and his might, and the wonders that he has done."* This responsibility to transmit faith to the next generation can be shared appropriately with grandparents while maintaining parental authority.

The Middle Years: Changing Parent Relationships

As both couples and their parents age, relationships often shift again. Parents may require increasing support, while couples typically have more established boundaries and family patterns.

Dennis Rainey describes the middle years as "a season when parent-child relationships often reverse gradually, with adult children providing increasing support to aging parents."[43] This role reversal requires sensitivity and ongoing adjustment.

Key focuses during this season include:

1. Monitoring parents' changing needs and capabilities: Pay attention to signs that parents may need additional support with health, finances, home maintenance, or other areas.

2. Having proactive conversations about future care needs: Discuss parents' preferences and plans for later years before crises force decisions.

3. Balancing parent care with other responsibilities: Develop approaches for meeting parent needs while maintaining appropriate focus on marriage, children, and other commitments.

4. Coordinating with siblings regarding parent support: Create collaborative approaches with siblings rather than allowing parent care to fall disproportionately on one child.

5. Preparing emotionally for parent decline: Process the emotional impact of seeing parents age and decline, seeking support when needed.

Proverbs 23:22 advises, *"Listen to your father who gave you life, and do not despise your mother when she is old."* This instruction recognizes the ongoing responsibility to honor parents even as relationships change with age.

The Later Years: Legacy and Loss

The later years of marriage often involve the loss of parents and a shift toward becoming the older generation in the family. This transition creates both grief and opportunity for legacy-building.

Billy Graham reflected that "the loss of parents, while painful, often prompts deeper appreciation for family legacy and more intentional investment in the next generation."[42] This perspective shift can enrich extended family relationships in the later years.

Key focuses during this season include:

1. Processing grief over parent loss individually and together: Create space to acknowledge and work through grief when parents die, recognizing that spouses may grieve differently.
2. Resolving any unfinished business with parents: Address any need for forgiveness, reconciliation, or closure in parent relationships before or after their death.
3. Preserving and transmitting family legacy: Identify values, stories, traditions, and faith elements from both families of origin that you want to preserve and pass on.
4. Becoming supportive rather than controlling in-laws: Develop healthy relationships with adult children and their spouses that offer support without interference.

261

5. Preparing your own end-of-life matters thoughtfully: Organize financial, legal, and personal matters to prevent burdening your children later.

Psalm 145:4 declares, *"One generation shall commend your works to another, and shall declare your mighty acts."* This passage highlights the opportunity in later years to focus on transmitting spiritual legacy to future generations.

Conclusion: Building Extended Family Relationships That Last

Extended family relationships represent both significant challenges and tremendous blessings for married couples. The vulnerability required for healthy family relationships exposes our deepest insecurities and selfishness yet also creates the multigenerational connections our hearts long for.

As you apply the insights from this chapter, remember these key principles:

1. Biblical teaching establishes both the primacy of the marriage relationship and the ongoing responsibility to honor parents, creating a tension that requires wisdom to navigate.
2. Common challenges with extended family—boundary violations, different expectations, in-law tensions, and others—can be addressed through clear communication, appropriate boundaries, and mutual respect.
3. Building healthy extended family relationships requires intentional effort, including establishing boundaries, prioritizing marriage, developing effective communication, and creating new traditions.
4. Different seasons of marriage bring unique extended family challenges and opportunities that require adaptation and renewed commitment.

5. Special circumstances such as unbelieving family members, toxic relationships, blended families, or international distance create additional challenges that can be navigated with wisdom and grace.

The journey toward healthy extended family relationships continues throughout marriage, with each stage offering opportunities for growth and renewed commitment. As Dennis Rainey observes, "Extended family relationships, when navigated with wisdom and grace, provide one of God's greatest gifts—a multigenerational community of love and support."[43]

May your marriage become increasingly characterized by healthy extended family relationships that honor God, support your marriage, and create a legacy of faith for future generations.

Chapter 11

Maintaining A Healthy Marriage

Nurturing Your Relationship for a Lifetime

"Let your fountain be blessed, and rejoice in the wife of your youth." (Proverbs 5:18)

Marriage is not merely an event but a lifelong journey. While the previous chapters have addressed specific aspects of marriage—communication, conflict resolution, intimacy, and others—this chapter focuses on the ongoing maintenance required to keep your marriage healthy and vibrant through changing seasons and circumstances.

Just as a garden requires consistent attention rather than occasional intense effort, a thriving marriage needs regular nurture and intentional care. This chapter explores biblical principles and practical approaches for maintaining a healthy marriage throughout the various seasons and challenges of life together.

The Biblical Vision for Marriage Longevity

Scripture presents a vision of marriage as a lifelong covenant relationship that grows deeper and richer with time. This vision contrasts sharply with cultural perspectives that often view marriage as disposable or primarily focused on personal fulfillment.[1]

Marriage as a Covenant Relationship

The biblical concept of covenant provides the foundation for understanding marriage longevity. Unlike a contract based on mutual benefit that can be broken when benefits diminish, a covenant represents an unconditional commitment that persists through changing circumstances.

Malachi 2:14 describes marriage as a "covenant" relationship, emphasizing its binding nature: *"The LORD was witness between you and the wife of your youth, to whom you have been faithless, though she is your companion and your wife by covenant."* This passage highlights God's role as a witness to the marriage covenant, adding divine significance to the commitment.

Timothy Keller explains that "the covenant concept means that marriage is more than a private arrangement between two individuals; it is a binding relationship witnessed by God and the community."[2] This covenant understanding provides stability through the inevitable challenges of married life.

Key elements of the covenant concept include:

1. Unconditional commitment that persists regardless of changing feelings or circumstances
2. Public declaration and community accountability rather than merely private arrangement
3. God as witness and participant in the relationship
4. Binding obligations that transcend personal preference or convenience
5. Expectation of faithfulness and permanence

As Gary Thomas observes, "Understanding marriage as a covenant rather than contract transforms how couples approach difficulties—from asking 'Is this meeting my needs?' to asking 'How can I fulfill my covenant obligations?'"[3] This perspective shift supports marriage longevity through challenging seasons.

The Blessing of Lifelong Companionship

Scripture presents lifelong marriage as a blessing rather than a burden, emphasizing the joy and fulfillment found in enduring companionship. This positive vision motivates the effort required for marriage maintenance.

Proverbs 5:18 encourages, *"Let your fountain be blessed, and rejoice in the wife of your youth."* This passage envisions continued joy and delight in one's spouse throughout life rather than diminishing satisfaction over time.

Ecclesiastes 9:9 similarly advises, *"Enjoy life with the wife whom you love, all the days of your vain life that he has given you under the sun because that is your portion in life and in your toil at which you toil under the sun."* This passage frames lifelong marriage as a gift that brings meaning and joy amid life's challenges.

The biblical vision includes:

1. Growing intimacy and knowledge of one another over time
2. Shared history and memories that enrich the relationship
3. Mutual support through life's challenges and transitions
4. The security and comfort of enduring commitment
5. Witness to God's faithfulness through human relationship

Dennis Rainey notes that "Scripture presents marriage longevity not merely as endurance but as increasing blessing as couples grow together through various seasons."[4] This positive vision provides motivation for the consistent effort marriage maintenance requires.

Marriage as Spiritual Formation

The biblical perspective frames marriage not merely as a source of personal happiness but as a context for spiritual growth and character formation. This understanding helps couples persevere through difficulties by recognizing their spiritual purpose.

Gary Thomas explains that "God designed marriage to make us holy more than to make us happy—though the holiness often leads to happiness."[5] This perspective reframes marriage challenges as opportunities for spiritual growth rather than merely obstacles to personal fulfillment.

Ephesians 5:25-27 describes Christ's relationship with the church as a model for marriage: *"Husbands, love your wives, as Christ loved the church and gave himself up for her, that he might sanctify her, having cleansed her by the washing of water with the word, so that he might present the church to himself in splendor, without spot or wrinkle or any such thing, that she might be holy and without blemish."* This passage connects marriage to sanctification and spiritual transformation.

The spiritual formation aspects of marriage include:

1. Learning selflessness through serving another's needs
2. Developing patience and forbearance through conflict
3. Growing in forgiveness and grace through failure
4. Building faithfulness through temptation and testing
5. Experiencing unconditional love that reflects God's love

As Timothy Keller observes, "Marriage is a major vehicle for the gospel's remaking of your heart from the inside out and your life from the ground up."[6] This understanding helps couples maintain their marriage through difficulties by recognizing the spiritual growth occurring through challenges.

Essential Practices for Marriage Maintenance

Maintaining a healthy marriage requires consistent practices rather than occasional grand gestures. These foundational habits create the conditions for ongoing relationship health and growth.[7]

Cultivating Spiritual Intimacy

Spiritual connection provides the deepest foundation for marriage longevity. Couples who share spiritual practices and growth experience greater relationship satisfaction and stability over time.

Dennis Rainey emphasizes that *"spiritual intimacy creates a three-strand cord* (Ecclesiastes 4:12) *that strengthens marriage against the inevitable pressures and challenges of life."*[8] This shared spiritual dimension adds resilience to the relationship.

Practices that cultivate spiritual intimacy include:

1. Praying together regularly: Sharing prayer concerns and approaching God together creates vulnerability and unity. Even brief daily prayer establishes a pattern of spiritual connection.

2. Studying Scripture together: Reading and discussing biblical passages allows couples to grow in their understanding of God's design for marriage and life. This shared learning creates a common spiritual language and perspective.

3. Worshiping together: Participating in corporate worship as a couple reinforces shared faith and connects the marriage to the larger body of Christ. This regular practice aligns the marriage with God's purposes.

4. Serving others together: Engaging in ministry or service as a couple creates shared purpose and experiences that strengthen spiritual connection. These experiences often become significant relationship memories.

5. Discussing spiritual insights and questions: Creating space for open conversation about faith, doubts, and spiritual growth builds intellectual and spiritual intimacy. These discussions deepen mutual understanding.

Hebrews 10:24-25 encourages believers to *"consider how to stir up one another to love and good works, not neglecting to meet together."* This principle applies powerfully within marriage, where spouses have unique opportunities to encourage one another's spiritual growth.

As Gary Thomas notes, "Couples who pray together regularly report significantly higher marital satisfaction and are much less likely to divorce than those who don't."[9] This simple practice creates both spiritual and relational benefits.

Maintaining Emotional Connection

Emotional connection requires ongoing attention and investment. Without regular emotional maintenance, couples can drift apart despite living in the same home and sharing daily activities.

H. Norman Wright observes that "emotional disconnection often occurs gradually through neglect rather than through major conflict or crisis."[10] This gradual nature makes proactive maintenance particularly important.

Practices that maintain emotional connection include:

1. Daily check-in conversations: Brief but focused conversations about each person's experiences, feelings, and thoughts maintain awareness of one another's inner lives. These conversations prevent emotional distance from developing.

2. Expressing appreciation regularly: Noticing and verbalizing specific things you appreciate about your spouse counteracts negativity bias and builds emotional goodwill. This practice prevents taking one another for granted.

3. Physical affection beyond sexual intimacy: Regular non-sexual touch—holding hands, hugging, sitting close—maintains the physical and emotional connection. These small gestures communicate care and a desire for closeness.

4. Creating shared experiences: Intentionally building memories through shared activities, adventures, or projects strengthens emotional bonds. These experiences become relationship anchors during difficult seasons.

5. Emotional presence during stress: Making extra effort to connect during busy or stressful periods prevents drift when couples might

naturally withdraw. This intentionality maintains connection when it's most needed.

Proverbs 27:19 observes that **"as water reflects the face, so one's life reflects the heart."** This principle applies to marriage, where emotional connection allows spouses to reflect and understand one another's hearts.

As John Gottman's research demonstrates, "Small moments of emotional connection have greater impact on marriage satisfaction than occasional grand gestures."[11] These daily interactions build the emotional bank account that sustains the relationship.

Practicing Effective Communication

Communication patterns established early in marriage often become habitual, requiring intentional maintenance and occasional recalibration to remain healthy. Effective communication prevents misunderstanding and disconnection.

Gary Chapman emphasizes that "communication skills require ongoing practice and refinement rather than one-time learning."[12] This ongoing development maintains this crucial aspect of relationship health.

Practices that maintain healthy communication include:

1. Regular time for uninterrupted conversation: Creating space for meaningful dialogue without distractions allows deeper connection than communication squeezed between other activities. This dedicated time communicates relationship priority.
2. Listening to understand rather than respond: Practicing active listening—seeking to understand your spouse's perspective before formulating your response—prevents defensive communication patterns. This approach demonstrates respect and care.

3. Addressing issues before resentment builds: Discussing concerns or hurts when they first arise prevents accumulation of unresolved issues that damage the relationship. This practice maintains emotional safety.

4. Using "I" statements rather than accusations: Expressing your feelings and needs without blame or criticism creates space for productive conversation rather than defensive responses. This approach invites connection rather than conflict.

5. Checking understanding through reflection: Verifying that you've understood your spouse's meaning by restating what you heard prevents misunderstanding and demonstrates engagement. This practice builds communication accuracy.

Ephesians 4:29 instructs believers to speak words *"that give grace to those who hear."* This principle applies particularly to marriage communication, where words have profound impact on relationship health.

As H. Norman Wright notes, "Couples who maintain healthy communication adapt their approach as circumstances change rather than relying on patterns that may have worked in earlier seasons."[13] This flexibility allows communication to evolve with the relationship.

Nurturing Physical and Sexual Intimacy

Physical and sexual connection requires intentional maintenance throughout marriage as bodies change, circumstances shift, and familiarity develops. This aspect of marriage provides unique bonding that supports overall relationship health.

Ed Wheat observes that "sexual intimacy serves as both a barometer of the overall relationship and a bonding agent that strengthens it."[14] This dual function makes sexual health an important aspect of marriage maintenance.

Practices that maintain physical and sexual intimacy include:

1. Prioritizing regular sexual connection: Making sexual intimacy a priority rather than an afterthought communicates value for this aspect of the relationship. This prioritization prevents neglect during busy seasons.

2. Communicating openly about needs and desires: Discussing preferences, concerns, and changes in sexual needs prevents misunderstanding and frustration. This communication allows adaptation to changing circumstances.

3. Addressing physical or emotional barriers: Proactively addressing issues that interfere with sexual connection—whether physical health problems, emotional wounds, or external stressors—prevents long-term disconnection. This approach treats sexual health as important rather than optional.

4. Maintaining non-sexual physical affection: Continuing affectionate touch that doesn't lead to sexual intimacy maintains physical connection and prevents touch becoming solely sexual. This broader physical connection supports sexual intimacy.

5. Creating romantic atmosphere and anticipation: Investing in romance through date nights, thoughtful gestures, and playful interaction prevents sexual routine and maintains excitement. This intentionality communicates desire and appreciation.

1 Corinthians 7:3-5 instructs, *"The husband should give to his wife her conjugal rights, and likewise the wife to her husband. For the wife does not have authority over her own body, but the husband does. Likewise, the husband does not have authority over his own body, but the wife does. Do not deprive one another, except perhaps by agreement for a limited time, that you may devote yourselves to prayer; but then come together again, so that Satan may not tempt you because of your lack of self-control."* This passage establishes the importance of ongoing sexual connection in marriage.

As Kevin Leman notes, "Sexual intimacy provides unique emotional and physical bonding that supports overall marriage health when maintained as a regular priority."[15] This connection strengthens the marriage against various challenges and temptations.

Managing Conflict Constructively

Conflict patterns tend to become entrenched without intentional maintenance and adjustment. Healthy conflict management prevents damage while allowing growth through disagreement.

John Gottman's research demonstrates that "it's not the presence of conflict that predicts marriage failure but how conflict is handled."[16] This finding highlights the importance of maintaining healthy conflict patterns.

Practices that maintain constructive conflict management include:

1. Addressing issues when calm rather than escalated: Choosing appropriate timing for difficult conversations prevents emotion from overwhelming productive discussion. This timing choice demonstrates respect for the relationship.

2. Focusing on understanding before problem-solving: Taking time to fully understand each other's perspectives before moving to solutions prevents premature closure and unresolved feelings. This approach honors both people's experiences.

3. Maintaining respect during disagreement: Committing to respectful language and behavior, even during an intense disagreement, prevents damage that outlasts the conflict. This boundary protects the relationship while allowing honest discussion.

4. Recognizing and interrupting negative patterns: Identifying destructive conflict cycles and intentionally choosing different responses prevents habitual negative interactions. This awareness allows growth rather than repetition.

5. Seeking resolution rather than victory: Approaching conflict with the goal of mutual understanding and relationship strengthening rather than winning prevents competitive dynamics. This perspective maintains unity through disagreement.

Ephesians 4:26-27 advises, *"Do not let the sun go down on your anger, and give no opportunity to the devil."* This principle encourages timely resolution of conflicts rather than allowing issues to fester and damage the relationship.

As Emerson Eggerichs observes, "Couples who maintain healthy conflict patterns recognize that the goal is understanding and connection rather than agreement on every issue."[17] This perspective allows couples to navigate differences while maintaining relationship health.

Practicing Forgiveness and Grace

Marriage inevitably involves hurt, disappointment, and failure, making forgiveness and grace essential maintenance practices rather than occasional responses. These practices prevent bitterness and resentment from damaging the relationship.

Timothy Keller explains that "a marriage without regular forgiveness and grace quickly becomes a scorekeeping arrangement that damages both partners."[18] This transactional approach undermines the covenant nature of marriage.

Practices that maintain forgiveness and grace include:

1. Acknowledging hurt without minimizing: Recognizing and validating the impact of hurtful actions creates space for authentic forgiveness rather than superficial dismissal. This acknowledgment demonstrates respect for the injured person's experience.
2. Taking responsibility without defensiveness: Accepting responsibility for your contribution to problems without excuse or

blame-shifting demonstrates maturity and creates possibility for healing. This responsibility allows genuine reconciliation.

3. Extending forgiveness as a decision: Choosing to forgive even when feelings haven't fully healed prevents bitterness from taking root. This decision begins the healing process rather than waiting for feelings to change first.

4. Avoiding bringing up forgiven issues: Resisting the temptation to resurrect past forgiven hurts during new conflicts demonstrates genuine forgiveness. This boundary prevents accumulated grievances from overwhelming the relationship.

5. Extending grace for weaknesses and failures: Accepting your spouse's humanity and imperfection creates safety and allows growth rather than performance pressure. This grace reflects God's approach to human weakness.

Colossians 3:13 instructs believers to *"bear with one another and, if one has a complaint against another, forgiving each other; as the Lord has forgiven you, so you also must forgive."* This passage connects human forgiveness to divine forgiveness, providing both motivation and model.

As Gary Thomas notes, "Forgiveness in marriage isn't a one-time event but an ongoing practice that maintains relationship health through inevitable hurts and disappointments."[19] This ongoing nature makes forgiveness a maintenance practice rather than merely a crisis response.

Navigating Life Transitions Together

Marriage spans numerous life transitions that can either strengthen the relationship or create disconnection. Intentional navigation of these transitions maintains relationship health through changing circumstances.

Dennis Rainey observes that "major life transitions create both challenge and opportunity for marriages, requiring intentional adaptation rather than passive drift."[20] This intentionality prevents transitions from becoming relationship crises.

Practices that maintain connection through transitions include:

1. Communicating openly about expectations and fears: Discussing hopes, concerns, and expectations regarding transitions creates shared understanding and prevents misalignment. This communication allows couples to support one another through change.

2. Adjusting roles and responsibilities intentionally: Explicitly discussing and agreeing on changing roles during transitions prevents confusion and resentment. This clarity supports smooth adaptation to new circumstances.

3. Maintaining relationship rituals during change: Preserving important relationship practices—date nights, bedtime routines, shared activities—during transitions provides stability amid change. These constants anchor the relationship through shifting circumstances.

4. Processing grief and loss together: Acknowledging and sharing the losses that often accompany transitions—even positive ones— prevents isolation and supports emotional connection. This shared processing deepens intimacy through difficulty.

5. Creating new shared vision for each season: Developing explicit understanding of how each new season aligns with your overall marriage purpose prevents drift and disconnection. This shared vision maintains unity through changing circumstances.

Ecclesiastes 3:1 observes that *"for everything, there is a season and a time for every matter under heaven."* This principle applies to marriage, where different seasons require different approaches while maintaining core commitment.

As H. Norman Wright notes, "Couples who navigate transitions well recognize that the relationship itself must adapt to new circumstances rather than merely trying to maintain previous patterns."[21] This flexibility allows the marriage to evolve while maintaining its essential character.

Maintaining Marriage Through Different Seasons

Marriage passes through predictable seasons that present unique challenges and opportunities. Understanding these seasons helps couples maintain their relationship appropriately through changing circumstances.[22]

The Early Years: Building Foundation

The early years of marriage establish patterns and expectations that often persist throughout the relationship. This formative period requires particular attention to building healthy foundations rather than merely responding to immediate circumstances.

Gary Chapman observes that "patterns established in the first five years of marriage often determine the trajectory of the relationship for decades to come."[23] This reality makes intentional foundation-building particularly important.

Key maintenance focuses during this season include:

1. Establishing healthy communication patterns: Developing effective approaches for both everyday conversation and conflict resolution creates foundation for ongoing connection. These patterns often become habitual and difficult to change later.
2. Navigating family of origin differences: Addressing differences in background, expectations, and family culture prevents these differences from creating ongoing tension. This navigation establishes your unique family identity.

3. Building friendship alongside romance: Developing shared interests, activities, and friendships creates relationship durability beyond initial romantic attraction. This friendship becomes increasingly important over time.

4. Creating financial management systems: Establishing approaches to budgeting, spending, saving, and financial decision-making prevents money conflicts that damage many marriages. These systems support financial partnerships.

5. Developing shared spiritual practices: Building habits of prayer, worship, and spiritual growth together creates foundation for spiritual intimacy throughout marriage. These practices connect the relationship to its ultimate purpose.

Proverbs 24:3-4 observes that *"by wisdom, a house is built, and through understanding, it is established; through knowledge, its rooms are filled with rare and beautiful treasures."* This passage highlights the importance of intentionally building relationship foundations with wisdom.

As Dennis Rainey notes, "The investment couples make in establishing healthy patterns during early marriage yields dividends throughout the relationship's lifetime."[24] This long-term perspective motivates the effort required during this formative season.

The Parenting Years: Maintaining Connection Amid Demands

The arrival of children transforms marriage in profound ways, creating both new joy and significant stress. This season requires intentional maintenance to preserve the marriage relationship amid competing demands.

Kevin Leman explains that "the transition to parenthood represents one of the most challenging periods for marriage maintenance, requiring deliberate effort to preserve couple identity."[25] This challenge makes intentional connection particularly important.

Key maintenance focuses during this season include:

1. Protecting couple time amid family demands: Establishing regular date nights, daily connection rituals, and occasional getaways maintains the primary relationship amid parenting responsibilities. This prioritization prevents parent-only identity.

2. Maintaining teamwork in parenting: Developing unified approaches to discipline, routines, and child-raising philosophy prevents parenting differences from creating marital conflict. This unity strengthens both marriage and parenting.

3. Continuing sexual connection despite fatigue: Making physical intimacy a priority despite exhaustion and limited privacy maintains this crucial aspect of marriage during challenging years. This connection supports overall relationship health.

4. Supporting one another through parenting challenges: Providing emotional support, practical help, and encouragement through difficult parenting seasons prevents these challenges from damaging the marriage. This mutual support strengthens partnership.

5. Continuing growth as individuals: Maintaining individual identity, interests, and development alongside parenting roles prevents resentment and supports long-term relationship health. This continued growth enriches the marriage relationship.

Psalm 127:3 declares that *"children are a heritage from the LORD, offspring a reward from him."* This perspective frames children as blessings rather than burden while maintaining awareness of their impact on marriage.

As Gary Thomas observes, "Couples who maintain strong marriages during the parenting years recognize that the best gift they can give their children is a healthy relationship between their parents."[26] This understanding motivates the effort required to maintain marriage during this demanding season.

The Middle Years: Renewal and Recommitment

The middle years of marriage—often coinciding with midlife transitions, launching children, and career shifts—provide opportunity for relationship renewal and deepening. This season requires intentional recommitment rather than passive continuation.

Timothy Keller notes that "the middle years offer unique opportunity for marriage renewal as external demands often decrease and couples have opportunity to rediscover one another."[27] This rediscovery requires intentional engagement rather than assumption.

Key maintenance focuses during this season include:

1. Rediscovering one another beyond roles: Taking time to know one another as individuals beyond functional roles as parents, providers, or homemakers deepens intimacy in this season. This rediscovery prevents growing apart despite years together.

2. Addressing accumulated issues or resentments: Resolving long-standing conflicts or hurts that may have been set aside during busier seasons prevents these issues from damaging the relationship's future. This resolution allows genuine renewal.

3. Reimagining shared purpose and dreams: Developing new shared vision and goals as earlier ones are accomplished creates forward momentum for the relationship. This shared future orientation prevents stagnation.

4. Revitalizing sexual intimacy: Investing in physical connection as bodies change and circumstances shift maintains this important aspect of marriage. This revitalization often requires new approaches and communication.

5. Preparing for upcoming life transitions: Discussing and planning for future changes—retirement, aging parents, grandchildren—prevents

these transitions from creating crises later. This preparation strengthens partnership for future seasons.

Isaiah 43:19 declares, *"Behold, I am doing a new thing; now it springs forth, do you not perceive it? I will make a way in the wilderness and rivers in the desert."* This passage encourages openness to new possibilities even after established patterns.

As Dennis Rainey observes, "The middle years provide opportunity for marriage to move from good to great as couples intentionally invest in relationship renewal rather than merely maintaining status quo."[28] This perspective motivates the effort required for genuine renewal.

The Later Years: Legacy and Finishing Well

The later years of marriage offer unique opportunity for deep companionship and legacy-building. This season requires adaptation to changing circumstances while maintaining core connections.

Gary Thomas explains that "the later years can represent the most rewarding season of marriage for couples who have maintained their relationship through earlier challenges."[29] This potential makes continued maintenance worthwhile despite changing circumstances.

Key maintenance focuses during this season include:

1. Adapting to health changes and limitations: Adjusting expectations and approaches as health changes occur prevents these limitations from unnecessarily restricting relationship quality. This adaptation allows continued connection despite changes.
2. Maintaining physical and emotional intimacy: Finding new ways to express affection and connection as bodies change preserves this important aspect of a relationship. This maintenance prevents unnecessary loss of intimacy.

3. Supporting one another through losses: Providing comfort and presence through the increasing losses of aging—friends, family members, and abilities—strengthens partnership during vulnerability. This mutual support deepens connection through difficulty.

4. Building meaningful legacy together: Identifying values, faith, wisdom, and resources you want to pass on to future generations creates shared purpose in later years. This legacy-building provides meaning beyond self-focus.

5. Preparing for eventual separation: Discussing end-of-life wishes, handling practical matters, and processing grief about eventual separation prevents these realities from becoming taboo topics. This preparation demonstrates care for one another.

Psalm 92:14 promises that *"they still bear fruit in old age; they are ever full of sap and green."* This passage encourages continued growth and fruitfulness even in later years rather than merely surviving.

As Billy Graham reflected near the end of his life, "The later years of marriage can be the most precious, as couples experience the fulfillment of promises made decades earlier and witness God's faithfulness through every season."[30] This perspective frames the later years as culmination rather than decline.

Addressing Common Threats to Marriage Health

Every marriage faces challenges that can damage relationship health without proper maintenance. Recognizing and addressing these common threats helps couples maintain their relationship through various challenges.[31]

Busyness and Neglect

The demands of work, parenting, community involvement, and other responsibilities often lead to relationship neglect despite good intentions. This common threat requires intentional counteraction rather than assuming the relationship will maintain itself.

Kevin Leman observes that "more marriages die from neglect than from conflict—the slow drift of busyness gradually eroding connection until couples barely know one another."[32] This gradual nature makes this threat particularly dangerous.

Signs of busyness damage include:

1. Conversation limited to logistics and scheduling
2. Physical intimacy becoming infrequent or routine
3. Important decisions made without meaningful discussion
4. Decreasing awareness of each other's inner lives
5. Relationships taking the lowest priority when time is limited

Ecclesiastes 4:9-12 reminds us that *"two are better than one because they have a good return for their labor: If either of them falls down, one can help the other up. But pity anyone who falls and has no one to help them up. Also, if two lie down together, they will keep warm. But how can one keep warm alone? Though one may be overpowered, two can defend themselves. A cord of three strands is not quickly broken."* This passage highlights the practical benefits of maintained connection.

Counteracting busyness requires:

1. Scheduling relationship time with the same priority as other commitments
2. Creating boundaries around work and technology
3. Simplifying commitments when necessary to protect marriage

4. Developing brief connection rituals that maintain relationships amid busyness

5. Periodically evaluating how time allocation reflects stated priorities

As Gary Chapman notes, "Couples who successfully navigate busyness recognize that time together isn't found but made through deliberate choices and boundaries."[33] These choices demonstrate that the relationship remains a genuine priority despite competing demands.

Digital Distraction and Technology

Digital technology and social media present unique challenges to relationship attention and connection. These modern realities require intentional management to prevent relationship damage.

Sherry Turkle's research demonstrates that "the constant presence of digital devices often creates 'alone together' dynamics where couples are physically present but mentally elsewhere."[34] This divided attention undermines meaningful connection.

Signs of technology damage include:

1. Devices regularly interrupting conversation or intimacy
2. More engagement with screens than with each other
3. Sharing significant news or feelings with online communities before spouse
4. Comparing relationships to idealized versions seen on social media
5. Developing separate digital lives with limited sharing or transparency

1 Corinthians 7:35 speaks of *"undivided devotion to the Lord."* While addressing a different context, this principle of undivided attention applies to marriage as well, where divided focus damages connection.

Healthy technology management includes:

1. Establishing tech-free zones and times in your home
2. Developing clear expectations about device use during couple time
3. Practicing full attention during conversation (devices down, notifications off)
4. Creating transparency about online activities and relationships
5. Using technology to enhance connection when apart rather than diminish it when together

As John Gottman's research indicates, "Brief moments of bids for attention either met or rejected accumulate over time to create either connection or distance."[35] Digital devices often prevent even noticing these bids, making intentional management essential.

Financial Stress and Conflict

Financial challenges create significant stress in many marriages, requiring intentional management to prevent damage to the relationship. Money conflicts often reflect deeper values and security issues rather than merely practical disagreements.

Dave Ramsey notes that "financial stress ranks among the top reasons for divorce, yet most couples spend more time planning their wedding than developing shared financial approaches."[36] This planning gap creates vulnerability to relationship damage.

Signs of financial stress damage include:

1. Recurring arguments about spending or saving
2. Secretive financial behavior or hidden purchases
3. Blame and criticism regarding money decisions
4. Anxiety or tension when financial topics arise
5. Different financial values creating ongoing conflict

Hebrews 13:5 advises, *"Keep your lives free from the love of money and be content with what you have because God has said, 'Never will I leave you; never will I forsake you.'"* This passage addresses the heart issues often underlying financial conflicts.

Healthy financial management includes:

1. Developing shared financial goals and values
2. Creating transparent systems for tracking spending and saving
3. Establishing agreed boundaries for individual discretionary spending
4. Communicating regularly about financial matters before problems develop
5. Seeking outside help when financial conflicts seem unresolvable

As Dave Ramsey observes, "Couples who successfully navigate financial challenges recognize that money management is primarily about shared values and communication rather than merely numbers."[37] This perspective elevates financial discussions from technical disagreements to meaningful value alignment.

Extended Family Challenges

Relationships with parents, in-laws, and other family members often create stress in marriages. These relationships require thoughtful navigation to prevent damage to the primary marriage bond.

H. Norman Wright explains that "extended family relationships often create loyalty conflicts that damage marriage when not addressed with clear boundaries and priorities."[38] These conflicts require intentional management rather than hoping they resolve themselves.

Signs of extended family damage include:

1. One spouse consistently prioritizing parents over partner
2. In-law criticism or interference creating tension

3. Different expectations about family involvement causing conflict

4. Holidays and celebrations creating recurring stress

5. Triangulation, where family members are involved in marital issues

Genesis 2:24 establishes that *"a man shall leave his father and his mother and hold fast to his wife, and they shall become one flesh."* This passage establishes the primacy of the marriage relationship over family of origin.

Healthy extended family management includes:

1. Establishing clear boundaries regarding visits, advice, and involvement

2. Presenting unified decisions to family members rather than allowing triangulation

3. Each spouse taking primary responsibility for addressing issues with their own family

4. Creating holiday and celebration approaches that balance different family expectations

5. Building positive relationships with in-laws while maintaining appropriate boundaries

As Dennis Rainey notes, "Couples who successfully navigate extended family challenges recognize that honoring parents doesn't mean allowing inappropriate influence or control."[39] This distinction allows both appropriate honor and appropriate boundaries.

Career Demands and Transitions

Work demands and career transitions create significant stress for many marriages. These challenges require intentional navigation to prevent career from damaging relationship health.

Timothy Keller observes that "career often becomes a primary identity competing with rather than supporting marriage, particularly when work demands increase or transitions occur."[40] This competition requires deliberate counterbalance.

Signs of career damage include:

1. Work consistently taking priority over relationship needs

2. Career decisions made without considering impact on marriage

3. Work stress regularly spilling into home relationship

4. Identity and worth primarily derived from professional role

5. Significant time apart due to work with limited connection maintenance

Ecclesiastes 4:8 warns, *"There was a man all alone; he had neither son nor brother. There was no end to his toil, yet his eyes were not content with his wealth. 'For whom am I toiling,' he asked, 'and why am I depriving myself of enjoyment?' This, too, is meaningless—a miserable business!"* This passage highlights the emptiness of work success without relational connection.

Healthy career management includes:

1. Making major career decisions as a couple rather than individually

2. Establishing clear boundaries between work and home time

3. Developing transition rituals between work and home roles

4. Creating realistic expectations about work hours and availability

5. Supporting career development while maintaining relationship priority

As Gary Chapman advises, "Couples who successfully navigate career challenges recognize that work serves the relationship rather than the relationship serving work."[41] This perspective maintains appropriate priorities amid professional demands.

Maintaining Marriage in Special Circumstances

Some marriages face particular challenges that require specific maintenance approaches. These special circumstances don't exempt couples from basic maintenance practices but require additional attention to specific issues.[42]

Navigating Chronic Illness or Disability

Chronic illness or disability creates unique stresses that can either strengthen or damage a marriage. These circumstances require specific maintenance approaches beyond general relationship practices.

Joni Eareckson Tada, who has navigated marriage with quadriplegia, observes that "disability or chronic illness tests the 'in sickness and health' vow in ways couples never anticipated, requiring intentional adaptation rather than merely enduring."[43] This adaptation allows continued connection despite changed circumstances.

Special maintenance needs include:

1. Grieving losses together while avoiding chronic grief: Acknowledging the real losses illness creates while not remaining stuck in grief allows couples to adapt to new realities. This balanced grieving prevents bitterness while honoring genuine loss.

2. Preventing caregiver/patient dynamics from overwhelming marriage: Maintaining husband/wife identity alongside caregiver/care-receiver roles prevents the relationship from becoming primarily functional. This balance preserves intimacy amid practical demands.

3. Finding new ways to connect intimately: Adapting approaches to physical and emotional intimacy as abilities change maintains this

crucial aspect of marriage. This adaptation prevents unnecessary loss of connection.

4. Building support systems beyond the marriage: Developing appropriate outside help prevents exhaustion and resentment from overwhelming the relationship. This support allows the marriage to be more than a care arrangement.

5. Finding meaning and purpose within limitations: Discovering how your marriage can still fulfill meaningful purpose despite limitations prevents hopelessness and gives shared vision. This meaning-making transforms suffering into opportunity for witness.

2 Corinthians 12:9 promises, *"My grace is sufficient for you, for my power is made perfect in weakness."* This passage offers hope that limitation becomes opportunity for experiencing God's strength rather than merely enduring hardship.

As Joni Eareckson Tada reflects, "Marriages that thrive despite illness or disability focus on what remains possible rather than only what has been lost."[44] This perspective allows continued growth and connection despite significant challenges.

Rebuilding After Betrayal

Serious betrayal—whether infidelity, addiction, or other trust violations—creates trauma that requires specific healing approaches. Recovery is possible but requires intentional rebuilding rather than merely continuing previous patterns.

Gary Thomas explains that "rebuilding after betrayal requires more than forgiveness—it involves reconstructing the relationship foundation with new patterns and safeguards."[45] This reconstruction takes significant time and effort from both partners.

Special maintenance needs include:

1. Establishing safety before expecting intimacy: Creating trustworthy patterns and appropriate transparency provides foundation for rebuilding connection. This safety must precede expectations of emotional or physical intimacy.

2. Allowing full expression of hurt without vengeance: Creating space for the betrayed spouse to express pain without the relationship becoming defined by punishment allows healing to begin. This expression acknowledges the genuine trauma created.

3. The offending spouse taking full responsibility: Acknowledging the betrayal without minimization, excuse, or blame-shifting demonstrates genuine repentance necessary for rebuilding. This responsibility creates possibility for genuine reconciliation.

4. Identifying and addressing root issues: Understanding the personal and relationship factors that contributed to the betrayal prevents recurrence and supports genuine healing. This understanding goes beyond the presenting issue to deeper patterns.

5. Establishing appropriate accountability and boundaries: Creating safeguards that rebuild trust while avoiding controlling or punitive dynamics supports healthy recovery. These boundaries demonstrate commitment to change.

Hosea 14:4 records God's promise to Israel after betrayal: *"I will heal their waywardness and love them freely, for my anger has turned away from them."* This passage offers hope that genuine healing and renewed love remain possible after serious breach.

As Gary Thomas observes, "Marriages that successfully rebuild after betrayal often become stronger than before, as couples develop deeper understanding, more authentic connection, and healthier patterns."[46] This potential for growth provides hope during the difficult rebuilding process.

291

Maintaining Connection During Separation

Work requirements, military service, or other circumstances sometimes require physical separation that challenges marriage connection. These situations demand intentional maintenance approaches to prevent emotional distance from accompanying physical distance.

Dennis Rainey notes that "physical separation need not create emotional separation when couples develop intentional connection practices despite distance."[47] These practices maintain relationship health despite challenging circumstances.

Special maintenance needs include:

1. Establishing consistent communication rhythms: Creating regular patterns for phone calls, video chats, or other communication prevents disconnection and provides stability amid separation. These rhythms maintain awareness of each other's lives.

2. Sharing daily experiences despite distance: Exchanging details about ordinary activities and feelings maintains shared life despite physical separation. This sharing prevents developing separate lives that exclude one another.

3. Continuing to make decisions together: Including one another in significant choices despite distance maintains partnership rather than independence. This inclusion prevents drift toward separate lives.

4. Creating meaningful rituals despite separation: Developing special practices—reading the same book, watching the same show, praying at the same time—creates shared experience despite distance. These rituals maintain connection beyond conversation.

5. Managing expectations about reunion: Discussing hopes and realities about time together prevents disappointment when

reunions don't match idealized expectations. This realism allows genuine connection rather than performance pressure.

Song of Solomon 8:6 declares that *"love is as strong as death... Many waters cannot quench love; rivers cannot sweep it away."* This passage affirms that genuine love can endure despite separation and challenge.

As military chaplain Peter Wherry observes, "Couples who maintain strong connection during separation focus on emotional and spiritual intimacy when physical presence isn't possible."[48] This focus prevents distance from creating permanent disconnection.

Blending Families Successfully

Remarriage involving children from previous relationships creates unique challenges requiring specific maintenance approaches. Blended family dynamics add complexity to marriage maintenance.

Ron Deal, blended family expert, explains that "blended families must simultaneously build couple unity while navigating complex parent-child and step-relationships."[49] This dual focus requires particular intentionality and patience.

Special maintenance needs include:

1. Maintaining strong couple relationships amid competing loyalties: Prioritizing marriage connections while respecting existing parent-child bonds prevents the relationship from being overwhelmed by blended family stress. This prioritization provides stability for all relationships.

2. Developing realistic expectations about family integration: Recognizing that blended family bonding typically takes years rather than months prevents discouragement when instant harmony doesn't occur. This realism allows appropriate patience.

3. Supporting biological parent leadership with children: Allowing biological parents to maintain primary discipline roles, especially initially, prevents stepparent rejection and loyalty conflicts. This approach builds relationships before authority.

4. Creating new family traditions while respecting history: Developing unique family practices while honoring important traditions from both previous families builds shared identity without erasing significant history. This balance respects all family members.

5. Maintaining appropriate boundaries with ex-spouses: Developing businesslike co-parenting relationships without emotional entanglement protects the marriage while supporting children's needs. These boundaries prevent past relationships from damaging current marriages.

Joshua 24:15 declares, *"As for me and my household, we will serve the LORD."* This passage offers unifying purpose for blended families seeking shared identity and values amid complexity.

As Ron Deal advises, "Successful blended families recognize that cooking a blended family stew takes longer than microwaving a biological family—patience and persistence allow integration to develop naturally."[50] This perspective prevents discouragement when blending takes significant time.

Conclusion: The Lifelong Journey of Marriage Maintenance

Marriage maintenance isn't a one-time project but a lifelong journey requiring consistent attention and care. The effort this maintenance requires yields tremendous blessings as your relationship deepens and matures through changing seasons and circumstances.

As you apply the principles from this chapter, remember these key insights:

1. Biblical teaching establishes marriage as a covenant relationship designed for lifelong growth and blessing rather than merely personal fulfillment or convenience.

2. Essential maintenance practices—spiritual intimacy, emotional connection, effective communication, physical intimacy, conflict management, forgiveness, and navigating transitions—require ongoing attention rather than occasional focus.

3. Different seasons of marriage present unique maintenance challenges and opportunities, from the foundation-building early years through the legacy-building later years.

4. Common threats to marriage health—busyness, technology distraction, financial stress, extended family challenges, and career demands—require specific counteraction to prevent relationship damage.

5. Special circumstances such as illness, betrayal, separation, or blended families create unique maintenance needs beyond general relationship practices.

The maintenance your marriage requires may seem demanding at times, but the rewards of a deeply connected, spiritually vibrant relationship that endures through life's challenges make every effort worthwhile. As Gary Thomas observes, "A marriage well-maintained becomes not burden but blessing, not merely obligation but opportunity for experiencing God's faithfulness through human relationship."[51]

May your marriage become increasingly characterized by the joy, intimacy, and mutual support God designed it to provide as you faithfully maintain this precious relationship through every season of life together.

Chapter 12

Summary And Application

Putting It All Together: Preparing for a God-Honoring Marriage

"Unless the LORD builds the house, those who build it labor in vain." (Psalm 127:1)

Throughout this book, we have explored the biblical foundations, practical skills, and spiritual dimensions of marriage. As we conclude, this chapter draws together the key principles from each area into a cohesive framework for preparing for and building a God-honoring marriage. Rather than introducing new concepts, we will synthesize what we've learned and provide practical application steps for implementing these truths in your relationship.

The journey toward marriage is both exciting and sobering—a path that requires thoughtful preparation rather than merely emotional enthusiasm. As you consider the principles we've discussed, remember that marriage preparation is not primarily about planning a wedding but about building a foundation for a lifetime relationship that honors God and blesses both partners.

The Biblical Vision for Marriage

Throughout this book, we have emphasized that a biblical understanding of marriage must form the foundation for all other aspects of relationship preparation. Without this foundation, couples build on shifting cultural ideas rather than enduring truth.[1]

Marriage as God's Design for Human Flourishing

From the beginning, God designed marriage as the fundamental human relationship—the foundation for family, society, and the continuation of humanity. Genesis 2:18 establishes that "it is not good for the man to be alone," highlighting God's intention for human companionship and partnership.

This divine design means that marriage is not merely a human invention or social construct but a relationship established by God with specific purposes:

1. Companionship and mutual support: Marriage provides the deepest human relationship of friendship, intimacy, and partnership.
2. Reflection of God's image: Together, husband and wife display aspects of God's character that neither can fully reflect alone.
3. Context for sexual intimacy: Marriage provides the exclusive relationship for the expression of sexual intimacy as God designed it.
4. Foundation for family: Marriage establishes the secure relationship for bearing and raising children when God grants them.
5. Witness to God's covenant love: Marriage displays to the world a picture of Christ's faithful love for His church.

Understanding these purposes helps couples approach marriage not merely as a path to personal happiness but as participation in God's larger purposes. As Timothy Keller observes, "Marriage is glorious but hard. It's a burning joy and strength, and yet it is also blood, sweat, and tears; humbling defeats and exhausting victories."[2]

Marriage as a Covenant Relationship

Throughout Scripture, marriage is consistently presented as a covenant relationship rather than merely a contractual arrangement. This covenant

297

nature establishes marriage as a binding commitment witnessed by God and community rather than merely a private arrangement between individuals.

Malachi 2:14 describes marriage as a "covenant" relationship: *"The LORD was witness between you and the wife of your youth, to whom you have been faithless, though she is your companion and your wife by covenant."* This passage highlights both the binding nature of marriage and God's role as witness to the commitment.

The covenant understanding of marriage includes several key elements:

1. Unconditional commitment that persists regardless of changing feelings or circumstances
2. Public declaration and community accountability rather than merely private arrangement
3. God as witness and participant in the relationship
4. Binding obligations that transcend personal preference or convenienc
5. Expectation of faithfulness and permanence

This covenant understanding provides stability through the inevitable challenges of married life. As Gary Thomas notes, "When we understand marriage as covenant rather than contract, we approach difficulties differently—asking 'How can I fulfill my covenant obligations?' rather than 'Is this meeting my needs?'"[3]

Marriage as Spiritual Formation

Throughout this book, we have emphasized that marriage serves not merely as a source of personal happiness but as a context for spiritual growth and character formation. This understanding helps couples persevere through difficulties by recognizing their spiritual purpose.

Gary Thomas explains that "God designed marriage to make us holy more than to make us happy—though the holiness often leads to happiness." This perspective reframes marriage challenges as opportunities for spiritual growth rather than merely obstacles to personal fulfillment.

The spiritual formation aspects of marriage include:

1. Learning selflessness through serving another's needs
2. Developing patience and forbearance through conflict
3. Growing in forgiveness and grace through failure
4. Building faithfulness through temptation and testing
5. Experiencing unconditional love that reflects God's love

This understanding of marriage as spiritual formation helps couples maintain perspective during difficulties, recognizing that God is working through the relationship to conform both partners more fully to the image of Christ.[4]

Essential Relationship Skills for Marriage

While a biblical foundation provides the "why" of marriage, practical relationship skills provide the "how" of daily married life. Throughout this book, we have explored several essential skill areas that couples must develop for a healthy marriage.

Communication: The Lifeblood of Relationship

Effective communication serves as the foundation for all other aspects of marriage relationship. Without healthy communication patterns, couples cannot resolve conflicts, build intimacy, or navigate life's challenges together.

Key communication principles include:

1. Speaking truth in love: Ephesians 4:15 instructs believers to *"speak the truth in love,"* providing the balanced approach of honesty with kindness that healthy marriage communication requires.

2. Listening to understand: James 1:19 advises, *"Everyone should be quick to listen, slow to speak, and slow to become angry."* This principle establishes the priority of understanding before responding.

3. Guarding words carefully: Proverbs 18:21 observes that *"the tongue has the power of life and death,"* highlighting the significant impact of our words on relationship health.

4. Addressing issues promptly: Ephesians 4:26-27 instructs, *"Do not let the sun go down while you are angry, and do not give the devil a foothold."* This principle encourages timely resolution rather than allowing issues to fester.

As you prepare for marriage, assess your communication patterns honestly. Do you listen well? Can you express feelings appropriately? Do you address issues directly or tend to avoid conflict? Identifying growth areas now allows you to develop healthier patterns before marriage.[5]

Conflict Resolution: Turning Differences into Growth

Every marriage experiences conflict due to differences in personality, background, expectations, and preferences. The question is not whether you will experience conflict but how you will handle it when it occurs.

Key conflict resolution principles include:

1. Addressing issues rather than attacking character: Focusing on specific behaviors or situations rather than making character judgments creates space for resolution rather than defensiveness.

2. Seeking understanding before solutions: Taking time to fully understand each other's perspectives before moving to problem-solving prevents premature closure and unresolved feelings.

3. Maintaining respect during disagreement: Committing to respectful language and behavior, even during intense disagreement, prevents damage that outlasts the conflict.

4. Working toward mutual benefit: Approaching conflict with the goal of finding solutions that address both partners' concerns rather than "winning" maintains relationship unity.

As you prepare for marriage, observe how you currently handle disagreements. Do you tend toward aggression, withdrawal, or healthy engagement? Practice addressing differences constructively now to establish healthy patterns for marriage.[6]

Intimacy: Connection Beyond the Physical

Throughout this book, we have emphasized that intimacy encompasses far more than physical connection, including emotional, intellectual, and spiritual dimensions. Developing multifaceted intimacy creates relationship depth and resilience.

Key intimacy principles include:

1. Emotional intimacy through vulnerability: Creating safe space for sharing feelings, fears, hopes, and needs builds deep emotional connection that supports all other aspects of intimacy.

2. Intellectual intimacy through shared learning: Discussing ideas, beliefs, and perspectives creates mental connection that enriches the relationship beyond practical matters.

3. Spiritual intimacy through shared faith practices: Praying together, studying Scripture, and discussing spiritual insights builds the deepest level of relationship connection.

4. Physical intimacy within God's boundaries: Reserving sexual intimacy for marriage while developing appropriate physical connection during engagement honors God's design.

As you prepare for marriage, assess which dimensions of intimacy come naturally to you and which require more intentional development. Building balanced intimacy creates a relationship that connects at multiple levels rather than depending on just one dimension.[7]

Practical Steps for Marriage Preparation

As you apply the principles from this book to your relationship, consider these practical steps for comprehensive marriage preparation.

Spiritual Preparation

The foundation for Christian marriage begins with individual spiritual health and shared faith commitment. Consider these spiritual preparation steps:

1. Assess your individual relationship with Christ: Healthy marriage flows from personal spiritual vitality rather than depending on your partner for spiritual nourishment.
2. Clarify theological understanding and church commitment: Discuss your beliefs about essential doctrines, church involvement, and spiritual practices to ensure alignment on fundamental faith issues.
3. Develop shared spiritual practices: Begin habits of prayer, Scripture reading, and spiritual conversation that can continue into marriage.
4. Seek spiritual mentorship: Connect with a mature Christian couple who can provide guidance and accountability during your engagement and early marriage.

5. Pray specifically about your relationship: Invite God's wisdom, direction, and blessing on your relationship, submitting your plans and timeline to His guidance.

Remember that spiritual preparation isn't merely about agreement on religious practices but about establishing Christ as the center and foundation of your relationship. As Jesus taught in Matthew 7:24-25, "*Everyone who hears these words of mine and puts them into practice is like a wise man who built his house on the rock. The rain came down, the streams rose, and the winds blew and beat against that house, yet it did not fall because it had its foundation on the rock.*"[8]

Final Encouragement: God's Faithfulness in Your Marriage

As we conclude this book, remember that marriage success ultimately depends not on perfect technique but on God's faithfulness working through your imperfect commitment. While the principles we've discussed provide important guidance, your ultimate hope rests in God's presence and power in your relationship.

Philippians 1:6 promises that "*he who began a good work in you will carry it on to completion until the day of Christ Jesus.*" This assurance applies not only to individual spiritual growth but to the marriage relationship God has called you to build. He remains faithful even when you struggle, providing grace for the journey and strength beyond your own resources.

As you prepare for marriage, remember these final encouragements:

1. God's design provides the blueprint: Trust the Creator's design for marriage rather than cultural patterns or personal preference. His ways lead to flourishing even when they differ from popular approaches.

2. God's Word provides guidance: Return regularly to Scripture for wisdom, correction, and encouragement rather than relying primarily

on feelings or opinions. Truth provides a stable foundation amid changing circumstances.

3. God's Spirit provides the power: Recognize your dependence on the Holy Spirit for the character transformation marriage requires. Human effort alone cannot produce the love, patience, kindness, and faithfulness marriage demands.

4. God's community provides the support: Remain connected to the body of Christ rather than isolating your relationship. The church provides wisdom, accountability, and encouragement for the marriage journey.

5. God's grace provides hope: Rest in God's forgiveness and restoration when you fail rather than allowing guilt or shame to define your relationship. His mercies are new every morning, providing a fresh start when you stumble.

May your marriage become a testimony to God's faithfulness, a source of mutual joy and growth, and a witness to the world of Christ's covenant love for His church? As you apply the principles from this book, remember that *"unless the LORD builds the house, those who build it labor in vain"* (Psalm 127:1). With Him as your foundation and strength, you can build a marriage that honors Him and blesses you both for a lifetime.[9]

Marriage by the Book: What Prospective Couples Should Know Before They Say I Do

This study guide is designed to help prospective couples and individuals deeply engage with the principles and insights presented in "Marriage by the Book: What Prospective Couples Should Know Before They Say I Do" by Mark Hobafcovich.

Each section of this guide corresponds to a chapter in the book, offering four thought-provoking questions to facilitate reflection, discussion, and application of the material. Our aim is to provide a valuable resource for those preparing for marriage, encouraging a thorough understanding of biblical foundations and practical wisdom for a lifelong covenant.

Introduction: The Purpose and Importance of Marriage Preparation

1. According to the manuscript, what are some key reasons why many modern marriages face significant challenges or end in dissolution?

2. How does the manuscript contrast the cultural view of marriage with the biblical vision for marriage, particularly regarding commitment and purpose?

3. What are the main arguments presented in this section for why intentional marriage preparation is essential for couples?

4. Describe the key components that this section outlines for effective marriage preparation. How does the church play a role in this process?

Chapter 1: God's Purpose for Creation and Marriage

1. How does the chapter explain marriage as an integral part of God's original design for creation, as opposed to merely a human institution?

2. What are the key biblical foundations of marriage discussed in this chapter, and how do they establish marriage as a covenant relationship?

3. According to the text, what is the significance of the "one flesh" union in marriage, and how does it relate to leaving and cleaving?

4. How does understanding God's purpose for marriage influence a couple's perspective on the challenges and joys they may encounter?

Chapter 2: Understanding Biblical Love

1. What are the different types of love discussed in this chapter, and how does the manuscript differentiate between them in the context of marriage?

2. How does the chapter define "agape" love, and why is it presented as foundational for a lasting biblical marriage?

3. In what ways does the manuscript suggest that biblical love is more about action and commitment than fleeting emotions?

4. What practical implications does this chapter offer for prospective couples seeking to cultivate a love that aligns with God's design?

Chapter 3: Biblical Foundations for Marriage

1. How does the chapter elaborate on marriage as a reflection of Christ and the Church, and what are the practical implications of this metaphor for a married couple?

2. Discuss the biblical roles within marriage as presented in this chapter. How are these roles understood in the context of mutual submission and servant leadership?

3. What specific biblical principles or passages does the chapter highlight as foundational for building a strong, God-honoring marriage?

4. How can prospective couples apply the teachings on biblical foundations to prepare for a marriage that aligns with God's design and purpose?

Chapter 4: Communication in Marriage

1. What are the foundational principles of effective communication in marriage, as outlined in this chapter?

2. Discuss the importance of active listening skills in marital communication and what are some practical ways to develop them.

3. What common barriers to communication in marriage does the chapter identify, and how does it suggest overcoming them biblically?

4. How can couples apply the communication principles from this chapter to foster deeper understanding and intimacy in their relationship?

Chapter 5: Resolving Conflict in Marriage

1. What is the chapter's perspective on the inevitability of conflict in marriage, and how does it suggest couples should approach disagreements?

2. Discuss the biblical principles for conflict resolution presented in this chapter. How do these principles differ from secular approaches?

3. How does the manuscript emphasize the importance of forgiveness and reconciliation in resolving marital conflicts?

4. What practical steps or strategies does the chapter provide for couples to navigate and resolve conflicts in a healthy, God-honoring way?

Chapter 6: Intimacy in Marriage

1. How does this chapter define intimacy in marriage, encompassing emotional, spiritual, and physical dimensions?

2. What does the manuscript teach about God's design for sexual intimacy within the confines of marriage?

3. Discuss the practical ways the chapter suggests for building and maintaining intimacy throughout a marriage.

4. How can couples prioritize and nurture all forms of intimacy to strengthen their bond according to biblical principles?

Chapter 7: Premarital Counseling

1. What are the primary purposes and benefits of engaging in premarital counseling, as presented in this chapter?

2. Identify and discuss the key topics that the manuscript suggests should be addressed during premarital counseling sessions.

3. How does this chapter emphasize the importance of setting realistic expectations for marriage through premarital counseling?

4. In what ways can premarital counseling help couples identify and address potential areas of conflict or misunderstanding before marriage?

Chapter 8: Parenting in Marriage

1. What biblical principles for parenting are emphasized in this chapter, and how do they apply to a married couple's approach to raising children?

2. How does the manuscript advocate for unified parenting approaches within a marriage, and what are the benefits of such unity?

3. Discuss the challenges and strategies for balancing the demands of parenting with the needs of the marital relationship, as presented in this chapter.

4. How can prospective couples prepare to integrate biblical parenting principles into their future marriage and family life?

Chapter 9: Spiritual Growth in Marriage

1. How does the chapter define and emphasize the importance of developing spiritual intimacy within a marriage?

2. What specific practices or disciplines does the manuscript suggest for fostering spiritual growth as a couple?

3. In what ways can a couple serve together in ministry, and how does this contribute to their spiritual growth and marital bond?

4. How does the chapter illustrate that a marriage centered on Christ provides the strongest foundation for navigating challenges and sustaining the relationship?

Chapter 10: Dealing with Extended Family

1. What is the importance of establishing healthy boundaries with extended family members, as discussed in this chapter, and why is it crucial for a healthy marriage?

2. How does the manuscript advise couples on honoring their parents while simultaneously prioritizing their marital relationship?

3. What strategies does the chapter offer for navigating family traditions and expectations that may differ between spouses or from their own preferences?

4. How can couples proactively address potential challenges with extended family to foster unity and minimize conflict in their marriage?

Chapter 11: Maintaining a Healthy Marriage

1. What practices does the chapter highlight as essential for the long-term health and vitality of a marriage?

2. How does the manuscript suggest couples navigate significant life transitions together while preserving their marital bond?

3. Discuss the importance of continually renewing commitment through different seasons of marriage, as presented in this chapter.

4. What practical advice does the chapter offer for couples to proactively work on maintaining a strong and healthy marriage throughout their lives?

Chapter 12: Summary and Application

1. What are the key biblical principles for marriage that this chapter summarizes, and how are they intended to be applied in daily married life?

2. Discuss the practical steps and actionable advice provided in this chapter for couples to implement the teachings of the entire manuscript.

3. What resources for ongoing marriage growth does the chapter suggest, and why are they important for long-term marital health?

4. How does the chapter emphasize God's faithfulness in the marriage journey, and what encouragement does it offer to couples as they apply these principles?

Notes by Chapters

Notes Introduction

[1] Bradford Wilcox, "The Evolution of Divorce," National Affairs 35 (2018): 81-94.

[2] Timothy Keller and Kathy Keller, The Meaning of Marriage (New York: Penguin Books, 2013), 28-30.

[3] Andreas J. Köstenberger, God, Marriage, and Family: Rebuilding the Biblical Foundation (Wheaton: Crossway, 2010), 73-75.

[4] Les and Leslie Parrott, Saving Your Marriage Before It Starts (Grand Rapids: Zondervan, 2015), 15-17.

[5] Albert Mohler, We Cannot Be Silent (Nashville: Thomas Nelson, 2015), 22-24.

[6] All Scripture quotations are from the English Standard Version (ESV) unless otherwise noted.

[7] Raymond C. Ortlund, Marriage and the Mystery of the Gospel (Wheaton: Crossway, 2016), 93-95.

[8] Bruce K. Waltke, The Book of Proverbs: Chapters 1-15 (Grand Rapids: Eerdmans, 2004), 127-129.

[9] Tremper Longman III, Song of Songs (Grand Rapids: Eerdmans, 2001), 55-58.

[10] D.A. Carson, Matthew (Grand Rapids: Eerdmans, 2010), 415-417.

[11] Scott M. Stanley, "Making a Case for Premarital Education," Family Relations 50 (2001): 272-280.

[12] Howard Markman and Scott Stanley, "Assessing Couples," Journal of Family Psychology 11 (1997): 176-190.

[13] Wayne Mack, Preparing for Marriage God's Way (Phillipsburg: P&R Publishing, 2013), 11-13.

[14] Paul David Tripp, What Did You Expect?: Redeeming the Realities of Marriage (Wheaton: Crossway, 2012), 21-23.

[15] John Piper, This Momentary Marriage: A Parable of Permanence (Wheaton: Crossway, 2012), 75-77.

[16] Gary Chapman, Now You're Speaking My Language (Nashville: B&H Books, 2014), 42-44.

[17] Gary Thomas, Sacred Marriage (Grand Rapids: Zondervan, 2015), 22-24.

[18] Norman Wright, Communication: Key to Your Marriage (Ventura: Regal Books, 2000), 33-35.

[19] Dennis Rainey, Preparing for Marriage (Minneapolis: Bethany House Publishers, 2010), 45-47.

[20] Larry Crabb, Connecting: Healing for Ourselves and Our Relationships (Nashville: Thomas Nelson, 2005), 140-142.

[21] Gary Chapman, The Four Seasons of Marriage (Carol Stream: Tyndale House Publishers, 2012), 187-189.

[22] Andreas J. Köstenberger and David W. Jones, Marriage and Family: Biblical Essentials (Wheaton: Crossway, 2012), 110-112.

[23] Timothy Keller, "Marriage as Ministry," in The Gospel-Centered Ministry (New York: Redeemer City to City, 2003), 15-17.

[24] H. Norman Wright, Before You Say "I Do" (Eugene: Harvest House Publishers, 2015), 9-11.

[25] Dietrich Bonhoeffer, Life Together (New York: Harper & Row, 1954), 83-85.

[26] Gary Chapman, The 5 Love Languages (Chicago: Northfield Publishing, 2015), 185-187.

[27] Dave Harvey, When Sinners Say "I Do" (Wapwallopen: Shepherd Press, 2007), 19-21.

[28] Emerson Eggerichs, Love and Respect (Nashville: Thomas Nelson, 2004), 15-17.

[29] Les and Leslie Parrott, The Good Fight (Nashville: Worthy Publishing, 2013), 28-30.

[30] C.S. Lewis, The Four Loves (New York: Harcourt Brace, 1960), 131-133.

[31] John Piper and Wayne Grudem, Recovering Biblical Manhood and Womanhood (Wheaton: Crossway, 2006), 31-33.

[32] Wayne Grudem, Systematic Theology: An Introduction to Biblical Doctrine (Grand Rapids: Zondervan, 2000), 515-517.

[33] Gary Smalley, The Marriage You've Always Wanted (Carol Stream: Tyndale House Publishers, 2005), 25-27.

[34] Henry Cloud and John Townsend, Boundaries in Marriage (Grand Rapids: Zondervan, 2002), 85-87.

[35] Ken Sande, The Peacemaker (Grand Rapids: Baker Books, 2004), 42-44.

[36] Richard J. Foster, Celebration of Discipline: The Path to Spiritual Growth (New York: HarperOne, 2018), 95-97.

[37] Gary Chapman, Things I Wish I'd Known Before We Got Married (Chicago: Northfield Publishing, 2010), 33-35.

[38] Dennis and Barbara Rainey, Two Hearts Praying as One (Colorado Springs: Multnomah Books, 2002), 18-20.

Notes Chapter 1

[1]John Piper, This Momentary Marriage: A Parable of Permanence (Crossway, 2012), 19.

[2]R. Albert Mohler, We Cannot Be Silent: Speaking Truth to a Culture Redefining Sex, Marriage, and the Very Meaning of Right and Wrong (Thomas Nelson, 2015), 32.

[3]Wayne Grudem, Christian Ethics: An Introduction to Biblical Moral Reasoning (Crossway, 2018), 215.

[4]R.C. Sproul, The Intimate Marriage: A Practical Guide to Building a Great Marriage (P&R Publishing, 2003), 23.

[5]John Piper, This Momentary Marriage: A Parable of Permanence (Crossway, 2012), 25.

[6]John Piper and Wayne Grudem, Recovering Biblical Manhood and Womanhood (Crossway, 2006), 33.

[7]Gary Thomas, Sacred Marriage: What If God Designed Marriage to Make Us Holy More Than to Make Us Happy? (Zondervan, 2015), 22.

[8]Timothy Keller and Kathy Keller, The Meaning of Marriage: Facing the Complexities of Commitment with the Wisdom of God (Penguin Books, 2013), 37.

[9]R.C. Sproul, The Intimate Marriage: A Practical Guide to Building a Great Marriage (P&R Publishing, 2003), 28.

[10]John Piper, This Momentary Marriage: A Parable of Permanence (Crossway, 2012), 42.

[11]Timothy Keller and Kathy Keller, The Meaning of Marriage: Facing the Complexities of Commitment with the Wisdom of God (Penguin Books, 2013), 45.

[12]Gary Thomas, Sacred Marriage: What If God Designed Marriage to Make Us Holy More Than to Make Us Happy? (Zondervan, 2015), 35.

[13]Timothy Keller and Kathy Keller, The Meaning of Marriage: Facing the Complexities of Commitment with the Wisdom of God (Penguin Books, 2013), 47.

[14]Wayne Grudem, Christian Ethics: An Introduction to Biblical Moral Reasoning (Crossway, 2018), 312.

[15]Andreas J. Köstenberger and David W. Jones, God, Marriage, and Family: Rebuilding the Biblical Foundation (Crossway, 2010), 25.

[16]Andreas J. Köstenberger and David W. Jones, God, Marriage, and Family: Rebuilding the Biblical Foundation (Crossway, 2010), 27.

[17]John MacArthur, Divine Design: God's Complementary Roles for Men and Women (David C Cook, 2010), 33.

[18]Quoted in Dennis Rainey and Barbara Rainey, Building Your Marriage to Last (FamilyLife Publishing, 2007), 42.

[19]Andreas J. Köstenberger and David W. Jones, God, Marriage, and Family: Rebuilding the Biblical Foundation (Crossway, 2010), 34.

[20]Timothy Keller and Kathy Keller, The Meaning of Marriage: Facing the Complexities of Commitment with the Wisdom of God (Penguin Books, 2013), 52.

[21]James Dobson, Marriage Under Fire: Why We Must Win This Battle (Multnomah, 2004), 28.

[22]Dennis Rainey and Barbara Rainey, Building Your Marriage to Last (FamilyLife Publishing, 2007), 45.

[23]R. Albert Mohler, We Cannot Be Silent: Speaking Truth to a Culture Redefining Sex, Marriage, and the Very Meaning of Right and Wrong (Thomas Nelson, 2015), 45.

[24]Herman Bavinck, Reformed Dogmatics: Holy Spirit, Church, and New Creation (Baker Academic, 2008), 118.

[25]Wayne Grudem, Christian Ethics: An Introduction to Biblical Moral Reasoning (Crossway, 2018), 325.

[26]R. Albert Mohler, We Cannot Be Silent: Speaking Truth to a Culture Redefining Sex, Marriage, and the Very Meaning of Right and Wrong (Thomas Nelson, 2015), 52.

[27]Andreas J. Köstenberger and David W. Jones, God, Marriage, and Family: Rebuilding the Biblical Foundation (Crossway, 2010), 42.

[28]Wayne Grudem, Christian Ethics: An Introduction to Biblical Moral Reasoning (Crossway, 2018), 332.

[29]R. Albert Mohler, We Cannot Be Silent: Speaking Truth to a Culture Redefining Sex, Marriage, and the Very Meaning of Right and Wrong (Thomas Nelson, 2015), 58.

[30]John Stott, Issues Facing Christians Today (Zondervan, 2006), 25.

[31]Wayne Grudem, Christian Ethics: An Introduction to Biblical Moral Reasoning (Crossway, 2018), 340.

[32]Bryan Chapell, Each for the Other: Marriage as It's Meant to Be (Baker Books, 2006), 32.

[33]Bryan Chapell, Each for the Other: Marriage as It's Meant to Be (Baker Books, 2006), 35.

[34]Andreas J. Köstenberger and David W. Jones, God, Marriage, and Family: Rebuilding the Biblical Foundation (Crossway, 2010), 48.

[35]R. Albert Mohler, We Cannot Be Silent: Speaking Truth to a Culture Redefining Sex, Marriage, and the Very Meaning of Right and Wrong (Thomas Nelson, 2015), 65.

[36]Dennis Rainey and Barbara Rainey, Building Your Marriage to Last (FamilyLife Publishing, 2007), 52.

[37]Ray Ortlund, Marriage and the Mystery of the Gospel (Crossway, 2016), 22.

[38]John MacArthur, Divine Design: God's Complementary Roles for Men and Women (David C Cook, 2010), 45.

[39]Michael Horton, Covenant, and Salvation: Union with Christ (Westminster John Knox Press, 2007), 125.

[40]Jim Newheiser, Marriage, Divorce, and Remarriage: Critical Questions and Answers (P&R Publishing, 2017), 38.

[41]Andreas J. Köstenberger and David W. Jones, God, Marriage, and Family: Rebuilding the Biblical Foundation (Crossway, 2010), 55.

[42]Ed Wheat and Gaye Wheat, Intended for Pleasure: Sex Technique and Sexual Fulfillment in Christian Marriage (Revell, 2010), 25.

[43] R. Albert Mohler, We Cannot Be Silent: Speaking Truth to a Culture Redefining Sex, Marriage, and the Very Meaning of Right and Wrong (Thomas Nelson, 2015), 72.

[44] James Dobson, Marriage Under Fire: Why We Must Win This Battle (Multnomah, 2004), 35.

Notes Chapter 2

[1]Keller, Timothy. The Meaning of Marriage. Penguin Books, 2013, p. 15.

[2]Piper, John. This Momentary Marriage: A Parable of Permanence. Crossway, 2012, p. 41.

[3]Lewis, C.S. The Four Loves. Harcourt Brace, 1960, p. 3.

[4]MacArthur, John. Divine Design: God's Complementary Roles for Men and Women. David C. Cook, 2010, p. 56.

[5]Thomas, Gary. Sacred Marriage. Zondervan, 2015, p. 45.

[6]Lewis, C.S. The Four Loves. Harcourt Brace, 1960, p. 57.

[7]Keller, Timothy. The Meaning of Marriage. Penguin Books, 2013, p. 125.

[8]Lewis, C.S. The Four Loves. Harcourt Brace, 1960, p. 71.

[9]Wheat, Ed, and Gaye Wheat. Intended for Pleasure. Revell, 2010, p. 15.

[10]Wheat, Ed, and Gaye Wheat. Intended for Pleasure. Revell, 2010, p. 30.

[11]Sproul, R.C. The Holiness of God. Tyndale House Publishers, 2000, p. 167.

[12]Piper, John. This Momentary Marriage: A Parable of Permanence. Crossway, 2012, p. 97.

[13]Piper, John. Desiring God: Meditations of a Christian Hedonist. Multnomah, 2011, p. 201.

[14]Thomas, Gary. Sacred Marriage. Zondervan, 2015, p. 72.

[15]Keller, Timothy. The Meaning of Marriage. Penguin Books, 2013, p. 78.

[16]Chan, Francis. You and Me Forever: Marriage in Light of Eternity. Claire Love Publishing, 2014, p. 37.

[17]Thomas, Gary. Sacred Marriage. Zondervan, 2015, p. 89.

[18]Keller, Timothy. The Meaning of Marriage. Penguin Books, 2013, p. 64.

[19]Keller, Timothy. The Meaning of Marriage. Penguin Books, 2013, p. 71.

[20]Cloud, Henry, and John Townsend. Boundaries in Marriage. Zondervan, 2002, p. 24.

[21]Cloud, Henry, and John Townsend. Boundaries in Marriage. Zondervan, 2002, p. 31.

[22]Sproul, R.C. The Holiness of God. Tyndale House Publishers, 2000, p. 178.

[23]Dobson, James. Love for a Lifetime. Multnomah, 1993, p. 42.

[24]Chapman, Gary. The Five Love Languages. Northfield Publishing, 2015, p. 118.

[25]Keller, Timothy. The Meaning of Marriage. Penguin Books, 2013, p. 83.

[26]Lewis, C.S. Mere Christianity. HarperOne, 2001, p. 122.

[27]Eggerichs, Emerson. Love and Respect. Thomas Nelson, 2004, p. 67.

[28]MacArthur, John. The Gospel According to Jesus. Zondervan, 2008, p. 118.

[29]Thomas, Gary. Sacred Marriage. Zondervan, 2015, p. 103.

[30]Smedes, Lewis. Forgive and Forget. HarperOne, 2007, p. 39.

[31]Sproul, R.C. The Consequences of Ideas. Crossway, 2009, p. 143.

[32]Piper, John. This Momentary Marriage: A Parable of Permanence. Crossway, 2012, p. 112.

[33]Piper, John. Desiring God: Meditations of a Christian Hedonist. Multnomah, 2011, p. 215.

[34]Keller, Timothy. The Meaning of Marriage. Penguin Books, 2013, p. 95.

[35]Keller, Timothy. The Meaning of Marriage. Penguin Books, 2013, p. 102.

[36]Piper, John. Desiring God: Meditations of a Christian Hedonist. Multnomah, 2011, p. 225.

[37]Sproul, R.C. The Holiness of God. Tyndale House Publishers, 2000, p. 192.

[38]Chapman, Gary. The Five Love Languages. Northfield Publishing, 2015, p. 143.

[39]Rainey, Dennis. Preparing for Marriage. Bethany House Publishers, 2010, p. 87.

Notes Chapter 3

[1]Keller, Timothy. The Meaning of Marriage. Penguin Books, 2013, p. 13.

[2]Grudem, Wayne. Systematic Theology: An Introduction to Biblical Doctrine. Zondervan, 2000, p. 454.

[3]Köstenberger, Andreas J. God, Marriage, and Family: Rebuilding the Biblical Foundation. Crossway, 2010, p. 31.

[4]Piper, John and Wayne Grudem. Recovering Biblical Manhood and Womanhood. Crossway, 2006, p. 35.

[5]Köstenberger, Andreas J. God, Marriage, and Family: Rebuilding the Biblical Foundation. Crossway, 2010, p. 33.

[6]Keller, Timothy. The Meaning of Marriage. Penguin Books, 2013, p. 47.

[7]Thomas, Gary. Sacred Marriage. Zondervan, 2015, p. 27.

[8]Ortlund, Raymond C. Marriage and the Mystery of the Gospel. Crossway, 2016, p. 19.

[9]Keller, Timothy. The Meaning of Marriage. Penguin Books, 2013, p. 71.

[10]MacArthur, John. Divine Design: God's Complementary Roles for Men and Women. David C. Cook, 2010, p. 45.

[11]Köstenberger, Andreas J. God, Marriage, and Family: Rebuilding the Biblical Foundation. Crossway, 2010, p. 38.

[12]Piper, John. This Momentary Marriage: A Parable of Permanence. Crossway, 2012, p. 32.

[13]Allender, Dan and Tremper Longman III. Intimate Allies. Tyndale House Publishers, 1999, p. 43.

[14]Mohler, R. Albert. We Cannot Be Silent. Thomas Nelson, 2015, p. 73.

[15]Thomas, Gary. Sacred Marriage. Zondervan, 2015, p. 52.

[16]Keller, Timothy. The Meaning of Marriage. Penguin Books, 2013, p. 59.

[17]Ortlund, Raymond C. Marriage and the Mystery of the Gospel. Crossway, 2016, p. 28.

[18]Piper, John and Wayne Grudem. Recovering Biblical Manhood and Womanhood. Crossway, 2006, p. 103.

[19]Ortlund, Raymond C. Marriage and the Mystery of the Gospel. Crossway, 2016, p. 31.

[20]Köstenberger, Andreas J. God, Marriage, and Family: Rebuilding the Biblical Foundation. Crossway, 2010, p. 53.

[21]DeYoung, Kevin. What Does the Bible Really Teach about Homosexuality? Crossway, 2015, p. 78.

[22]Keller, Timothy. The Meaning of Marriage. Penguin Books, 2013, p. 83.

[23]Ortlund, Raymond C. Marriage and the Mystery of the Gospel. Crossway, 2016, p. 37.

[24]MacArthur, John. Divine Design: God's Complementary Roles for Men and Women. David C. Cook, 2010, p. 62.

[25]Piper, John. This Momentary Marriage: A Parable of Permanence. Crossway, 2012, p. 48.

[26]Keller, Timothy. The Meaning of Marriage. Penguin Books, 2013, p. 47.

[27]Piper, John and Wayne Grudem. Recovering Biblical Manhood and Womanhood. Crossway, 2006, p. 165.

[28]Keller, Timothy. The Meaning of Marriage. Penguin Books, 2013, p. 110.

[29]Ortlund, Raymond C. Marriage and the Mystery of the Gospel. Crossway, 2016, p. 83.

[30]Keller, Timothy. The Meaning of Marriage. Penguin Books, 2013, p. 47.

[31]Tripp, Paul David. What Did You Expect?: Redeeming the Realities of Marriage. Crossway, 2012, p. 87.

[32]Tripp, Paul David. What Did You Expect?: Redeeming the Realities of Marriage. Crossway, 2012, p. 95.

[33]Tripp, Paul David. What Did You Expect?: Redeeming the Realities of Marriage. Crossway, 2012, p. 102.

[34]Piper, John. This Momentary Marriage: A Parable of Permanence. Crossway, 2012, p. 173.

[35]Ortlund, Raymond C. Marriage and the Mystery of the Gospel. Crossway, 2016, p. 92.

[36]Lewis, C.S. The Four Loves. Harcourt Brace, 1960, p. 137.

[37]Piper, John. This Momentary Marriage: A Parable of Permanence. Crossway, 2012, p. 182.

[38]Keller, Timothy. The Meaning of Marriage. Penguin Books, 2013, p. 132.

[39]Thomas, Gary. Sacred Marriage. Zondervan, 2015, p. 13.

[40]Piper, John and Wayne Grudem. Recovering Biblical Manhood and Womanhood. Crossway, 2006, p. 186.

[41]Grudem, Wayne. Systematic Theology: An Introduction to Biblical Doctrine. Zondervan, 2000, p. 464.

[42]Horton, Michael. Covenant and Salvation: Union with Christ. Westminster John Knox Press, 2007, p. 126.

[43]Wheat, Ed, and Gaye Wheat. Intended for Pleasure. Revell, 2010, p. 19.

Notes Chapter 4

[1]Chapman, Gary. The Five Love Languages. Northfield Publishing, 2015, p. 47.

[2]Chapman, Gary. Now You're Speaking My Language. B&H Books, 2014, p. 11.

[3]Keller, Timothy. The Meaning of Marriage. Penguin Books, 2013, p. 162.

[4]Tripp, Paul David. What Did You Expect?: Redeeming the Realities of Marriage. Crossway, 2012, p. 139.

[5]Keller, Timothy. The Meaning of Marriage. Penguin Books, 2013, p. 165.

[6]Eggerichs, Emerson. Love and Respect. Thomas Nelson, 2004, p. 118.

[7]Tripp, Paul David. What Did You Expect?: Redeeming the Realities of Marriage. Crossway, 2012, p. 142.

[8]Thomas, Gary. Sacred Marriage. Zondervan, 2015, p. 135.

[9]Eggerichs, Emerson. Love and Respect. Thomas Nelson, 2004, p. 125.

[10]Keller, Timothy. The Meaning of Marriage. Penguin Books, 2013, p. 172.

[11]Rainey, Dennis. Preparing for Marriage. Bethany House Publishers, 2010, p. 103.

[12]Chapman, Gary. The Five Love Languages. Northfield Publishing, 2015, p. 37.

[13]Rainey, Dennis. Preparing for Marriage. Bethany House Publishers, 2010, p. 107.

[14]Feldhahn, Shaunti. For Women Only. Multnomah, 2013, p. 26.

[15]Eggerichs, Emerson. Love and Respect. Thomas Nelson, 2004, p. 132.

[16]Tripp, Paul David. What Did You Expect?: Redeeming the Realities of Marriage. Crossway, 2012, p. 147.

[17]Gottman, John. Why Marriages Succeed or Fail. Simon & Schuster, 1994, p. 72.

[18]Powell, John. Why Am I Afraid to Tell You Who I Am? Zondervan, 1999, p. 54.

[19]Keller, Timothy. The Meaning of Marriage. Penguin Books, 2013, p. 175.

[20]Crouch, Andy. The Tech-Wise Family. Baker Books, 2017, p. 41.

[21]Crouch, Andy. The Tech-Wise Family. Baker Books, 2017, p. 43.

[22]Parrott, Les and Leslie. The Good Fight. Worthy Publishing, 2013, p. 35.

[23]Chapman, Gary. Now You're Speaking My Language. B&H Books, 2014, p. 89.

[24]Doherty, William. Take Back Your Marriage. Guilford Press, 2013, p. 67.

[25]Chapman, Gary. Now You're Speaking My Language. B&H Books, 2014, p. 95.

[26]Parrott, Les and Leslie. The Good Fight. Worthy Publishing, 2013, p. 42.

[27]Gottman, John. The Seven Principles for Making Marriage Work. Harmony, 2015, p. 100.

[28]Keller, Timothy. The Meaning of Marriage. Penguin Books, 2013, p. 178.

[29]Tripp, Paul David. What Did You Expect?: Redeeming the Realities of Marriage. Crossway, 2012, p. 152.

[30]Chapman, Gary. Now You're Speaking My Language. B&H Books, 2014, p. 103.

[31]Keller, Timothy. The Meaning of Marriage. Penguin Books, 2013, p. 181.

[32]Gottman, John. The Seven Principles for Making Marriage Work. Harmony, 2015, p. 112.

[33]Thomas, Gary. Sacred Marriage. Zondervan, 2015, p. 152.

[34]Chapman, Gary. The Five Love Languages. Northfield Publishing, 2015, p. 42.

[35]Feldhahn, Shaunti. The Surprising Secrets of Highly Happy Marriages. Multnomah, 2013, p. 73.

[36]Rainey, Dennis. Preparing for Marriage. Bethany House Publishers, 2010, p. 112.

[37]Thomas, Gary. Sacred Marriage. Zondervan, 2015, p. 157.

[38]Deal, Ron. The Smart Stepfamily. Bethany House Publishers, 2014, p. 89.

[39]Thomas, Gary. Sacred Marriage. Zondervan, 2015, p. 162.

[40]Keller, Timothy. The Meaning of Marriage. Penguin Books, 2013, p. 185.

[41]Graham, Billy. Just As I Am. HarperOne, 2007, p. 173.

[42]Thomas, Gary. Sacred Marriage. Zondervan, 2015, p. 168.

Notes Chapter 5

[1]Thomas, Gary. Sacred Marriage. Zondervan, 2015, p. 128.

[2]Keller, Timothy. The Meaning of Marriage. Penguin Books, 2013, p. 158.

[3]Tripp, Paul David. What Did You Expect?: Redeeming the Realities of Marriage. Crossway, 2012, p. 121.

[4]Keller, Timothy. The Meaning of Marriage. Penguin Books, 2013, p. 160.

[5]Tripp, Paul David. What Did You Expect?: Redeeming the Realities of Marriage. Crossway, 2012, p. 125.

[6]Tripp, Paul David. What Did You Expect?: Redeeming the Realities of Marriage. Crossway, 2012, p. 21.

[7]Keller, Timothy. The Meaning of Marriage. Penguin Books, 2013, p. 163.

[8]Thomas, Gary. Sacred Marriage. Zondervan, 2015, p. 13.

[9]Keller, Timothy. The Meaning of Marriage. Penguin Books, 2013, p. 165.

[10]Tripp, Paul David. What Did You Expect?: Redeeming the Realities of Marriage. Crossway, 2012, p. 132.

[11]Parrott, Les and Leslie. The Good Fight. Worthy Publishing, 2013, p. 27.

[12]Keller, Timothy. The Meaning of Marriage. Penguin Books, 2013, p. 168.

[13]Chapman, Gary. The Four Seasons of Marriage. Tyndale House Publishers, 2012, p. 68.

[14]Blue, Ron. Master Your Money. Moody Publishers, 2016, p. 42.

[15]Keller, Timothy. The Meaning of Marriage. Penguin Books, 2013, p. 170.

[16]Leman, Kevin. Sheet Music: Uncovering the Secrets of Sexual Intimacy in Marriage. Tyndale House Publishers, 2003, p. 21.

[17]Wheat, Ed, and Gaye Wheat. Intended for Pleasure. Revell, 2010, p. 19.

[18]Chapman, Gary. The Four Seasons of Marriage. Tyndale House Publishers, 2012, p. 73.

[19]Dobson, James. The New Dare to Discipline. Tyndale House Publishers, 2014, p. 78.

[20]Gottman, John. Why Marriages Succeed or Fail. Simon & Schuster, 1994, p. 68.

[21]Tripp, Paul David. What Did You Expect?: Redeeming the Realities of Marriage. Crossway, 2012, p. 138.

[22]Gottman, John. Why Marriages Succeed or Fail. Simon & Schuster, 1994, p. 73.

[23]Eggerichs, Emerson. Love and Respect. Thomas Nelson, 2004, p. 49.

[24]Tripp, Paul David. What Did You Expect?: Redeeming the Realities of Marriage. Crossway, 2012, p. 142.

[25]Gottman, John. Why Marriages Succeed or Fail. Simon & Schuster, 1994, p. 79.

[26]Parrott, Les and Leslie. The Good Fight. Worthy Publishing, 2013, p. 53.

[27]Chapman, Gary. Now You're Speaking My Language. B&H Books, 2014, p. 103.

[28]Tripp, Paul David. What Did You Expect?: Redeeming the Realities of Marriage. Crossway, 2012, p. 147.

[29]Thomas, Gary. Sacred Marriage. Zondervan, 2015, p. 145.

[30]Chapman, Gary. The Five Love Languages. Northfield Publishing, 2015, p. 157.

[31]Keller, Timothy. The Meaning of Marriage. Penguin Books, 2013, p. 181.

[32]Rainey, Dennis. Preparing for Marriage. Bethany House Publishers, 2010, p. 112.

[33]Thomas, Gary. Sacred Parenting. Zondervan, 2005, p. 72.

[34]Chapman, Gary. The Four Seasons of Marriage. Tyndale House Publishers, 2012, p. 95.

[35]Dobson, James. Love Must Be Tough. Tyndale House Publishers, 2007, p. 83.

[36]Thomas, Gary. Sacred Marriage. Zondervan, 2015, p. 168.

[37]Keller, Timothy. The Meaning of Marriage. Penguin Books, 2013, p. 185.

[38]Chapman, Gary. The Four Seasons of Marriage. Tyndale House Publishers, 2012, p. 98.

Notes Chapter 6

[1]Köstenberger, Andreas J. God, Marriage, and Family: Rebuilding the Biblical Foundation. Crossway, 2010, p. 78.

[2]Keller, Timothy, and Kathy. The Meaning of Marriage. Penguin Books, 2013, p. 123.

[3]Köstenberger, Andreas J. God, Marriage, and Family: Rebuilding the Biblical Foundation. Crossway, 2010, p. 82.

[4]Wheat, Ed, and Gaye. Intended for Pleasure. Revell, 2010, p. 19.

[5]Ortlund, Ray. Marriage and the Mystery of the Gospel. Crossway, 2016, p. 47.

[6]Thomas, Gary. Sacred Marriage. Zondervan, 2015, p. 204.

[7]Chapman, Gary. The 5 Love Languages. Northfield Publishing, 2015, p. 149.

[8]Wheat, Ed, and Gaye. Intended for Pleasure. Revell, 2010, p. 25.

[9]Leman, Kevin. Sheet Music: Uncovering the Secrets of Sexual Intimacy in Marriage. Tyndale House, 2008, p. 37.

[10]Chapman, Gary. The 5 Love Languages. Northfield Publishing, 2015, p. 153.

[11]Parrott, Les and Leslie. The Good Fight. Worthy Publishing, 2013, p. 172.

[12]Keller, Timothy, and Kathy. The Meaning of Marriage. Penguin Books, 2013, p. 128.

[13]Thomas, Gary. Sacred Marriage. Zondervan, 2015, p. 211.

[14]Rainey, Dennis. Preparing for Marriage. Bethany House Publishers, 2010, p. 98.

[15]Chapman, Gary. The 5 Love Languages. Northfield Publishing, 2015, p. 158.

[16]Wright, H. Norman. Before You Say "I Do". Harvest House Publishers, 2015, p. 67.

[17]Eggerichs, Emerson. Love and Respect. Thomas Nelson, 2004, p. 219.

[18]Chapman, Gary. The 5 Love Languages. Northfield Publishing, 2015, p. 162.

[19]Leman, Kevin. Sheet Music: Uncovering the Secrets of Sexual Intimacy in Marriage. Tyndale House, 2008, p. 43.

[20]Parrott, Les and Leslie. The Good Fight. Worthy Publishing, 2013, p. 178.

[21]Thomas, Gary. Sacred Marriage. Zondervan, 2015, p. 217.

[22]Rainey, Dennis. Preparing for Marriage. Bethany House Publishers, 2010, p. 104.

[23]Wright, H. Norman. Before You Say "I Do". Harvest House Publishers, 2015, p. 72.

[24]Cloud, Henry, and John Townsend. Boundaries in Marriage. Zondervan, 2002, p. 187.

[25]Eggerichs, Emerson. Love and Respect. Thomas Nelson, 2004, p. 224.

[26]Chapman, Gary. The 5 Love Languages. Northfield Publishing, 2015, p. 167.

[27]Thomas, Gary. Sacred Marriage. Zondervan, 2015, p. 223.

[28]Rainey, Dennis. Preparing for Marriage. Bethany House Publishers, 2010, p. 109.

[29]Chapman, Gary. The 5 Love Languages. Northfield Publishing, 2015, p. 171.

[30]Leman, Kevin. Sheet Music: Uncovering the Secrets of Sexual Intimacy in Marriage. Tyndale House, 2008, p. 49.

[31]Keller, Timothy, and Kathy. The Meaning of Marriage. Penguin Books, 2013, p. 134.

[32]Rainey, Dennis. Preparing for Marriage. Bethany House Publishers, 2010, p. 115.

[33]Wright, H. Norman. Before You Say "I Do". Harvest House Publishers, 2015, p. 78.

[34]Wright, H. Norman. Before You Say "I Do". Harvest House Publishers, 2015, p. 81.

[35]Chapman, Gary. The 5 Love Languages. Northfield Publishing, 2015, p. 176.

[36]Rainey, Dennis. Preparing for Marriage. Bethany House Publishers, 2010, p. 121.

[37]Graham, Billy. Nearing Home: Life, Faith, and Finishing Well. Thomas Nelson, 2011, p. 87.

[38]Wright, H. Norman. The Complete Guide to Crisis and Trauma Counseling. Bethany House Publishers, 2011, p. 243.

[39]Tada, Joni Eareckson, and Ken. Joni and Ken: An Untold Love Story. Zondervan, 2013, p. 154.

[40]Penner, Clifford and Joyce. The Gift of Sex. Thomas Nelson, 2003, p. 67.

[41]Shriver, Gary, and Mona. Unfaithful: Hope and Healing After Infidelity. David C. Cook, 2009, p. 112.

Notes Chapter 7

[1]Rainey, Dennis. Preparing for Marriage. Bethany House Publishers, 2010, p. 15.

[2]Stanley, Scott M., et al. "Premarital Education, Marital Quality, and Marital Stability." Journal of Family Psychology, vol. 20, 2006, pp. 117-126.

[3]Mack, Wayne. Preparing for Marriage God's Way. P&R Publishing, 2013, p. 23.

[4]Tripp, Paul David. Marriage: 6 Gospel Commitments Every Couple Needs to Make. Crossway, 2021, p. 42.

[5]Parrott, Les and Leslie. Saving Your Marriage Before It Starts. Zondervan, 2015, p. 29.

[6]Köstenberger, Andreas J. God, Marriage, and Family. Crossway, 2010, p. 78.

[7]Larson, Jeffry H. "Premarital Predictors of Marital Quality and Stability." Family Relations, vol. 43, 1994, pp. 228-237.

[8]Thomas, Gary. Sacred Marriage. Zondervan, 2015, p. 87.

[9]Trent, John, and Gary Smalley. The Blessing. Thomas Nelson, 2011, p. 103.

[10]Eggerichs, Emerson. Love and Respect. Thomas Nelson, 2004, p. 65.

[11]Chapman, Gary. The 5 Love Languages. Northfield Publishing, 2015, p. 42.

[12]Sande, Ken. The Peacemaker. Baker Books, 2004, p. 31.

[13]Blue, Ron. Master Your Money. Moody Publishers, 2016, p. 57.

[14]Keller, Timothy. The Meaning of Marriage. Penguin Books, 2013, p. 168.

[15]Leman, Kevin. Sheet Music. Tyndale House Publishers, 2003, p. 25.

[16]Dobson, James. The New Dare to Discipline. Tyndale House Publishers, 2014, p. 83.

[17]Rainey, Dennis. Preparing for Marriage. Bethany House Publishers, 2010, p. 124.

[18]Carroll, Jason S., and William J. Doherty. "Evaluating the Effectiveness of Premarital Prevention Programs." Family Relations, vol. 52, 2003, pp. 105-118.

[19]Keller, Timothy. The Meaning of Marriage. Penguin Books, 2013, p. 193.

[20]Vernick, Leslie. The Emotionally Destructive Relationship. Harvest House Publishers, 2007, p. 45.

[21]Rainey, Dennis. Preparing for Marriage. Bethany House Publishers, 2010, p. 156.

[22]Parrott, Les and Leslie. Saving Your Marriage Before It Starts. Zondervan, 2015, p. 47.

[23]Wright, H. Norman. Before You Say "I Do". Harvest House Publishers, 2015, p. 12.

[24]Larson, Jeffry H., and Thomas B. Holman. "Premarital Predictors of Marital Quality and Stability." Family Relations, vol. 43, 1994, pp. 228-237.

[25]Tripp, Paul David. Marriage: 6 Gospel Commitments Every Couple Needs to Make. Crossway, 2021, p. 58.

[26]Gottman, John, and Nan Silver. The Seven Principles for Making Marriage Work. Harmony Books, 2015, p. 39.

[27]Chapman, Gary. The 5 Love Languages. Northfield Publishing, 2015, p. 53.

[28]Parrott, Les and Leslie. Saving Your Marriage Before It Starts. Zondervan, 2015, p. 62.

[29]Clinton, Tim, and John Trent. The Quick-Reference Guide to Marriage & Family Counseling. Baker Books, 2009, p. 47.

[30]Markman, Howard J., et al. "Preventing Marital Distress Through Communication and Conflict Management Training." Journal of Consulting and Clinical Psychology, vol. 61, 1993, pp. 70-77.

[31]Olson, David H., and Amy Olson-Sigg. Empowering Couples: Building on Your Strengths. Life Innovations, 2000, p. 28.

[32]Thomas, Gary. Sacred Marriage. Zondervan, 2015, p. 102.

[33]Rainey, Dennis. Preparing for Marriage. Bethany House Publishers, 2010, p. 178.

[34]Thomas, Gary. Sacred Marriage. Zondervan, 2015, p. 115.

[35]Gottman, John, and Nan Silver. The Seven Principles for Making Marriage Work. Harmony Books, 2015, p. 52.

[36]Wright, H. Norman. Before You Say "I Do". Harvest House Publishers, 2015, p. 87.

[37]Tripp, Paul David. Marriage: 6 Gospel Commitments Every Couple Needs to Make. Crossway, 2021, p. 73.

[38]Wright, H. Norman. Before You Say "I Do". Harvest House Publishers, 2015, p. 95.

[39]Rainey, Dennis. Preparing for Marriage. Bethany House Publishers, 2010, p. 203.

Notes Chapter 8

[1]Dobson, James. The New Dare to Discipline. Tyndale House Publishers, 2014, p. 15.

[2]Keller, Timothy, and Kathy. The Meaning of Marriage. Penguin Books, 2013, p. 212.

[3]Köstenberger, Andreas J. God, Marriage, and Family: Rebuilding the Biblical Foundation. Crossway, 2010, p. 97.

[4]Köstenberger, Andreas J. God, Marriage, and Family: Rebuilding the Biblical Foundation. Crossway, 2010, p. 98.

[5]Tripp, Paul David. Parenting: 14 Gospel Principles That Can Radically Change Your Family. Crossway, 2016, p. 23.

[6]Clarkson, Sally. The Mission of Motherhood. WaterBrook Press, 2003, p. 42.

[7]Rainey, Dennis. Preparing for Marriage. Bethany House Publishers, 2010, p. 178.

[8]Rainey, Dennis and Barbara. Two Hearts Praying as One. Multnomah Books, 2002, p. 87.

[9]Dobson, James. The New Dare to Discipline. Tyndale House Publishers, 2014, p. 28.

[10]Baucham, Voddie. Family Driven Faith. Crossway, 2007, p. 93.

[11]Tripp, Tedd. Shepherding a Child's Heart. Shepherd Press, 1995, p. 52.

[12]McDowell, Josh. Set Free to Choose Right. Harvest House Publishers, 2018, p. 74.

[13]Thomas, Gary. Sacred Parenting. Zondervan, 2005, p. 38.

[14]Leman, Kevin. Making Children Mind Without Losing Yours. Revell, 2017, p. 63.

[15]Kimmel, Tim. Grace-Based Parenting. Thomas Nelson, 2005, p. 29.

[16]Tripp, Tedd. Shepherding a Child's Heart. Shepherd Press, 1995, p. 67.

[17]Baucham, Voddie. Family Driven Faith. Crossway, 2007, p. 97.

[18]Ezzo, Gary and Robert Bucknam. On Becoming Childwise. Parent-Wise Solutions, 2001, p. 42.

[19]Dobson, James. The New Dare to Discipline. Tyndale House Publishers, 2014, p. 53.

[20]Mueller, Walt. Understanding Today's Youth Culture. Tyndale House Publishers, 2016, p. 118.

[21]Rainey, Dennis. Preparing for Marriage. Bethany House Publishers, 2010, p. 183.

[22]Thomas, Gary. Sacred Parenting. Zondervan, 2005, p. 45.

[23]Thomas, Gary. Sacred Marriage. Zondervan, 2015, p. 172.

[24]Leman, Kevin. Making Children Mind Without Losing Yours. Revell, 2017, p. 78.

[25]Eggerichs, Emerson. Love and Respect. Thomas Nelson, 2004, p. 215.

[26]McDowell, Josh. Set Free to Choose Right. Harvest House Publishers, 2018, p. 82.

[27]Crouch, Andy. The Tech-Wise Family. Baker Books, 2017, p. 39.

[28]Smalley, Gary. The Marriage You've Always Wanted. Tyndale House Publishers, 2005, p. 143.

[29]Lewis, Robert. Raising a Modern-Day Knight. Tyndale House Publishers, 2007, p. 92.

[30]Deal, Ron. The Smart Stepfamily. Bethany House Publishers, 2014, p. 57.

[31]Moore, Russell. Adopted for Life. Crossway, 2015, p. 68.

[32]Colson, Emily. Dancing with Max. Zondervan, 2012, p. 93.

[33]Tripp, Paul David. Parenting: 14 Gospel Principles That Can Radically Change Your Family. Crossway, 2016, p. 37.

[34]Dobson, James. The New Dare to Discipline. Tyndale House Publishers, 2014, p. 67.

[35]Neufeld, Gordon and Gabor Maté. Hold On to Your Kids. Ballantine Books, 2014, p. 112.

[36]Tobias, Cynthia. You Can't Make Me (But I Can Be Persuaded). WaterBrook Press, 2012, p. 43.

[37]Chapman, Gary and Ross Campbell. The 5 Love Languages of Children. Northfield Publishing, 2016, p. 58.

[38]Kimmel, Tim. Raising Kids Who Turn Out Right. Thomas Nelson, 2005, p. 72.

[39]Thomas, Gary. Sacred Parenting. Zondervan, 2005, p. 53.

[40]Rienow, Rob. Visionary Parenting. Randall House Publications, 2013, p. 84.

[41]Joiner, Reggie. Think Orange. David C. Cook, 2009, p. 47.

[42]Powell, Kara, and Chap Clark. Sticky Faith. Zondervan, 2011, p. 73.

Notes Chapter 9

[1]Köstenberger, Andreas J. God, Marriage, and Family: Rebuilding the Biblical Foundation. Crossway, 2010, p. 78.

[2]Keller, Timothy, and Kathy. The Meaning of Marriage. Penguin Books, 2013, p. 123.

[3]Köstenberger, Andreas J. God, Marriage, and Family: Rebuilding the Biblical Foundation. Crossway, 2010, p. 82.

[4]Thomas, Gary. Sacred Marriage. Zondervan, 2015, p. 13.

[5]Chan, Francis, and Lisa. You and Me Forever: Marriage in Light of Eternity. Claire Love Publishing, 2014, p. 42.

[6]Ortlund, Ray. Marriage and the Mystery of the Gospel. Crossway, 2016, p. 47.

[7]Thomas, Gary. Sacred Marriage. Zondervan, 2015, p. 21.

[8]Rainey, Dennis. Preparing for Marriage. Bethany House Publishers, 2010, p. 98.

[9]Rainey, Dennis. Preparing for Marriage. Bethany House Publishers, 2010, p. 102.

[10]Chapman, Gary. The 5 Love Languages. Northfield Publishing, 2015, p. 153.

[11]Wright, H. Norman. Before You Say "I Do". Harvest House Publishers, 2015, p. 67.

[12]Rainey, Dennis. Preparing for Marriage. Bethany House Publishers, 2010, p. 107.

[13]Thomas, Gary. Sacred Marriage. Zondervan, 2015, p. 211.

[14]Chan, Francis, and Lisa. You and Me Forever: Marriage in Light of Eternity. Claire Love Publishing, 2014, p. 48.

[15]Rainey, Dennis. Preparing for Marriage. Bethany House Publishers, 2010, p. 112.

[16]Wright, H. Norman. Before You Say "I Do". Harvest House Publishers, 2015, p. 72.

[17]Wright, H. Norman. Before You Say "I Do". Harvest House Publishers, 2015, p. 75.

[18]Thomas, Gary. Sacred Marriage. Zondervan, 2015, p. 217.

[19]DeYoung, Kevin. Crazy Busy: A (Mercifully) Short Book about a (Really) Big Problem. Crossway, 2013, p. 83.

[20]Rainey, Dennis. Preparing for Marriage. Bethany House Publishers, 2010, p. 118.

[21]Eggerichs, Emerson. Love and Respect. Thomas Nelson, 2004, p. 219.

[22]Chapman, Gary. The 5 Love Languages. Northfield Publishing, 2015, p. 162.

[23]Rainey, Dennis. Preparing for Marriage. Bethany House Publishers, 2010, p. 124.

[24]Keller, Timothy, and Kathy. The Meaning of Marriage. Penguin Books, 2013, p. 134.

[25]Whitney, Donald S. Spiritual Disciplines for the Christian Life. NavPress, 2014, p. 237.

[26]Foster, Richard J. Celebration of Discipline: The Path to Spiritual Growth. HarperOne, 2018, p. 12.

[27]Thomas, Gary. Sacred Marriage. Zondervan, 2015, p. 223.

[28]Thomas, Gary. Sacred Marriage. Zondervan, 2015, p. 226.

[29]Chan, Francis, and Lisa. You and Me Forever: Marriage in Light of Eternity. Claire Love Publishing, 2014, p. 53.

[30]Rainey, Dennis. Preparing for Marriage. Bethany House Publishers, 2010, p. 129.

[31]Chapman, Gary. The 5 Love Languages. Northfield Publishing, 2015, p. 171.

[32]Keller, Timothy, and Kathy. The Meaning of Marriage. Penguin Books, 2013, p. 139.

[33]Thomas, Gary. Sacred Marriage. Zondervan, 2015, p. 231.

[34]Chan, Francis, and Lisa. You and Me Forever: Marriage in Light of Eternity. Claire Love Publishing, 2014, p. 58.

[35]Rainey, Dennis. Preparing for Marriage. Bethany House Publishers, 2010, p. 135.

[36]Wright, H. Norman. Before You Say "I Do". Harvest House Publishers, 2015, p. 81.

[37]Wright, H. Norman. Before You Say "I Do". Harvest House Publishers, 2015, p. 84.

[38]Thomas, Gary. Sacred Marriage. Zondervan, 2015, p. 237.

[39]Rainey, Dennis. Preparing for Marriage. Bethany House Publishers, 2010, p. 141.

[40]Graham, Billy. Nearing Home: Life, Faith, and Finishing Well. Thomas Nelson, 2011, p. 87.

Notes Chapter 10

[1]Köstenberger, Andreas J. God, Marriage, and Family: Rebuilding the Biblical Foundation. Crossway, 2010, p. 103.

[2]Köstenberger, Andreas J. God, Marriage, and Family: Rebuilding the Biblical Foundation. Crossway, 2010, p. 105.

[3]Keller, Timothy, and Kathy. The Meaning of Marriage. Penguin Books, 2013, p. 171.

[4]Rainey, Dennis. Preparing for Marriage. Bethany House Publishers, 2010, p. 156.

[5]Chapman, Gary. The 5 Love Languages. Northfield Publishing, 2015, p. 192.

[6]Keller, Timothy, and Kathy. The Meaning of Marriage. Penguin Books, 2013, p. 174.

[7]Rainey, Dennis. Preparing for Marriage. Bethany House Publishers, 2010, p. 159.

[8]Wright, H. Norman. Before You Say "I Do". Harvest House Publishers, 2015, p. 112.

[9]Wright, H. Norman. Before You Say "I Do". Harvest House Publishers, 2015, p. 115.

[10]Chapman, Gary. The 5 Love Languages. Northfield Publishing, 2015, p. 197.

[11]Eggerichs, Emerson. Love and Respect. Thomas Nelson, 2004, p. 252.

[12]Cloud, Henry, and John Townsend. Boundaries in Marriage. Zondervan, 2002, p. 146.

[13]Rainey, Dennis. Preparing for Marriage. Bethany House Publishers, 2010, p. 163.

[14]Chapman, Gary. The 5 Love Languages. Northfield Publishing, 2015, p. 201.

[15]Wright, H. Norman. Before You Say "I Do". Harvest House Publishers, 2015, p. 118.

[16]Thomas, Gary. Sacred Marriage. Zondervan, 2015, p. 267.

[17]Ramsey, Dave. Financial Peace Revisited. Viking, 2003, p. 127.

[18]Ramsey, Dave. Financial Peace Revisited. Viking, 2003, p. 131.

[19]Rainey, Dennis. Preparing for Marriage. Bethany House Publishers, 2010, p. 168.

[20]Chapman, Gary. The 5 Love Languages. Northfield Publishing, 2015, p. 205.

[21]Thomas, Gary. Sacred Marriage. Zondervan, 2015, p. 271.

[22]Cloud, Henry, and John Townsend. Boundaries in Marriage. Zondervan, 2002, p. 152.

[23]Cloud, Henry. Necessary Endings. HarperCollins, 2010, p. 89.

[24]Keller, Timothy, and Kathy. The Meaning of Marriage. Penguin Books, 2013, p. 178.

[25]Chapman, Gary. The 5 Love Languages. Northfield Publishing, 2015, p. 209.

[26]Wright, H. Norman. Before You Say "I Do". Harvest House Publishers, 2015, p. 121.

[27]Rainey, Dennis. Preparing for Marriage. Bethany House Publishers, 2010, p. 172.

[28]Thomas, Gary. Sacred Marriage. Zondervan, 2015, p. 275.

[29]Keller, Timothy, and Kathy. The Meaning of Marriage. Penguin Books, 2013, p. 182.

[30]Rainey, Dennis. Preparing for Marriage. Bethany House Publishers, 2010, p. 176.

[31]Chapman, Gary. The 5 Love Languages. Northfield Publishing, 2015, p. 213.

[32]Wright, H. Norman. Before You Say "I Do". Harvest House Publishers, 2015, p. 124.

[33]Thomas, Gary. Sacred Marriage. Zondervan, 2015, p. 279.

[34]Ramsey, Dave. Financial Peace Revisited. Viking, 2003, p. 135.

[35]Ramsey, Dave. Financial Peace Revisited. Viking, 2003, p. 138.

[36]Keller, Timothy, and Kathy. The Meaning of Marriage. Penguin Books, 2013, p. 186.

[37]Wright, H. Norman. Before You Say "I Do". Harvest House Publishers, 2015, p. 127.

[38]Rainey, Dennis. Preparing for Marriage. Bethany House Publishers, 2010, p. 179.

[39]Thomas, Gary. Sacred Marriage. Zondervan, 2015, p. 283.

[40]Wright, H. Norman. Before You Say "I Do". Harvest House Publishers, 2015, p. 130.

[41]Wright, H. Norman. Before You Say "I Do". Harvest House Publishers, 2015, p. 133.

[42]Thomas, Gary. Sacred Marriage. Zondervan, 2015, p. 287.

[43]Rainey, Dennis. Preparing for Marriage. Bethany House Publishers, 2010, p. 183.

Notes Chapter 11

[1]Keller, Timothy, and Kathy. The Meaning of Marriage. Penguin Books, 2013, p. 45.

[2]Keller, Timothy, and Kathy. The Meaning of Marriage. Penguin Books, 2013, p. 48.

[3]Thomas, Gary. Sacred Marriage. Zondervan, 2015, p. 42.

[4]Rainey, Dennis. Preparing for Marriage. Bethany House Publishers, 2010, p. 201.

[5]Thomas, Gary. Sacred Marriage. Zondervan, 2015, p. 13.

[6]Keller, Timothy, and Kathy. The Meaning of Marriage. Penguin Books, 2013, p. 52.

[7]Chapman, Gary. The 5 Love Languages. Northfield Publishing, 2015, p. 167.

[8]Rainey, Dennis. Preparing for Marriage. Bethany House Publishers, 2010, p. 205.

[9]Thomas, Gary. Sacred Marriage. Zondervan, 2015, p. 47.

[10]Wright, H. Norman. Before You Say "I Do". Harvest House Publishers, 2015, p. 142.

[11]Gottman, John. The Seven Principles for Making Marriage Work. Harmony Books, 2015, p. 79.

[12]Chapman, Gary. The 5 Love Languages. Northfield Publishing, 2015, p. 172.

[13]Wright, H. Norman. Before You Say "I Do". Harvest House Publishers, 2015, p. 145.

[14]Wheat, Ed. Intended for Pleasure. Fleming H. Revell, 2010, p. 18.

[15]Leman, Kevin. Sheet Music: Uncovering the Secrets of Sexual Intimacy in Marriage. Tyndale House Publishers, 2003, p. 25.

[16]Gottman, John. The Seven Principles for Making Marriage Work. Harmony Books, 2015, p. 96.

[17]Eggerichs, Emerson. Love and Respect. Thomas Nelson, 2004, p. 207.

[18]Keller, Timothy, and Kathy. The Meaning of Marriage. Penguin Books, 2013, p. 57.

[19]Thomas, Gary. Sacred Marriage. Zondervan, 2015, p. 53.

[20]Rainey, Dennis. Preparing for Marriage. Bethany House Publishers, 2010, p. 209.

[21]Wright, H. Norman. Before You Say "I Do". Harvest House Publishers, 2015, p. 148.

[22]Chapman, Gary. The 4 Seasons of Marriage. Tyndale House Publishers, 2012, p. 31.

[23]Chapman, Gary. The 4 Seasons of Marriage. Tyndale House Publishers, 2012, p. 35.

[24]Rainey, Dennis. Preparing for Marriage. Bethany House Publishers, 2010, p. 213.

[25]Leman, Kevin. Sheet Music: Uncovering the Secrets of Sexual Intimacy in Marriage. Tyndale House Publishers, 2003, p. 31.

[26]Thomas, Gary. Sacred Marriage. Zondervan, 2015, p. 59.

[27]Keller, Timothy, and Kathy. The Meaning of Marriage. Penguin Books, 2013, p. 63.

[28]Rainey, Dennis. Preparing for Marriage. Bethany House Publishers, 2010, p. 217.

[29]Thomas, Gary. Sacred Marriage. Zondervan, 2015, p. 65.

[30]Graham, Billy. Nearing Home: Life, Faith, and Finishing Well. Thomas Nelson, 2011, p. 103.

[31]Chapman, Gary. The 4 Seasons of Marriage. Tyndale House Publishers, 2012, p. 42.

[32]Leman, Kevin. Sheet Music: Uncovering the Secrets of Sexual Intimacy in Marriage. Tyndale House Publishers, 2003, p. 37.

[33]Chapman, Gary. The 5 Love Languages. Northfield Publishing, 2015, p. 178.

[34]Turkle, Sherry. Alone Together: Why We Expect More from Technology and Less from Each Other. Basic Books, 2017, p. 157.

[35]Gottman, John. The Seven Principles for Making Marriage Work. Harmony Books, 2015, p. 112.

[36]Ramsey, Dave. Financial Peace Revisited. Viking, 2003, p. 115.

[37]Ramsey, Dave. Financial Peace Revisited. Viking, 2003, p. 118.

[38]Wright, H. Norman. Before You Say "I Do". Harvest House Publishers, 2015, p. 151.

Notes Chapter 12

[1] Keller, Timothy, and Kathy. The Meaning of Marriage. Penguin Books, 2013, p. 13.

[2] Keller, Timothy, and Kathy. The Meaning of Marriage. Penguin Books, 2013, p. 21.

[3] Thomas, Gary. Sacred Marriage. Zondervan, 2015, p. 42.

[4] Rainey, Dennis. Preparing for Marriage. Bethany House Publishers, 2010, p. 28.

[5] Chapman, Gary. The Five Love Languages. Northfield Publishing, 2015, p. 15.

[6] Gottman, John, and Nan Silver. The Seven Principles for Making Marriage Work. Harmony Books, 2015, p. 87.

[7] Wheat, Ed, and Gaye Wheat. Intended for Pleasure. Revell, 2010, p. 19.

[8] Parrott, Les and Leslie. Saving Your Marriage Before It Starts. Zondervan, 2015, p. 33.

[9] Tripp, Paul David. Marriage: 6 Gospel Commitments Every Couple Needs to Make. Crossway, 2021, p. 217.

Bibliography and Further Study

Allender, Dan and Tremper Longman III. Intimate Allies. Tyndale House Publishers, 1999.

Andreas, J. God, Marriage, and Family: Rebuilding the Biblical Foundation. Crossway, 2010.

Baucham, Voddie. Family Driven Faith. Crossway, 2007.

Blue, Ron. Master Your Money. Moody Publishers, 2016.

Chan, Francis, and Lisa. You and Me Forever: Marriage in Light of Eternity. Claire Love Publishing, 2014.

Chapman, Gary and Ross Campbell. The 5 Love Languages of Children. Northfield Publishing, 2016.

Chapman, Gary. Now You're Speaking My Language. B&H Books, 2014.

Chapman, Gary. The Five Love Languages. Northfield Publishing, 2015.

Chapman, Gary. The Four Seasons of Marriage. Tyndale House Publishers, 2012.

Chapman, Gary. Things I Wish I'd Known Before We Got Married. Northfield Publishing, 2010.

Clarkson, Sally. The Mission of Motherhood. WaterBrook Press, 2003.

Clinton, Tim, and John Trent. The Quick-Reference Guide to Marriage & Family Counseling. Baker Books, 2009.

Cloud, Henry, and John Townsend. Boundaries in Marriage. Zondervan, 2002.

Cloud, Henry. Necessary Endings. HarperCollins, 2010.

Colson, Emily. Dancing with Max. Zondervan, 2012.

Crouch, Andy. The Tech-Wise Family. Baker Books, 2017.

Deal, Ron. The Smart Stepfamily. Bethany House Publishers, 2014.

DeYoung, Kevin. Crazy Busy: A (Mercifully) Short Book about a (Really) Big Problem. Crossway, 2013.

DeYoung, Kevin. What Does the Bible Really Teach about Homosexuality? Crossway, 2015.

Dobson, James. Love for a Lifetime. Multnomah, 1993.

Dobson, James. Love Must Be Tough. Tyndale House Publishers, 2007.

Dobson, James. The New Dare to Discipline. Tyndale House Publishers, 2014.

Doherty, William. Take Back Your Marriage. Guilford Press, 2013.

Eggerichs, Emerson. Love and Respect. Thomas Nelson, 2004.

Ezzo, Gary and Robert Bucknam. On Becoming Childwise. Parent-Wise Solutions, 2001.

Feldhahn, Shaunti. For Women Only. Multnomah, 2013.

Feldhahn, Shaunti. The Surprising Secrets of Highly Happy Marriages. Multnomah, 2013.

Foster, Richard J. Celebration of Discipline: The Path to Spiritual Growth. HarperOne, 2018.

Gottman, John, and Nan Silver. The Seven Principles for Making Marriage Work. Harmony Books, 2015.

Gottman, John. The Seven Principles for Making Marriage Work. Harmony Books, 2015.

Gottman, John. Why Marriages Succeed or Fail. Simon & Schuster, 1994.

Graham, Billy. Just As I Am. HarperOne, 2007.

Graham, Billy. Nearing Home: Life, Faith, and Finishing Well. Thomas Nelson, 2011.

Grudem, Wayne. Systematic Theology: An Introduction to Biblical Doctrine. Zondervan, 2000.

Horton, Michael. Covenant and Salvation: Union with Christ. Westminster John Knox Press, 2007.

Joiner, Reggie. Think Orange. David C. Cook, 2009.

Journal of Consulting and Clinical Psychology, vol. 61, 1993.

Journal of Family Psychology, vol. 20, 2006.

Keller, Timothy, and Kathy. The Meaning of Marriage. Penguin Books, 2013.

Kimmel, Tim. Grace-Based Parenting. Thomas Nelson, 2005.

Kimmel, Tim. Raising Kids Who Turn Out Right. Thomas Nelson, 2005.

Leman, Kevin. Making Children Mind Without Losing Yours. Revell, 2017.

Leman, Kevin. Sheet Music: Uncovering the Secrets of Sexual Intimacy in Marriage. Tyndale House Publishers, 2003.

Lewis, C.S. Mere Christianity. HarperOne, 2001.

Lewis, C.S. The Four Loves. Harcourt Brace, 1960.

Lewis, Robert. Raising a Modern-Day Knight. Tyndale House Publishers, 2007.

MacArthur, John. Divine Design: God's Complementary Roles for Men and Women. David C. Cook, 2010.

MacArthur, John. The Gospel According to Jesus. Zondervan, 2008.

Mack, Wayne. Preparing for Marriage God's Way. P&R Publishing, 2013.

McDowell, Josh. Set Free to Choose Right. Harvest House Publishers, 2018.

Mohler, R. Albert. We Cannot Be Silent. Thomas Nelson, 2015.

Moore, Russell. Adopted for Life. Crossway, 2015.

Mueller, Walt. Understanding Today's Youth Culture. Tyndale House Publishers, 2016.

Neufeld, Gordon and Gabor Maté. Hold On to Your Kids. Ballantine Books, 2014.

Olson, David H., and Amy Olson-Sigg. Empowering Couples: Building on Your Strengths. Life Innovations, 2000.

Ortlund, Raymond C. Marriage and the Mystery of the Gospel. Crossway, 2016.

Parrott, Les and Leslie. Saving Your Marriage Before It Starts. Zondervan, 2015.

Parrott, Les and Leslie. The Good Fight. Worthy Publishing, 2013.

Penner, Clifford and Joyce. The Gift of Sex. Thomas Nelson, 2003.

Piper, John and Wayne Grudem. Recovering Biblical Manhood and Womanhood. Crossway, 2006.

Piper, John. Desiring God: Meditations of a Christian Hedonist. Multnomah, 2011.

Piper, John. This Momentary Marriage: A Parable of Permanence. Crossway, 2012.

Powell, John. Why Am I Afraid to Tell You Who I Am? Zondervan, 1999.

Powell, Kara, and Chap Clark. Sticky Faith. Zondervan, 2011.

Rainey, Dennis and Barbara. Two Hearts Praying as One. Multnomah Books, 2002.

Rainey, Dennis. Preparing for Marriage. Bethany House Publishers, 2010.

Ramsey, Dave. Financial Peace Revisited. Viking, 2003.

Rienow, Rob. Visionary Parenting. Randall House Publications, 2013.

Sande, Ken. The Peacemaker. Baker Books, 2004.

Shriver, Gary, and Mona. Unfaithful: Hope and Healing After Infidelity. David C. Cook, 2009.

Smalley, Gary. The Marriage You've Always Wanted. Tyndale House Publishers, 2005.

Smedes, Lewis. Forgive and Forget. HarperOne, 2007.

Sproul, R.C. The Consequences of Ideas. Crossway, 2009.

Sproul, R.C. The Holiness of God. Tyndale House Publishers, 2000.

Tada, Joni Eareckson, and Ken. Joni and Ken: An Untold Love Story. Zondervan, 2013.

Thomas, Gary. Sacred Marriage. Zondervan, 2015.

Thomas, Gary. Sacred Parenting. Zondervan, 2005.

Tobias, Cynthia. You Can't Make Me (But I Can Be Persuaded). WaterBrook Press, 2012.

Trent, John, and Gary Smalley. The Blessing. Thomas Nelson, 2011.

Tripp, Paul David. Marriage: 6 Gospel Commitments Every Couple Needs to Make. Crossway, 2021.

Tripp, Paul David. Parenting: 14 Gospel Principles That Can Radically Change Your Family. Crossway, 2016.

Tripp, Paul David. What Did You Expect?: Redeeming the Realities of Marriage. Crossway, 2012.

Tripp, Tedd. Shepherding a Child's Heart. Shepherd Press, 1995.

Turkle, Sherry. Alone Together: Why We Expect More from Technology and Less from Each Other. Basic Books, 2017.

Vernick, Leslie. The Emotionally Destructive Relationship. Harvest House Publishers, 2007.

Wheat, Ed, and Gaye. Intended for Pleasure. Revell, 2010.

Whitney, Donald S. Spiritual Disciplines for the Christian Life. NavPress, 2014.

Wright, H. Norman. Before You Say "I Do". Harvest House Publishers, 2015.

Meet Mark Hobafcovich

Mark Hobafcovich is a pastor, author, and Christian leader passionate about advancing God's kingdom around the world. For nearly three decades, he served with the Southern Baptist Convention's North American Mission Board—the largest network of evangelical churches in the United States—equipping churches and leaders to embrace the Great Commission. His ministry has impacted North America, Europe, Australia, South America, and beyond, inspiring many to live lives marked by disciple-making and kingdom impact. Married to Christine since 1985, Mark lives near Atlanta, Georgia, where they continue to live on a mission—trusting God, encouraging the next generation, and making Christ's last command their first priority.

MarkHobafcovich.com

X @MarkHobafcovich

www.ingramcontent.com/pod-product-compliance
Lightning Source LLC
Chambersburg PA
CBHW071706120626
46550CB00001B/126